PRAISE FOR

COMMON CORE FOR THE NOT-SO-COMMON LEARNER, GRADES 6–12

"With this book the authors provide just the kind of resource that secondary teachers are yearning for as they navigate implementation of the Common Core State Standards. The emphasis on 'not-so-common' learners validates the unique needs these students bring to our schools and provides teachers with tools for assisting all students in becoming college and career ready. The specific ideas and strategies presented are invaluable!"

—Jana Echevarria
Professor Emerita
California State University, Long Beach, CA

"Honigsfeld and Dove artfully interweave a myriad of strategies derived from and related to the Common Core State Standards for English Language Arts. . . . In bridging theory to classroom practice, the authors consider the characteristics of a spectrum of adolescent students who are challenged by the linguistic and conceptual expectations of these rigorous standards in hopes of directing them onto pathways to success."

—Margo Gottlieb
Director, Assessment & Evaluation
Illinois Resource Center, and
Lead Developer, WIDA Consortium

"Educators can turn to this book for theoretically sound and eminently practical information about approaches and strategies to support English Learners' complex language use, critical thinking, and deep engagement with the Common Core."

—Rita MacDonald
Academic English Language Researcher
WIDA Consortium

"From the first quote in Chapter 1 to the final word, this book struck a chord. A veritable treasure trove of useful classroom practices and scaffolding techniques are identified and carefully explained. . . . The valuable information in this book provides the suggestions teachers have been seeking to be successful at implementing the Common Core with their diverse, not-so-common, learners."

—Susan Lafond
National Board Certified Teacher, ESL
Teacher, Advocate, and Member of the
Common Core State Standards Initiative
K–12 Standards Development Team

"For years, teachers who teach in Grades 6–12 have had little to choose from in terms of ESL professional development, and little-to-nothing with regard to CCSS. This publication represents a significant advancement in the field on both counts. By combining research-based theory with specific classroom activities, the authors give their readers a comprehensive picture of the topic at hand with significant, useable strategies."

—N. Eleni Pappamihiel
Associate Professor
TESL Program Coordinator and ELMS Project Director
University of North Carolina Wilmington

"This is a must-have resource for every teacher. Andrea Honigsfeld and Maria Dove have 'connected the dots' between the Common Core State Standards and the tools to address the needs of diverse students in actual classrooms. This brilliantly straightforward framework is exactly what teachers have been pleading for."

—Annette Shideler
President
A-Net Consulting Services, Ltd., Mt. Sinai, NY

We dedicate this book to our respective families, who are our greatest source of support for all of our endeavors: Howie, Benjamin, Jacob, and Noah; Tim, Dave, Jason, Christine, Sara, Meadow Rose, and Gavin Joseph. We also dedicate this book to all educators who are committed to the success of the not-so-common learner.

Common Core

for the
Not-So-Common
Learner

English
Language Arts
Strategies
GRADES
6–12

ANDREA HONIGSFELD
MARIA G. DOVE

CORWIN
A SAGE Company

CORWIN
A SAGE Company

FOR INFORMATION:

Corwin
A SAGE Company
2455 Teller Road
Thousand Oaks, California 91320
(800) 233-9936
www.corwin.com

SAGE Publications Ltd.
1 Oliver's Yard
55 City Road
London EC1Y 1SP
United Kingdom

SAGE Publications India Pvt. Ltd.
B 1/I 1 Mohan Cooperative Industrial Area
Mathura Road, New Delhi 110 044
India

SAGE Publications Asia-Pacific Pte. Ltd.
3 Church Street
#10-04 Samsung Hub
Singapore 049483

Printed in the United States of America.

ISBN 978-1-4522-5781-5

This book is printed on acid-free paper.

Acquisitions Editor: Dan Alpert
Associate Editor: Kimberly Greenberg
Editorial Assistant: Heidi Arndt
Production Editor: Amy Schroller
Copy Editor: Linda Gray
Typesetter: C&M Digitals (P) Ltd.
Proofreader: Laura Webb
Cover Designer: Rose Storey

SFI Certified Sourcing
www.sfiprogram.org
SFI-00453

15 16 17 10 9 8 7 6 5 4

Content

Preface

One of the ways that teachers improve is by learning from other teachers. . . . Isolation is the enemy of all improvement.

—Andy Hargreaves, 2011, p. xx

The intention of this book along with its companion volume, *Common Core for the Not-So-Common Learner, Grades K–5: English Language Arts Strategies* is to provide a carefully selected sample of instructional strategies that address each anchor standard to help teachers meet the Common Core State Standards (CCSS) with diverse adolescent students. It is not a step-by-step prescriptive manual for successful implementation of the CCSS, nor does it attempt to provide a comprehensive guide to meet the academic, linguistic, social, and emotional needs of diverse learners. This book identifies the CCSS anchor standards for English language arts and literacy in content-area subjects, provides guidance on how to interpret those standards for Grades 6–12 diverse learners in terms of academic performance, and suggests possible strategies to achieve them. Teachers are encouraged to examine the strategies contained herein, experiment with them in their own classes, investigate as well as interpret their effectiveness, modify them to support their own instructional goals, and work collaboratively with fellow teachers to create methods, techniques, and activities that are most suitable for their own population of students.

It is our hope that some of the instructional and implementation strategies addressed in these pages will spark new ideas and begin conversations about teaching practices that are shared by many. In this way, this book should not be perceived as the definitive account of necessary strategies to use with diverse learners but as the impetus that compels all educators to better understand research-based best practices, to further search for answers to critical questions regarding the CCSS implementation with various student populations, and to collaboratively share their findings with colleagues.

It is no surprise that the CCSS will present many challenges for teachers who instruct diverse learners. Educators will read and try to interpret each individual standard for their grade and content area and will no doubt be faced with numerous questions, such as the following:

- *What does each standard actually require students to know and be able to do?*
- *How do I help struggling students meet the standards?*
- *Must I change what I normally do in my daily instructional practices in light of the CCSS?*
- *How can I develop and support students' literacy skills in my content-area classes?*
- *Where am I going to find the resources to create lessons that address individual standards?*

These questions are answered in detail in this book. We address the CCSS by first explaining what each anchor standard requires students to know and do in broad terms. We identify what we call an *Anchor Performance* for each of the 32 anchor standards, which represent a critical skill students should be able to develop in light of the CCSS. We further suggest both broad and specific strategies for helping diverse and struggling learners succeed with each of these standards, and we share our ideas for changing instructional practices. Furthermore, we offer a range of additional resources at the end of each chapter for readers to explore instructional ideas that are too numerous to contain within these pages.

What we suggest is considering the three *R*'s when implementing the CCSS with diverse learners: rigor, relevance, and research! Engaging students in both rigorous and challenging academic tasks that are relevant to their college and career readiness needs is a must and is well-supported in the literature (see Daggett, 2011, and the Rigor/Relevance Framework, a tool developed by the International Center for Leadership in Education at http://www.leadered.com/rrr.html). Yet teachers cannot forget about research-based best practices and the type of scaffolded, differentiated instruction that will support academically and linguistically diverse learners in achieving success.

In light of the complexity of implementing the CCSS, teachers can no longer work in isolation to overcome the various obstacles in order to initiate effective instructional practices. There are no quick fixes, and although it may be a starting point, adding a few instructional strategies to one's teaching repertoire will not bring about the systemic change that is vital for diverse learners to succeed. As *Washington Post* blogger Strauss

(2010) also noted, "No set of standards has much meaning without equitable resources to ensure that teachers are trained well enough to reach kids who live in widely different circumstances" (para. 11). We hope that this book, and its companion version for Grades K–5, will be added as a ready-to-use, practical resource to the professional libraries of schools across the country.

Further, we would like to invite our readers to reflect on their own teaching effectiveness, to engage colleagues in collaborative efforts to do so as well, to investigate new models of instruction, to review and revise curricula, and to go beyond the scope of this book to begin and sustain the essential collaborative conversations and interventions that are vital to school reform.

HOW THIS BOOK IS ORGANIZED

Chapter 1 establishes the framework for the rest of the book and discusses who the not-so-common learners are and what the CCSS mean for them and their teachers. Chapters 2 through 6 follow the same internal organization. Each chapter focuses on one strand of the Common Core State Standards in the following order: Language (Chapter 2); Reading Literature (Chapter 3); Reading Informational Text (Chapter 4); Writing (Chapter 5); and Speaking and Listening (Chapter 6). The order of the chapters follows the order in which the CCSS are presented (see www .corestandards.org), with one exception. Since academic language development is so critical for linguistically, culturally, and academically diverse students, we emphasized the importance of paying attention to language skills by intentionally disrupting the CCSS order and placing that chapter ahead of all others.

Within each chapter, we offer the rationale for explicit, strategy-based instruction related to the target Common Core anchor standards. Following the presentation of our recommended set of core strategies that are aligned to the CCSS and anchor performances, we discuss anticipated outcomes and instructional challenges readers may encounter. We close each of these five chapters by offering authentic classroom vignettes documenting promising practices from middle and high schools with diverse student populations. A list of key resources related to the chapter is also added to encourage further exploration of the topic.

Chapters 4 and 5 address not only reading informational texts and writing in English language arts, but they also examine the 6–12 grade-level literacy standards in history/social studies as well as science and technical subjects.

Chapter 7 stands apart from the previous six. As a continuation of our earlier work, *Collaboration and Coteaching: Strategies for English Learners* (Honigsfeld & Dove, 2010), here we outline the types of instructional and noninstructional collaborative practices that teachers may wish to engage in to support the successful implementation of the CCSS for all learners.

It is our hope that the CCSS will represent new windows of opportunity for consistency in grade-appropriate expectations, ensuring equitable education for and meaningful engagement of all learners, and enhance teacher collaboration in curriculum development and instructional delivery. We wish you an *uncommonly* productive time exploring this book!

Acknowledgments

We would like to express our sincere appreciation for all of those who made a contribution—either directly or indirectly—to this volume: Kelley Brown, Jim Burke, Jonathan Chiaramonte, Linda Chick, Debra Cole, Paula Dreyfuss, Elizabeth Gennosa, Karen Goyette, Victoria Klaassen-Chew, Susan Lafond, Kim Manfredi, Mike Markulis, Ann McCallum, Loraine K. McCray, Sunday Ogunsola, Elizabeth Oldendorp, Young Pahk, Tina Proulx, Lucille Purpura-Otto, Christine Rowland, Shaeley Santiago, and Jonna St. Croix.

Our gratitude goes to our graduate assistant Taylor Volpe for her technical assistance with the research for and organization of this text.

We would also like to thank our reviewers whose detailed and honest feedback enhanced the writing of this volume:

Angela Bell, Assistant Professor
University of Colorado, Colorado Springs
Colorado Springs, CO

Joanne Kilgour Dowdy, Professor
Kent State University
Kent, OH

Elizabeth Gennosa, Academic Intervention Services
Sachem, New York

Susan Lafond, National Board Certified Teacher
New York State United Teachers
Latham, New York

Rita MacDonald, Academic English Language Researcher
Wisconsin Center for Education Research
World-Class Instructional Design and Assessment (WIDA) Research
    Team
Madison, Wisconsin

Paul Chamness Miller, Associate Professor/English for Academic Purposes
Akita International University
Akita, Japan

Thomas DeVere Wolsey, Program Director: Master's of Science in Education—Literacy Specializations
Walden University
Minneapolis, MN

We cannot say enough about the unyielding support and the overwhelming confidence bestowed on us by our editor, Dan Alpert. For this and so much more, we sincerely thank you. We would also like to express our appreciation for the entire Corwin team, especially to Heidi Arndt, Linda Gray, and Amy Schroller, for their work on the manuscript preparation and production process.

A special thank you to Joanne Lufrano, whose insistence on the development of an inservice course on the Common Core State Standards for the Valley Stream Teacher Center not only led to the development of this project but also inspired the name of the two volumes—*Common Core for the Not-So-Common Learner.*

We would like to thank our friends and colleagues at Molloy College, Rockville Centre, New York, who continually support and encourage our scholarship efforts. We would like to offer a special thanks to Vicky Giouroukakis, who read and commented on earlier drafts of this manuscript, and Audrey Cohan for her professional dialogues and exchanges with us to enhance our understanding of special needs students.

Last but not least, to our families and friends who frequently cheer us on; your love and support for our work are paramount for us.

About the Authors

 **Andrea Honigsfeld, EdD,** is a professor in the Division of Education at Molloy College, Rockville Centre, New York. She teaches graduate education courses related to cultural and linguistic diversity, linguistics, ESL methodology, and action research. Before entering the field of teacher education, she was an English-as-a-foreign-language teacher in Hungary (Grades 5–8 and adult) and an English-as-a-second-language teacher in New York City (Grades K–3 and adult); she also taught Hungarian at New York University.

She was the recipient of a doctoral fellowship at St. John's University, New York, where she conducted research on individualized instruction and learning styles. She has published extensively on working with English language learners and providing individualized instruction based on learning style preferences. She received a Fulbright Award to lecture in Iceland in the fall of 2002. In the past ten years, she has been presenting at conferences across the United States, Great Britain, Denmark, Sweden, the Philippines, and the United Arab Emirates. She frequently offers staff development primarily focusing on effective differentiated strategies and collaborative practices for English-as-a-second-language and general education teachers. She coauthored *Differentiated Instruction for At-Risk Students* (2009) and coedited the five-volume *Breaking the Mold of Education* series (2010–2013), published by Rowman and Littlefield. With Maria Dove, she coedited *Coteaching and Other Collaborative Practices in the EFL/ESL Classroom: Rationale, Research, Reflections, and Recommendations* (2012) and coauthored *Collaboration and Co-Teaching: Strategies for English Learners* (2010)—a Corwin bestseller.

Maria G. Dove, EdD is Associate Professor and Coordinator of the TESOL Programs in the Division of Education at Molloy College, Rockville Centre, New York, where she teaches courses to preservice and inservice teachers on the research and best practices for developing effective programs and school policies for English learners. Before entering the field of higher education, she worked over thirty years as an English-as-a-second-language teacher in public school settings (Grades K–12) and in adult English language programs in Nassau County, New York.

In 2010, she received the Outstanding ESL Educator Award from New York State Teachers of English to Speakers of Other Languages (NYS TESOL). She frequently provides professional development throughout the United States for educators on the teaching of diverse students. She also serves as a mentor for new ESL teachers as well as an instructional coach for general education teachers and literacy specialists. She has published articles and book chapters on collaborative teaching practices, instructional leadership, and collaborative coaching. With Andrea Honigsfeld, she coauthored the companion volume to this work, *Common Core for the Not-So-Common Learner, Grades K-5: English Language Arts Strategies* (2013) and the best-selling book, *Collaboration and Co-Teaching: Strategies for English Learners* (2010), both published by Corwin. The same writing team also coedited, *Coteaching and Other Collaborative Practices in the EFL/ESL Classroom: Rationale, Research, Reflections, and Recommendations* (2012), published by Information Age Publishing.

1 Introduction

A well-educated person has a well-furnished mind, shaped by reading and thinking about history, science, literature, the arts, and politics.

—Diane Ravitch, 2010, p. 16

The challenges of teaching in secondary education have been amplified since the adoption of the Common Core State Standards (CCSS) initiative. More than ever before, teachers are being asked to examine their classroom practices and align them with the advancements in instruction as identified by the CCSS. Some of these advancements propose the inclusion of literacy skills and strategies in all areas of instruction with an overall expectation that these changes in classroom practices will bring about school reform.

For decades, school reform and the innovative approaches that lead to school improvement have been extensively examined (Hargreaves, 1994; Ravitch, 2000; Reeves, 2006), and the results have revealed that the implementation of many policies and practices have not been successful in improving student achievement even when educational change has been rigorously pursued (Fullan, 2007). In some instances, the improvement of teaching and learning has been viewed as an "only if" proposition—only if we had more qualified teachers, adequate funding, current technology, appropriate materials, better leadership . . . *only if*. Far worse is the impression that the fault lies somewhere among the perceived deficits in diverse student populations that more and more teachers find seated in their classrooms across our nation.

Of some concern is the notion that there are individual school entities that are lacking, their alteration will bring about desired educational outcomes, and the solution is for policymakers to mitigate circumstances through legislation such as student assessment practices, teacher evaluation, or the selection of a new set of standards. Although there is no panacea, standards-based instruction is an opportunity to set a meaningful context to build challenging curricula and uphold rigorous expectations for all students, even those who are perceived as struggling learners.

The Common Core State Standards (CCSS) clearly identify rigorous academic objectives and support teachers' high expectations for student performance. Yet in examining the Standards with a wide lens, we have found the CCSS challenge secondary teachers in numerous ways—to go beyond merely requiring students to receive information and recall content facts. The Standards emphasize a deeper understanding of text, including the development of students' abilities to collect, analyze, and synthesize information from a variety of sources as well as interpret data, infer meaning, and make connections among texts. In short, the development of these learning skills requires a different set of skills for teaching.

For the most part, the adoption of the CCSS alone is unlikely to bring about an increase in student achievement, and it remains to be seen how their implementation will fare with diverse learners. With broad concerns over the effectiveness of the CCSS as well as their implementation, Weingarten (2012) offered her opinion:

> The hard part is not the development of standards or their adoption, but the implementation. These standards must be supported by a comprehensive system that includes development of aligned curriculum; support and time for appropriate professional development; instructional materials and other resources including model lesson plans; collaborative planning efforts; and assessments that are aligned but must inform instruction and not be used excessively or punitively. (para. 2)

More than ever before, educational change in all its complexity rests within a teacher's classroom practices and the ability to collaborate concerning the materials and instructional resources chosen, the use of teaching approaches and strategies, and the alteration of pedagogical beliefs (Fullan, 2007; Honigsfeld & Dove, 2010). Nonetheless, the teaching process is impeded by the ways in which our schools are compartmentalized. Teachers concern themselves with their discipline-specific curriculum, and there may be limited opportunities to incorporate student learning from subject to subject. What is happening in the history class is vastly different from the English language arts class, yet both require students to listen, speak, read, and write.

In his argument for science literacy, Trefil (2008) identified a problem with the nature of secondary school design. He commented that all too often, the school day is divided into discipline-specific classes, in which each content area is taught exclusive of any other subject. As teachers, we do not take the opportunity to carry over the learning students accumulate from one class to another, and we almost never consider incorporating material from multiple classes so that courses such as chemistry, biology, art history, and mathematics have a common thread.

The practice of compartmentalized curricula may be detrimental to the learning of all students in that it does not foster students' abilities to draw on previously learned information across the disciplines or make complex, meaningful connections between content classes. This division of subject matter particularly impacts the success of diverse learners, who with their special learning needs are not only trying to make sense of academic content but also in some cases must navigate a mainstream American school culture due to ethnic, social, and language differences.

Overall, the CCSS present an unprecedented opportunity for secondary school educators to examine their current instructional practices and align them to the new standards. To assist with planning new types of instruction, we look to Fullan (2007) who identified three key features to establish new initiatives: (a) the adoption of new material resources for instructional purposes, (b) the application of different teaching strategies, and (c) the amendment of practitioners' pedagogical or theoretical beliefs; all three elements are necessary to successfully establish particular program implementation. However, despite the establishment of all three of these components, other issues can influence the effective foundation of new educational initiatives. What is needed is a comprehensive plan of implementation that incorporates leadership strategies, buy-in from the school community, alignment of the curricula, and adequate professional development.

With consideration for the academic, linguistic, ethnic, racial, cultural, and economic backgrounds of diverse learners, educators should approach the employment of the CCSS as a multidimensional task. School administrators in particular should take into account the complexities of implementation, encompass various approaches to the challenges, collaboratively analyze the issues, and develop an overall plan of action. From our perspective, successful implementation will require the following:

1. A shared vision and mission for all students reached through consensus along with the determination of measurable, achievable goals with an understanding of how to accomplish them

2. Curriculum mapping and alignment to ensure that instructional content and practices for academically and linguistically diverse pupils are consistent with the Standards and the learning outcomes for all students

3. Collaborative planning, instruction, and assessment among teams of teachers—content-area, English as a second language (ESL), special education, and literacy specialists, among others—to foster the use of teaching and learning strategies to make academic material comprehensible for all learners

4. Strategies to integrate language and content instruction to foster literacy and language development while acquiring content information (as well as professional development opportunities for teachers to become proficient with such strategies)

5. A direct focus on teaching academic language and literacy needed to access rigorous content and opportunities for students to apply newly learned language and content-based literacy skills through various modes of discourse

6. Explicitly teaching literacy and language-learning strategies to develop students' understanding of their own thinking and learning processes and help them develop as self-directed, independent learners who are college and career ready

By fostering a comprehensive plan for implementation of the CCSS with the needs of diverse learners in mind, school administrators will be better able to support teachers in their efforts to promote students' success in meeting the Standards.

WHO ARE OUR NOT-SO-COMMON LEARNERS?

It is no surprise that in the 21st century, U.S. classrooms are filled with students that are more culturally, ethnically, and linguistically diverse than ever before. Yet the nature of school systems, in particular, the way we assess our students, has a tendency to create segregated populations of learners in the same school building. The purpose of segregating diverse students—English learners, students with disabilities, or those in need of other instructional support services—is to target their instruction. Middle school and high school classes often support the learning of these diverse groups with specialized classes and curricula developed to help these students meet with success. However, all too often the curricula of tracked courses or stand-alone specialized secondary programs generally set particularly low expectations for these students to meet, and the curricula for these classes do not always offer the same rigor as those set for mainstream classes. Often coupled with low expectations for them, when diverse students are labeled and segregated from the mainstream classroom, their abilities, language, and culture are subject to "subtle forms of unintentional rejection" (Cummins, 2001, p. 2).

Our main objective for defining the *not-so-common learner* is not to add to the divisiveness or segregation of these pupils. In our inclusion and description of them, we hope that teachers and administrators will be better able to plan for the education of diverse students so that they may meet with success in their coursework and provide the appropriate resources, strategies, and techniques, many of which are outlined in this volume, to assist their learning.

The following are a list of the common characteristics and labels often associated with the not-so-common learner:

- English Learners (ELs). These are students who are either foreign-born immigrants or U.S.-born citizens of immigrant parents, speak a language other than English, and have yet to develop proficient skills (listening, speaking, reading, or writing) in English.
- Students With Interrupted or Limited Formal Education (SIFE). A subgroup of English learners, these school-age youngsters often have significant gaps in their education and, on the average, two years or less schooling than their same-age peers.
- Students With Disabilities. Pupils with special learning needs due to physical and/or mental impairments who require special assistance to meet with academic success.
- Nonstandard-English-Speaking Children. Often racially and/or ethnically diverse, these U.S.-born students speak a dialect of English in their communities and have yet to acquire standard American English skills.
- Children of Poverty. Youngsters under the age of 18 whose families have incomes below the U.S. poverty threshold. Approximately 16 million of America's poor are children who are often malnourished, live in substandard housing, and have unequal access to education opportunities.
- Struggling Learners. Students who are not performing at grade level in the core subject matters.

THE STANDARDS MOVEMENT

Thirty years after the publication of *A Nation at Risk* (National Commission on Excellence in Education, 1983), a comprehensive report concerning the quality of education in America, 46 U.S. states have joined together to adopt a foundation for educational reform with the CCSS initiative. However, there is frequent debate about the benefits of standards, particularly when so many variables affect educational reforms and student outcomes. One point of view is that standards are secondary to the issue of funding in that "arguing about what standards should be taught in school is of dubious value when the resources that teachers and students will have at their disposal will vary so deeply, district to district" (Lehman, 2012, para. 5). Funding certainly is crucial to educational reforms and to implementing positive systemic change. Monies are essential to employ highly qualified teachers, to provide effective professional development, to reduce class size, and to incorporate the latest instructional technology. Therefore, it is a simple conclusion that standards alone will not alter the learning outcomes.

Nevertheless, based on the research of quality standards found both in the United States and high-performing countries globally regarding what students need to know and be able to do to become college and career ready, the CCSS can be a strong foundation for school reform. Considering the overall benefits of well-established standards, Reeves (2000) stated the following:

> Although standards alone are clearly an insufficient instrument for the improvement of student achievement, the essence of standards— the clear articulation of what students should know and be able to do—forms the basis for the essential transformations necessary for school success. (p. 5)

Yet resistance to standards and certain accountability measures continues to surface as educators debate what might bring about lasting school success (Rowan, Correnti, Miller, & Camburn, 2009), along with other obstacles—cultural, traditional, political, and economic—that impede their implementation (Thomas, 2002).

The institution of educational reforms is a complex process, and it is vital that educational policies translate into sound classroom practices so that all children are supported in the learning process. Standards must be the framework that guides the inclusion and educational advancement of all students. To make educational reforms a reality, there must be an investment in quality teacher training (Elmore, 2008) and capacity building through collaborative practices (Honigsfeld & Dove, 2010) to foster the necessary skills for teachers and school-level administrators to undertake the challenge of meeting the needs of diverse learners.

COMMON CORE ADVANCES

The *Common Core State Standards for English Language Arts & Literacy in History/ Social Studies, Science, and Technical Subjects* (2010a)—the Standards—identify several advances in instruction for not only the teaching of English language arts but also for the teaching of literacy skills during content-area instruction, a considerable shift in classroom practices for many secondary school teachers. This advancement was developed to truly ensure that all students are college and career ready by the end of Grade 12. For this reason, the CCSS contain sets of anchor standards in reading, writing, speaking and listening, and language that are consistent across all grade levels and promote an integrated model of literacy, and in Grades 6–12 specify a separate set of grade-level standards that solely focus on building reading and writing skills in the content areas.

This major shift in classroom practices, the teaching of literacy as a shared responsibility, is an outstanding promotion for the teaching and learning of diverse students as all teachers are expected to foster students' reading and writing skills across the disciplines. Furthermore, in Grades 6–12, there is an increased emphasis on the reading of nonfiction texts in conjunction with an interdisciplinary approach to the teaching of literacy. This emphasis on reading is based on extensive research establishing the necessary skills to comprehend informational texts proficiently and prepare students to be college and career ready.

To advance students' facility with reading informational texts, teachers may no longer solely deliver content information to students through direct instruction. Teachers therefore must shift their practices to assist students in gathering their own information about subject content through thoughtful, deep reading as well as through guided and independent research, and by participating in meaningful academic conversations and sustained collaborations with peers. Furthermore, to enhance the content learning and literacy development of diverse students, teachers will determine how to scaffold instruction to support the reading and analysis of complex texts as well as written responses with those youngsters who are not yet able to read or express themselves on grade level.

Teachers will need to focus their instruction so students read more closely and deeply in order to participate in text-dependent conversations.

The CCSS specify that students' opinions, arguments, and conclusions must be grounded in text-based evidence. To support evidence-based conversations with diverse learners, teachers will need to activate students' prior knowledge, build background information from students' personal experiences, and motivate students through their personal connections with the topic in order to aid their comprehension of text and enhance their ability to participate in meaningful conversations. Or as a recent report indicated, "Some students, particularly those with LDs, require sustained and intensive combinations of classroom instruction, remediation, and accommodations that are individualized, explicit, systematic, and relevant" (National Joint Committee on Learning Disabilities, 2008, para. 27).

An additional advancement in instruction due to the CCSS is the level and complexity of student writing. Secondary students are expected to write arguments that are supported by ample text-based evidence and compose explanatory texts that convey complex ideas, compiling information obtained through multiple print and digital sources. Students must discern the value of information obtained from various sources and to develop a facility with using technology to generate and publish individually written work as well as codevelop shared writing projects.

One final broad-based shift in instruction initiated by the Standards is a direct emphasis on the explicit teaching of academic vocabulary. For students to consistently be able to comprehend complex texts, all content teachers should identify vocabulary that most frequently appears in text across disciplines and grade levels, carefully explain strategies for understanding new vocabulary during the different phases of reading (before, during, and after), associate new words with previously known or learned vocabulary, and focus students on key objectives for reading to emphasize clear tasks. With diverse learner needs in mind, the shared reading of short, complex texts is an invaluable opportunity for teachers to stress not only key academic vocabulary but also the understanding of content by analyzing meaning at both the sentence and text levels.

The changes in teaching responsibilities and instruction as identified by the CCSS will present a new set of challenges for secondary teachers and administrators. A comprehensive plan of implementation of the CCSS coupled with adequate ongoing support should be in place so that all teachers have the opportunity to develop their literacy-building skills across the disciplines. Additionally, curriculum should be mapped and aligned to the CCSS in order for teachers to have a usable guide that includes built-in time to conduct close, careful reading with grade-level text.

WHAT IS NOT COVERED IN THE COMMON CORE DOCUMENT

To better understand the implications of the CCSS for academically and linguistically diverse pupils, it is critical that all educators read the Introduction (pp. 3–7) of the *Common Core State Standards for English Language Arts & Literacy in History/Social Studies, Science and Technical Subjects* (2010a), even if their main instructional focus is not teaching English language arts. The beginning pages of the CCSS document contain information not only on the development of the Standards but also on what they are and are not. To this end, we would like to identify the design limitations or clear boundaries of the CCSS. Our main purpose for underscoring these boundaries is to eliminate any misinterpretations about the Standards:

- The CCSS were created to ensure that students are college and career ready. By design, they identify what students should know and be able to do. However, the Standards do not specify any particular curriculum to be taught or the techniques and strategies teachers must use to teach students.
- The Standards describe only the essential skills that must be taught; it is beyond the scope of the CCSS to identify "all that can and should be taught" (*Common Core State Standards*, 2010a, p. 6). Therefore, curriculum that addresses only the Standards, in our estimation, is not a complete curriculum.
- The methods, materials, and instructional interventions necessary to foster academic growth with students who are not yet working at grade level or the nature of assignments for students working above grade-level expectations are not specified by the Standards.
- The instructional supports necessary for English learners or students with disabilities to succeed are not specified by the Standards. In our opinion, teachers must continue to apply research-based strategies, best practices, and appropriate accommodations for working with these student populations while not compromising rigor and relevance.
- The Standards do not address the necessary social, emotional, physical, and cultural growth of students to be college and career ready.

It is clear that the CCSS outline essential skills and guidelines for educators to build curricula. However, they are limited in scope and should not be the sole guide for all that can and should be taught. Furthermore, teachers should be able to maintain a certain sense of autonomy when making instructional decisions concerning what is best for their students to meet with success.

APPLICATION OF THE COMMON CORE TO ADDRESS INDIVIDUAL DIFFERENCES

The structure and organization of the CCSS document can assist teachers to differentiate instruction for diverse learners. All grade-level standards are carefully aligned to a corresponding set of anchor standards. These anchor standards are the same for all grade levels. As a result of this congruence, students who may not yet be able to meet a particular standard on grade level may still develop the same skills and concepts as specified in the same standard on a lower grade level. In this way, teachers may maintain the same or similar lesson objectives for all students yet differentiate their instruction to meet the needs of individual learners.

We strongly believe the Standards are an opportunity for all learners to have access to rigorous curriculum and high-quality instruction, elements that may not have always been present in the teaching of special student populations. Be that as it may, it will not be an easy task for all educators to maintain high expectations and provide essential differentiated and individualized instruction to progress students working below grade level. In support of developing these much needed practices, Tomlinson and Imbeau (2010) identified a set of guidelines, which include the following:

- Teachers have a responsibility to ensure that all their students master important content.
- Teachers have to make specific and continually evolving plans to connect each learner with key content.
- Teachers are required to understand the nature of each of their students, in addition to the nature of the content they teach.
- A flexible approach to teaching "makes room" for student variance.
- Teachers should continually ask, "What does this student need at this moment in order to be able to progress with this key content, and what do I need to do to make it happen?" (p. 15)

As a part of strengthening instructional practices, teachers to some degree must reexamine their overall beliefs about the abilities, strengths, and value of the diverse learners they teach. If these students are perceived as limited, their progress will remain in jeopardy. Similarly, if teachers maintain that diverse learners are an integral part of both their school and overall community, then these students' differences will be celebrated as an opportunity for all stakeholders to learn from their varied cultural viewpoints, their personal struggles, and individual triumphs.

STUDENT DIVERSITY AND TEACHER CHALLENGES

We anticipate that all teachers will be challenged to some degree with the task of identifying, planning, and executing effective instruction to meet the Standards. Coupled with multiple competing initiatives being implemented in districts at the same time, much teacher anxiety about the onset of the CCSS is due to changes in the curriculum, service delivery, program models, instructional practices, adopted program materials, and state as well as local assessments, not to mention teacher evaluation that is tied to student progress. As if it were not overwhelming enough, enter into the mix the needs of special populations of youngsters.

It is certain that classroom practices in light of the Common Core may no longer remain status quo. However, to meet the ever-growing challenges of instructing diverse student groups, teachers can no longer afford to work in isolation. Teachers will need guidance as well as honest feedback on how to scaffold instruction in content-area classes so that struggling readers or those who have not yet gained grade-level academic proficiency in English can have access to complex texts. In addition, they will need support to provide the necessary strategies to assist students to write arguments based on textual evidence texts and teach essential academic vocabulary even though some students have yet to develop basic vocabulary and concepts.

There is little doubt why some teachers are apprehensive about the implementation of the CCSS, particularly with diverse learners. Teachers might perceive that much of the understanding of new initiatives is often left to them to investigate and execute on their own. Furthermore, those who experience a lack of support at the school or district level have great concerns in terms of the necessary resources or training to effectively achieve the Standards. Additionally, they need time to tackle the groundwork for the following:

- Identifying how to meet the grade-level Standards with diverse student populations
- Interpreting what the CCSS mean for severely learning disabled youngsters
- Understanding how to execute the CCSS with emergent bilingual students
- Applying the CCSS to students with interrupted formal education (SIFE)
- Creating CCSS-aligned units of learning for students working below grade level

The key to meeting the multiple challenges of diverse students is true collaboration (DuFour, 2003) in which teachers can engage in honest talk about their practices, take risks to apply new strategies, and foster collective accountability for all student learning. We discuss collaborative practices in greater detail in Chapter 7.

FOCUS ON RESEARCH-BASED STRATEGIES TO ADDRESS LEARNING NEEDS

The implementation of the CCSS is being interpreted in various ways by different state educational agencies, public school districts, private learning institutions, and individual educators. Some interpretations on how to incorporate the Standards into classroom practices may be misguided, especially when applying the Standards to working with diverse learners. It is therefore essential to note that the only course for adequately addressing the CCSS is through the examination and high-quality, rigorous implementation of research-based and evidence-based best practices for special student populations. As a result, we take this opportunity to identify some general guidelines and techniques for best practices in teaching diverse learners as follows:

- Base instruction not only on standards and curriculum but also on evidence of student learning.
- Implement instruction that is systematic and explicit, breaking down complex tasks and teaching with a step-by-step approach.
- Monitor students' progress and identify candidates for small-group instruction or individualized intervention in order to preteach and reteach information, skills, and strategies.
- Develop students' abilities to manage their own learning through organizational techniques (structured guides, graphic organizers, etc.).

- Provide information through alternative formats: audio, video, and multimedia presentations.
- Scaffold speech so that complex sentences and academic vocabulary are supported through the repetition of information using less complex sentences.
- Increase instructional time for students to process information.
- Increase student engagement by having students work in cooperative learning groups.
- Maintain a low-anxiety learning environment.
- Build on students' strengths instead of their perceived deficits.

Additionally, Fisher and Frey (2008) offered their own framework for delivering instruction to enhance student understanding and gradually increase student independence. Their model of structured teaching, based in part on the gradual release of responsibility model (Pearson & Gallagher, 1983), is as follows:

1. Focus lesson: Teachers begin by setting a purpose for the lesson and modeling a skill, strategy, or learning task.

2. Guided instruction: Students have the opportunity to practice alongside the teacher; instruction during this phase of the lesson can be differentiated.

3. Student collaboration: Students work in cooperative learning groups to engage in meaningful activities and problem solve to gain a clearer understanding of the purpose of the lesson.

4. Independent practice: Students are released to work on their own to apply what they have learned.

Classroom instruction that follows this framework provides diverse learners with various structured occasions to be exposed to information, vocabulary, and language practice before having to perform tasks on their own.

CONCLUDING THOUGHTS

Considering current educational trends, the inclusion of diverse learners in mainstream classes is far more likely to increase than decline, and the implementation of the CCSS will no doubt continue to be a challenging and multidimensional task for all educators. However, it is certain that with the onset of the CCSS, there needs to be multiple, collaborative discussions among all stakeholders and agreed-upon actions for how to best prepare teachers to foster success with diverse populations of youngsters—to carefully examine curricula, resources, materials, and classroom practices in order to afford the learning of all students and provide the necessary time and professional development to support teacher learning. To this end, the following chapters offer sets of essential strategies that address each anchor standard that furnish teachers in Grades 6–12 with the necessary tools for addressing the needs of diverse students.

2 Strategies for Academic Language Development

What is it that differentiates students who make it from those who do not? This list is long, but very prominent among the factors is mastery of academic language.

—Lily Wong Fillmore, 2004, p. 3

OVERVIEW

Researchers and practitioners are in agreement: Academic language skills are critical for student success in the content areas (see key resources on this topic at the end of the chapter). In a recent publication, O'Hara, Zwiers, and Pritchard (2012) identified core teaching practices for developing academic language and cautioned that "explicit attention to academic language instruction, coupled with extended opportunities for students to hear and use academic language, is needed in classrooms with English learners and other students who struggle to understand and use the language of school" (p. 1).

Academic language is commonly referred to as the language competence required for students to gain access to and master content taught in English. Connecting it to the Common Core State Standards (CCSS), academic language is the type of abstract and cognitively demanding language students need in order to be ready for college and careers. Along with new concepts and complex information presented in the content areas, students must recognize, internalize, and apply the unique ways language is used in English language arts, math, science, social studies, and all other technical subjects. As such, special attention must be paid to the following:

- Discipline-specific vocabulary
- Phrases and idiomatic expressions associated with the target academic content
- Typical sentence structures used in the lessons
- Grammatical constructs used in academic text
- Text-level features, such as organization and voice

Consider the following sample of linguistic features that will emerge while teaching a unit on the Civil War:

- Discipline-specific vocabulary: *to secede, tariff, state versus national sovereignty, to abolish, emancipation*
- Phrases and idiomatic expressions associated with the target academic content:
  o *Confederate States of America*
  o *Slave-holding South*
  o *Free-labor North*
  o *To enlist in the army*
  o *To strike a blow at the Confederates*
- Typical sentence structures used in the lessons:
  o *The Civil War resulted in almost as many deaths as the total of all other American Wars.*
  o *Slavery could not be abolished where it existed, but it should not be expanded.*
- Grammatical constructs used in academic text:
  o *One in every five military men died*
  o _____*leads to* _____
  o *Being protected by the Constitution*
- Text-level features, such as organization and voice: See the excerpt below for a close reading of Abraham Lincoln's June 26, 1858, speech, especially focusing on organization and rhetorical devices:

A house divided against itself cannot stand. I believe this government cannot endure, permanently half slave and half free. I do not expect the Union to be dissolved—I do not expect the house to fall—but I do expect it will cease to be divided. It will become all one thing or all the other.

(Excerpted from http://www.abrahamlincolnonline.org/lincoln/speeches/house.htm)

Now let's look at some examples of academic language that will have to be considered while teaching a unit on cellular respiration:

- Discipline-specific vocabulary: *glucose, glycolysis, cytoplasm, mitochondrion*
- Phrases and idiomatic expressions associated with the target academic content:
  - *A source of energy; cellular respiration; electron transport chain; lactic acid fermentation; chemical pathways; give off carbon, water, and oxygen*
- Typical sentence structures used in the lessons:
  - *"Cellular respiration is the process that releases energy by breaking down food molecules in the presence of oxygen"* (Miller & Levine, 2003, p. 222).
  - *"Lactic acid is produced in your muscles during rapid exercise when the body cannot supply enough oxygen to the tissues"* (Miller & Levine, 2003, p. 225).
- Grammatical constructs used in academic text:
  - *_____ is followed by _____*
  - *As a result of _____,*
- Text-level features, such as organization and voice: See the excerpt below from a biology text book, which lends itself to examining the use of linguistic markers (bold added) such as signal words, synonyms, pronouns, transition words, examples, and so on, to reveal the internal organization of the paragraph (see boxed explanations).

> **How linguistic markers work:**
>
> *Although* is a transition word connecting this paragraph to the previous one.
>
> *So fast, in just a few milliseconds,* and *besides speed* are all connected as synonyms or examples of the same idea
>
> *Does not require oxygen* is followed by an explanation with two linguistic markers: *this means* and *when oxygen is not available*

Although *the energy yield from glycolysis is small, the process is* **so fast** *that cells can produce thousands of ATP molecules* **in just a few milliseconds.** **Besides speed,** *another advantage is that glycolysis itself* **does not require oxygen.** **This means** *that glycolysis can supply chemical energy to cells* **when oxygen is not available.** (Miller & Levine, 2003, p. 223)

From these examples, it is clearly evident that all teachers are language teachers. Yet it is equally critical to acknowledge what is so astutely stated in the *Application of Common Core State Standards for English Language Learners* (2010) document: "Teachers should recognize that it is possible to achieve the standards for reading and literature, writing and research, language development and speaking and listening without manifesting native-like control of conventions and vocabulary" (para. 2).

For the purposes of this volume, we will use the definition of academic language offered by the World-Class Instructional Design and Assessment Consortium (2011), as follows: "The language required to succeed in school that includes deep understandings of content and communication of that language in the classroom environment. These understandings revolve around specific criteria related to discourse, sentence, and word/phrase levels of language" (p. 1). An overview of the three levels of academic language with their key features is presented in Table 2.1. When teachers are mindful of the complexity of academic language development, they quickly move beyond teaching words in isolation or presented as vocabulary lists; instead, they provide students with multiple, varied, and meaningful learning experiences for understanding, analyzing, and using academic language at the sentence level as well as the text (or discourse) level.

Table 2.1 Levels and Key Features of Academic Language

Level	Key Academic Language Features
Word/Phrase	• General academic words and phrases • Content-specific words and phrases • Collocations, figurative expressions, and multiple-meaning terms • Roots and affixes
Syntax	• Sentence types • Sentence structure, length, and complexity • Transitions/connectives • Verb tenses • Active versus passive voice • Pronouns and references
Text/Discourse	• Organization and text structure • Voice and register • Density • Clarity and coherence

Source: Adapted from O'Hara, S., Zwiers, J., & Pritchard, R. (2013). *Framing the development of complex language and literacy.* Retrieved from http://complexlanguage.org/sites/default/files/pictures/cln_brief.pdf

WHY DIVERSE ADOLESCENT LEARNERS NEED EXPLICIT INSTRUCTION IN ACADEMIC LANGUAGE

Diverse secondary students may have difficulties with developing academic language skills attributable to a range of out-of-school factors. Some adolescent learners are not completely familiar with Standard American English either because their families speak a dialect other than standard English or they may come from homes where little or no English is spoken. Poverty may limit access to out-of-school learning opportunities that incorporate more formal language use, examples of which may include visiting museums and art exhibits or attending theater performances and other cultural events. Thus, some of those students coming from low-income families with parents who sometimes also have limited formal education might be at a disadvantage; they may lack the background knowledge and firsthand, personally relevant learning experiences that can serve as a stepping stone for acquiring complex academic language. In addition, some students with disabilities are speech and language impaired and may also struggle with expressing their ideas, which can impede their learning in a less academically supportive environment.

Regardless of linguistic or scholastic abilities, most, if not all, adolescent learners belong to the *iGeneration* (Rosen, 2011). To a great extent, their lives have been shaped by technology, by "being online, using computers offline, listening to music, playing video games, talking on the telephone, instant messaging, texting, sending and receiving e-mail, and watching television" (p. 12). Due to the informal nature of these activities, schools play an even more essential role in teaching the formal, academic language critical for students to begin and successfully stay on a college and career path.

What are the central features of academic language? According to Snow (2010), they include "grammatical embeddings, sophisticated and abstract vocabulary, precision of word choice, and use of nominalizations to refer to complex processes" (p. 452), all of which are used in texts in science, social studies, and the technical subjects to express complex ideas efficiently. When discussing younger learners' literacy development, Olson and Torrance (2009) observed that

> children enter school with different linguistic, sociolinguistic, and pragmatic experiences, and not all of them have been exposed to the forms of communication valued at school. Strategies to make children feel comfortable in expressing who they are and what they bring to school should be at the core of any instructional program. At the same time, schools have the moral obligation to provide all

children with equal opportunities to participate in the discourse of academics that is a requisite for later academic success. (p. 129)

Within the secondary school context, students may be provided with more opportunities to develop receptive language skills—to aid them in comprehending discipline-specific academic English by listening to presentations or teacher-directed lessons or reading complex text. However, they also need to build their productive language skills by speaking in complete sentences, generating well-constructed paragraphs, and creating longer academic texts both orally and in writing that emulate key academic text features. Baker (2002), a Boston vocational high school English teacher, poignantly explained that her students, as do most Americans, need at least three forms of the English language—or need to be trilingual—to lead socially fulfilling and economically viable lives:

- "home" English or dialect, which most students learn at home, and recent immigrants often learn from peers, and which for first and second generation immigrants may be a combination of English and their mother tongue
- "formal" or academic English, which is learned by many in school, from reading, and from the media, although it may also be learned in well-educated families
- "professional" English, the particular language of one's profession, which is mostly learned in college or on the job, or . . . in vocational education. (pp. 51–52)

After a careful examination of textbooks written for elementary, middle, and high school students, Fang, Schleppegrell, and Cox (2006) concluded that "explicit, shared knowledge about the way language works can help students better handle academic texts" (p. 269) and engage them in academic discourse that is unlike the home language or home dialect, thus making its acquisition rather challenging for many.

In sum, students need both explicit instruction in academic language and sustained, meaningful opportunities to continue to acquire and develop essential language skills independently to be ready for life, college, and careers.

CORE LANGUAGE AND VOCABULARY STRATEGIES

The strategies we present in this chapter are aligned to the expectations of the six College and Career Readiness Anchor Standards (CCRAS) for Language (see Box 2.1). They are framed by the CCRAS strand-specific sets of *Conventions of Standard English, Knowledge and Application of*

Language, and *Vocabulary Acquisition and Use.* We must acknowledge that the language standards are found in the final section of the CCSS document following the reading, writing, and speaking and listening standards; however, when we focus on developing diverse learners' English language arts skills, we recognize the importance of discussing academic language prior to the four literacy skills. Not only do we place special emphasis on the language standards by putting them in a prominent place (Chapter 2), we will also present specific strategies to support the six language standards that address the needs of English learners as well as those who may come from bilingual or bidialectal homes, live in communities where a vernacular dialect of English is spoken, have learning disabilities that impact on standard academic language development and use, or may not use standard American English consistently.

Box 2.1 College and Career Readiness Anchor Standards for Language (CCRASL)

Conventions of Standard English

1. Demonstrate command of the conventions of standard English grammar and usage when writing or speaking.

2. Demonstrate command of the conventions of standard English capitalization, punctuation, and spelling when writing.

Knowledge and Application of Language

3. Apply knowledge of language to understand how language functions in different contexts, to make effective choices for meaning or style, and to comprehend more fully when reading or listening.

Vocabulary Acquisition and Use

4. Determine or clarify the meaning of unknown and multiple-meaning words and phrases by using context clues, analyzing meaningful word parts, and consulting general and specialized reference materials, as appropriate.

5. Demonstrate understanding of word relationships and nuances in word meanings.

6. Acquire and use accurately a range of general academic and domain-specific words and phrases sufficient for reading, writing, speaking, and listening at the college and career readiness level; demonstrate independence in gathering vocabulary knowledge when encountering an unknown term important to comprehension or expression.

From each of the six CCRAS for Language, we derived and aligned a series of related *Anchor Performances*—skill sets that all students need to develop—and suggest strategies to help diverse students build these skills in order to meet the language standards. Some strategies may be more appropriate than others depending upon the grade levels, language proficiency levels, challenges or learning difficulties students face, or learning disabilities they may have.

Conventions of Standard English

Anderson (2005) noted that grammar instruction must be intentional, integrated, and carefully planned. To facilitate this planning process, we created a *Grammar Lesson Planning Checklist* presented in Table 2.2, which teachers may use not only for lesson planning but for self-assessment or reflection purposes as well. It is especially critical to accept this challenge because of the changing focus of grammar instruction from grade to grade as presented in subsequent sections of this chapter.

Anchor Performance 1: Apply the Conventions of English Grammar and Usage in Writing and Speaking.

As students enter each secondary grade, they will find that special emphasis is placed on a different aspect of standard English grammar and usage. The focus of Grade 6 instruction is predominantly on proper pronoun usage; students in Grade 7 will be expected to explain and correctly

Table 2.2 Grammar Lesson Planning Checklist

Will my lesson provide:	✓
1. A simple explanation of the grammar point at issue?	☐
2. Students' immersion in correct models of grammar?	☐
3. A demonstration of the particular pattern in a piece of writing (model texts)?	☐
4. Multiple meaningful activities for better understanding of the grammar point?	☐
5. Examples posted in the classroom/posted online/incorporated in handouts and other resources?	☐
6. Ample student practice to apply new grammar knowledge?	☐
7. Time for students to edit their own writing?	☐

choose among phrases, clauses, and sentence types ranging from simple to compound and complex sentences. In Grade 8, the focus shifts to correct verb usage, whereas in Grades 9–10, sentence structure is revisited at a higher level to ensure that students use varied phrases and clauses with a specific intention in their writing or oral presentations. Finally, in Grades 11–12, students will apply the understanding that usage is "a matter of convention, can change over time, and is sometimes contested" (*Common Core State Standards*, 2010a, p. 54); when needed, they will use reference materials to amend or revise complex or contested usage.

Essential Strategy to Support Anchor Performance 1: Grammar Connections

The purpose of the next section is to present research-based strategies that connect grammar to subject matter texts, to literature and mentor texts, and to students' authentic experiences with varied linguistic input.

Sentence Dissection. Although sentences are no longer diagrammed, sentence-level language analysis can be helpful for diverse learners. Anderson (2005) publicly identified himself as a *sentence stalker*—using a phrase he borrowed from Spandel (2005)—and noted that he is "always on the lookout for great mentor texts, sentences, paragraphs, essays, articles, advertisements, and novels" (p. 17). During a structured session of no longer than eight to ten minutes a few times a week, offer students exposure to and guided exploration of a carefully selected, sufficiently complex sentence (or two). It is best if the excerpt comes from a text you are using for literacy or content-based instruction and is loaded with information as well as opportunities for discussing grammar and usage.

Teachers we worked with selected a range of different type of sentences for dissection, varying both by length and complexity. They followed these steps with a fair amount of individual variances based on their students' needs:

1. Selected a sentence from the target textbook or other assigned readings

2. Presented the sentence on chart paper, traditional blackboard, document camera, or SMART Board

3. Facilitated an in-depth discussion of what the sentence meant and how the author expressed his or her idea, inviting student input into meaning making first

4. Asked probing questions—about the deep structure and meaning or the *who, what, when,* and *where* of the sentence

5. Pinpointed one or more unique linguistic features of the sentence (passive voice, relative clauses, heavy noun phrases) to call students' attention to select language complexities

6. Used color coding or other visually engaging methods to chunk the sentence into clauses or phrases

7. Employed think alouds as they called attention to grammatical or stylistic choices in some (but not *all* of the) language chunks to keep the activity brief and engaging

8. Invited students to use the sentence as mentor text and to create similar sentences of their own to be able to internalize the language complexity, which is a key follow-up activity

The first sentence dissected in Table 2.3 is excerpted from a social studies text, and the second one analyzed in Table 2.4 is from a science journal article.

Although the sentence in Table 2.3 was short and relatively easy to comprehend, it contained a frequently appearing, challenging feature of academic English (a heavy noun phrase) that proved to be ideal for an introductory-level sentence dissection exercise. The sentence also served as mentor text when students produced heavy noun phrases similar to the example—*The first state to call for a vote on the Constitution . . .*:

Table 2.3 A Dissected Sentence From a Social Studies Textbook

Sentence: *"The first state to call for a vote on the Constitution was Delaware"* (Harcourt Horizons, 2003, p. 367).

Sentence Chunk	Possible Discussion Points	Linguistic Features
The first state to call	Let's reverse the word order. Can you finish this sentence starter: *Delaware was the first state to . . .*	Infinitive following a noun phrase
(call) for a vote	What does *"call for a vote"* mean?	Phrasal verb: *"call for"* *a vote*
(a vote) on the Constitution	*"Vote"* can be a verb and a noun. Which one is it in this sentence? Can we also say: What did they vote on?	Prepositional phrase: *"on the Constitution"*
was Delaware.	How do we know the entire phrase *"The first state to call for a vote on the Constitution"* is the subject of this sentence?	Heavy noun phrase

The first thing to do in case of a hurricane emergency is . . .

The first member of my family to go to college was . . .

The first step to take after a car accident is . . .

Sentence dissection can be performed on all text types on all grade levels. It is especially important to apply this strategy to content-based, academic text so students can gradually become independent readers of textbooks and other high-density, more complex informational texts. Introducing English language learners (ELLs) to one "juicy sentence" a day based on a shared text is a similar strategy also promoted by Fillmore (2009).

Table 2.4   A Dissected Sentence From a *Science News* Article

Sentence: *"Newly discovered viruses may be at fault in a disease that causes snakes to regurgitate their food, behave strangely, and even twist themselves into knots"* (Saey, 2012, p. 2).

Sentence Chunk	Possible Discussion Points	Linguistic Features
Newly discovered viruses	What kind of viruses is this sentence discussing?	Past participle used as an adjective (*discovered*) Collocation (words that frequently go together): *newly discovered*
may be at fault in a disease	Why is the author saying "may be" and *not* "are" or "must be"? How do you say "be at fault" in conversational English?	Auxiliary verbs to express degrees of certainty (*may* vs. *might* vs. *could* vs. *must*) Prepositional phrases: "at fault, in a disease"
that causes snakes to	What does *that* refer to in this sentence?	Defining relative clause introduced by the pronoun *that*
regurgitate their food, behave strangely, and even twist themselves into knots.	What are the three action verbs? How does the author use parallel structure in this sentence and why?	Parallel sentence structure; Tricolon (three items listed as examples)

Real Grammar, Real Life. The secondary school is a place for a range of extracurricular activities that often support learning academic language in their own unique ways: Going on field trips, participating in clubs, joining sport teams, running fundraisers for a good cause, or completing community service are just a few of these experiences. As a supplement or alternative to traditional grammar practice exercises, we suggest turning these authentic experiences into meaningful opportunities to learn about grammar rules as they apply to real situations. Have students analyze the posters and flyers created by clubs and sports teams for grammar points. Invite them to be critical readers of the school newspaper and make editorial suggestions for improvement. For example, students can analyze the possessive noun phrase (*Girls' and Boys' Friendships*) used in the title as opposed to in the first sentence of the following high school newspaper article and compare and contrast the two versions to decide which is correct (see Box 2.2).

Box 2.2 Excerpt From a High School Newspaper

The Gender Divide: A Look Into the Differences Between Girls' and Boys' Friendships
Stereotypes pervade girl's and boy's friendships at every age. Whether its elementary school when girls bond over dolls and drawing pictures, or middle school when boys associate themselves with the sport they play, there are certain notions that seem to hold true.

Excerpt from a March 15, 2013 article printed in the *Inklings* available at http://www.inklingsnews .com/b/2013/03/15/the-gender-divide-a-look-into-the-differences-between-girls-and-boys-friendships/

Anchor Performance 2: Apply the Conventions of Punctuation and Spelling When Writing.

As students progress from Grade 6 to Grade 12, the expectations for knowing how to spell words is consistently incorporated in the standards; however, how to use punctuation conventions of English and what types of punctuation marks students should be able to use correctly become incrementally more challenging. The following strategies are designed for acquiring and practicing the conventions of writing at the secondary level.

Essential Strategy to Support Anchor Performance 2: Hands-On Work With Words Using Reference Materials and Mentor Texts

Students must participate in meaningful, age-appropriate, engaging activities of increasing complexity. Authentic materials, reference books, and online resources will contribute to such learning opportunities.

Resourcing. To assist students with their spelling, provide them with explicit instruction on how to access and use available print resources; create regular opportunities to enhance their skills to be efficient and successful with reference materials such as monolingual and bilingual print and online dictionaries, glossaries, and other reference books. Some suggestions may include (a) scanning a dictionary page to develop ease of dictionary use, (b) exploring long entries and multiple meanings given for a word, and (c) searching for sample sentences given for correct usage. In addition to dictionaries, Rothstein, Rothstein, and Lauber (2007) suggested that middle schools and high schools provide the following types of materials to support successful writing programs:

- Books of word histories and origins
- Style manuals
- Globes and maps
- Alphabetical thesauri and topic thesauri
- Books of concise biographies
- Appropriate magazines, periodicals, and newspapers

Personal Dictionaries or Word Study Books. Turn a blank notebook or small spiral notebook into either an alphabetized personal dictionary or a subject-matter word study book by inserting appropriate tabs. Have students collect their own general academic words and phrases (ones that all disciplines use, such as *determine, categorize,* and *conclusion*) and discipline-specific words that are unique to each subject matter (such as *photosynthesis* and *ecosystem* in science; *equilateral* and *equiangular* in math; *imagery* and *personification* in English; and *indigenous people* and *manufactured goods* in social studies). Students develop ownership of the spelling and meaning of the words by doing one or more of the following: writing each target word, visualizing it, lifting a line from the text where the word was used, and using it in multiple meaningful ways, such as putting it into their own sentences. For additional activities to use with target words, see Chapter 3, *Word Analysis Framework.*

Mentor Texts. Mentor texts may be aligned to a range of core standards and anchor performances (also see Chapter 5 on writing). When students are asked to examine a mentor text for use of writing mechanics such as punctuation, they see an authentic example of how and where the author chose to insert a colon as opposed to a semicolon or use a dash instead of a comma. When grammar and mechanics are taught in the context of authentic reading and writing tasks, students learn how authors of fiction and nonfiction use language effectively to achieve their goals. An engaging way to use authentic literature is to explore one of the CCSS readings that more explicitly lend themselves to examining punctuation as well as offer teaching opportunities about a range of grammar points and conventions of English. See Box 2.3 for target texts we recommend—each representing carefully selected excerpts from the exemplar texts listed in Appendix B of the Common Core State Standards (*Common Core State Standards*, 2010c).

Box 2.3 Mentor Texts for Teaching Grammatical Conventions

Grades 6–8

Roll of Thunder, Hear My Cry by Mildred Taylor (1976)

The Diary of Anne Frank by Frances Goodrich and Albert Hackett (1958)

I, Too, Sing America by Langston Hughes (1925)

"Letter on Thomas Jefferson" by John Adams (1776)

Blood, Toil, Tears and Sweat: Address to the Parliament by Winston Churchill (1940)

Grades 9–10

The Book Thief by Marcus Zusak (2005)

In the Time of the Butterflies by Julia Alvarez (1994)

I Know Why the Caged Bird Sings by Maya Angelou (1969)

"I Have a Dream"—Address at the March on Washington by Martin Luther King Jr. (1963/1992)

"Hope, Despair and Memory"—Nobel Prize Acceptance Speech by Elie Wiesel (1986)

Grades 11–12

The Adventures of Augie March by Saul Bellow (1953)

The Namesake by Jhumpa Lahiri (2003)

"Song of Myself" from *Leaves of Grass* by Walt Whitman (c1860)

Mother Tongue by Amy Tan (1990)

The Tipping Point: How Little Things Can Make a Big Difference by Malcolm Gladwell (2002)

Knowledge and Application of Language

The grade-specific standard for knowledge and application of language shows a clear progression. In Grade 6, students are expected to use varied sentence patterns, but by Grade 7, students will make conscious choices of language patterns. In Grade 8, active and passive voice as well as the conditional and subjunctive mood is to be used. In high school, the expectations grow even higher: Students in Grades 9–10 are to adhere to the guidelines of a specific style manual based on the content area (APA or MLA). Finally, in Grades 11–12, students will vary their syntax to show affect and will consult appropriate style guides to further enhance their writing. As so accurately noted by Giouroukakis and Connelly (2012),

> The scaffolded nature of the grade-specific CCSS would please Bloom. In Grades 6–8, students are developing their *understanding* of specific elements of language (sentence variation, word choice, voice). They *apply* their understanding of language to a given context in Grades 9–10 and they *synthesize* their style with style choices recommended in reference guides in Grades 11–12. (p. 154)

Anchor Performance 3: Understand and Use Language in Different Genres and Styles

Diverse adolescent learners need exposure to language used in a variety of ways and in a variety of contexts—formally and informally, in written and spoken formats, and in varied genres and situations. If students internalize the knowledge they have about how language functions in different contexts, they are likely to comprehend more fully when reading and listening or to make more effective choices when speaking and writing.

Essential Strategy to Support Anchor Performance 3: Integrate Multiple Language Skills (Listening, Speaking, Reading, and/or Writing) Meaningfully and Intentionally

Students' knowledge and understanding of how language is used in various contexts will increase by listening to and reading texts in a variety of styles. At the same time, such understanding must be transferred to actual opportunities for students to produce language by making not only the grammatically correct word-, sentence-, and text-level choices but also by making the most appropriate and powerful choices for words and sentence structures when speaking and writing.

Read It, Speak, It, Write It. One effective way for students to recognize and use varied sentence structures is by reading target texts with appropriate complexity, selecting sample sentences as mentor texts, and encouraging students to create original sentences that parallel the target sentence structure. This activity reinforces for students that careful examination of what they read can help improve their speaking and writing. Among others, Oczkus (2007) also recognized the importance of borrowing from authors: "When students study the textual patterns in fiction and nonfiction, first analyzing and then borrowing another author's organizational pattern or word choice, their writing improves" (p. xiv). At the elementary level, using patterned writing and patterned speech are more commonly accepted practices; at the secondary level, sentence patterns can also be recognized both in fiction and nonfiction with the intention of helping academically and linguistically diverse learners become familiar with the way

(a) words are strung together to make meaning,

(b) verb tense is used appropriately,

(c) parts of speech fit together, and

(d) simple, compound, and complex sentences are formed.

We invite our readers to be *sentence pattern detectives* to introduce the strategy of *Read It, Speak It, Write It* into their teaching. The following sentences all represent selections from exemplar texts discussed in the Appendix B of the CCSS (*Common Core State Standards,* 2010c). Each quotation is followed by a sentence frame that may serve as inspiration or mentor text for students to complete on their own:

> "What they don't understand about birthdays and what they never tell you is that when you're eleven, you're also ten, and nine, and eight, and seven, and six, and five, and four, and three, and two, and one." (Cisneros, Sandra. "Eleven." In *Woman Hollering Creek and Other Stories.* New York: Random House, 1991. *Common Core State Standards,* 2010c, p. 87).

Students can use the following sentence frame borrowed from Cisneros to discuss their own experiences of being an adolescent, a member of a sports team, a new driver with a fresh permit, or any other challenges they face:

> *What they don't understand about* _____ *and what they never tell you is that* _____.

Here is another target sentence, this time representing a nonfiction selection.

"Despite his dramatic beginning, Vincent had an ordinary child-hood, giving no hint of the painter he would become." (Greenberg, Jan, and Sandra Jordan. *Vincent Van Gogh: Portrait of an Artist*. New York: Random House, 2001. From Chapter 1: "A Brabant Boy 1853–75." *Common Core State Standards*, 2010c, p. 94)

As students research and write about historical figures, politicians running for office in the election, artists, or any other actual person, they might start their biographical account using the following frame:

_____ *had an ordinary beginning, giving no hint of the* _____ *(s)he would become.*

In yet another example, Zusak's (2005) text can be used to help students describe what actions a character they choose to write about wants to take using vivid language:

"Apart from everything else, the book thief wanted desperately to go back to the basement, to write, or read through her story one last time." (Zusak, Marcus. *The Book Thief*. New York: Knopf, 2005. *Common Core State Standards*, 2010c, p. 110)

Apart from everything else, _____ *wanted to* _____*, to* _____*, or* _____ *one last time.*

A possible extension of this activity is to expose students to longer, more complex texts and engage them in more in-depth discussions about the same topic. Students can compare a news report on TV with a news article online or a newspaper or magazine article with a podcast about the same current event.

Text Analysis. Work through carefully selected text to complete the four-quadrant graphic organizer adapted from Gottlieb (2011) in Figure 2.1. Start by using a paragraph excerpted from the target text and build up to longer units of reading as the school year progresses. Identify the overall purpose of the text; highlight the key words and phrases that give the main idea of the selection and/or are essential for understanding the authors' message; focus on a few, select sentence-level grammatical features such as verb tense usage, active-passive voice; and finally, examine the overall characteristics of the text with special attention to transitional words or other linguistic markers that help identify the text type or genre. This activity supports the development of metalinguistic awareness about

Figure 2.1 Text Analysis Grid

The Overall Purpose	Key Words and Phrases
Grammatical Forms	Genre or Text Type

a text and the craft of writing; thus students will focus not only on what is being said but on how it is being said in the text.

To enhance your knowledge of standard American English grammar for instructional purposes, see recommended resources at the end of the chapter.

Theme Reading, Theme Listening Across Genres. Supporting several other Common Core standards, this strategy shows students how writing style changes when they read or listen to a range of resources about a topic represented by various genres. To address this Common Core language standard, compare how authors chose to write about a shared theme—using words and sentences as well as text-level organization—while operating within the framework of their chosen genres. In Box 2.4, see a collection of our favorite resources on the topics of *Evolution* and *The Great Depression*.

Box 2.4 Theme Reading/Listening Collection on Evolution and the Great Depression

On Evolution

PBS NOVA (http://www.pbs.org/wgbh/nova/evolution/):

- 18 articles
- 3 audio slide shows
- 7 audio stories
- 12 interactive digital tools and presentations
- 13 interviews
- 6 short videos

On the Great Depression

The History Channel (http://www.history.com/topics/great-depression):

- 21 videos
- 7 speeches
- 5 photo galleries
- 1 interactive digital tool

The Library of Congress (http://www.loc.gov/teachers/classroommaterials/themes/great-depression/):

- 2 primary source sets (specific artifacts such as photographs, posters, recorded music and other sound files, song lyrics, manuscripts and maps)
- 10 lesson plans
- 24 multimedia resources (including expert presentations, exhibitions, bibliographies, webcasts, and other online materials)

Vocabulary Acquisition and Use

Successful vocabulary learning and accurate vocabulary use in all content areas are considered strong predictors of academic success. Determining or clarifying the meaning of unknown words, deciphering multiple word meanings, using context clues, identifying and analyzing meaningful word parts, and consulting general and specialized reference materials are among the most daunting tasks that linguistically and academically diverse students face on a daily basis.

The challenge of working with difficult academic words is exacerbated by what Zwiers (2008) also described as a tendency in teacher practices: "Teachers sometimes do two things: (1) they do not use enough academic language when they model and scaffold content-area thinking and doing, and, (2) they too often accept oral and written responses that are not sufficiently academic in nature" (p. 50). Thus, students are not exposed to rigorous academic language, nor are they expected to use it consistently. For language to develop and flourish among diverse secondary learners, it must be recognized as a powerful tool that needs purposeful attention in all content areas by all teachers.

For over a decade, Beck, McKeown, and Kucan's (2002) publication *Bringing Words to Life* has been frequently cited both to provide a rationale for and also to create a manageable framework for robust vocabulary instruction. Some of the strategies presented next build on their suggestions, whereas others represent additional researchers' and practitioners' recommendations. Our work is informed by a range of scholars, among whom are Nagy and Townsend (2012), who recently noted that "vocabulary learning must occur in authentic contexts, with students having many opportunities to learn how target words interact with, garner meaning from, and support meanings of other words" (p. 98).

As students move through the secondary grades, the CCSS expectations for vocabulary acquisition and use remain consistent yet also become incrementally more challenging. Students will be expected to determine or clarify the meaning of unknown and multiple-meaning words and phrases based on the grade-appropriate reading *and content* and will choose flexibly from among the same set of strategies as required by the target learning outcomes. Also reflective of the increasing complexity of learning at each grade level, students are expected to demonstrate understanding of more challenging figurative language, word relationships, and nuances in word meanings. Finally, in support of the grade-level curricula, secondary students must acquire and use accurately both general academic and domain-specific words and phrases as well as build vocabulary knowledge to determine the importance of a word or phrase for comprehension or expression.

Anchor Performance 4: Determine or Clarify the Meaning of Unknown and Multiple-Meaning Words and Phrases Using a Variety of Strategies

Learning new words and figuring out word meaning often present an added challenge for struggling learners. If they are less than fluent speakers or competent readers in English, context clues and contextual understanding may not be as effective as they are for more proficient speakers and readers. Thus, scaffolding vocabulary acquisition and creating multiple meaningful opportunities to encounter and to actively use robust vocabulary should be a primary goal, closely followed by word-learning strategies that foster independent, self-directed academic language acquisition.

Essential Strategy Support Anchor Performance 4: Use Visual and Contextual Support

Pictures ranging from ad hoc line drawings to magnificent photographs, from quick sketches to intricate illustrations found in professional publications may all offer an appropriate context and much needed visual support for new and difficult words. Showing brief video clips and presenting realia (the real object you are teaching about) may further enhance students' understanding of complex word meanings. Additionally, providing a variety of authentic contexts in which the target words are used will lead to the type of rich instruction that gives students numerous meaningful experiences with the words.

Picture It. Marzano and Pickering (2005) suggested that "when you ask students to construct a picture, symbol or graphic representation of a term, they are forced to think of the term in a totally different way" (p. 21). When students are learning about various discipline-specific concepts and words—such as the digestive system, animal and plant cells, greenhouse effect—have them generate their own illustrations, with the expectation that the drawings are likely to look similar. On the other hand, when exploring big concepts—democracy, freedom, global economy, biodiversity—each student's conceptualization may vary considerably. These drawings can be used to spark rich conversations and lend themselves to opportunities for academic language use as part of classroom discourse. Student-created illustrations (with appropriate guidance and scaffolding) will contribute to internalizing word meaning while engaging learners in a multimodal task.

Student-Friendly Definitions and Concept Maps. The definition of *outrageous* as "exceeding the limits of what is usual" *or* "not conventional or matter-of-fact" as found in an online dictionary is *outrageously* difficult for struggling learners. Why? These dictionary definitions use sentence fragments and synonyms that would need to be defined and explained, so they are just as difficult as the target word. Presenting definitions to students written in an accessible, student-friendly way and then letting them use their own words to define new concepts is expected to lead to greater access and greater retention. So what would be a student-friendly definition of *outrageous*? Let's try this:

> *When something is outrageous, it shocks you. You can hardly believe it has happened. For example, if someone had broken into the school and vandalized the main office, that would be outrageous.*

When student-friendly definitions are augmented with visual or graphic support such as a concept map (Figure 2.2), a fourfold vocabulary tool (Figure 2.3), or the four-square Frayer model (Figure 2.4), the connections and associations that go with the target word will also be more readily revealed. (A resource for the guided use of the Frayer model is given at the end of this chapter.)

Look Inside and Outside of the Word. We are inspired by Frey and Fisher's (2009) framework for learning words "inside and out." To look *inside* a word, direct students to identify root words, prefixes, suffixes, or word parts of compound words they recognize. Invite them to also look

Figure 2.2 Concept Map for the Word *Health*

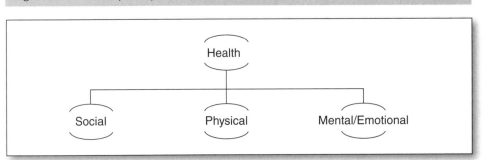

Figure 2.3 Fourfold Vocabulary Template

Word	Definition	Picture	Sentence

Figure 2.4 Frayer Diagram

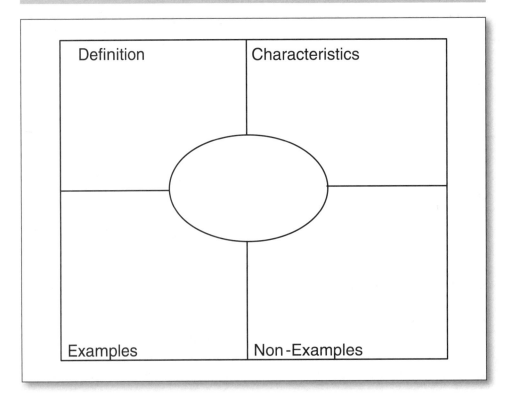

outside the word and try to figure out the meaning from the sentence or paragraph where they came across the word or look for any illustrations or other visuals that could help. Another take on the inside-outside strategy is to examine how the word is used inside the context of the subject matter or literacy task as opposed to outside in the students' own out-of-school, authentic experiences if applicable. For example, try the *Inside-Outside* strategy on non-subject-specific academic words, such as *conclusion*.

Anchor Performance 5: Recognize Word Relationships, Figurative Language, and Nuances in Word Meanings

Knowledge and application of vocabulary gets increasingly complicated when complex word relationships are introduced in each consecutive secondary grade or when more figurative language is used in ELA and other content-area classes. With increased text complexity facing learners in every discipline, they will need to be able to recognize or define nuances in word meanings to understand the target content.

Essential Strategy to Support Anchor Performance 5: Active Engagement With Challenging Language Segments Presented in Context

Although ELLs and at-risk students need support and scaffolding and although they highly benefit when difficult academic content is made accessible, teachers should not shy away from exposing them to the complexity of the English language. Diverse learners cannot afford to have less-than-robust language learning opportunities. Instead, they need engaging explorations of meaningful language segments as well as exposure to the complexity of carefully chosen whole text selections. Betsy Gennosa, AIS teacher in Sagamore Middle School, New York, understands that students participating in academic intervention services (AIS) need a lot of support, so she pairs a complex text with a simple text on the same topic. Once the concepts are gained through the simpler reading, students are ready to work with more rigorous language.

Word Sorts. Depending on the objective of the lesson, frequently engage students in sorting activities, in which they need to match single words or phrases to preestablished categories. Similar to a word sort, Fisher, Frey, and Rothenberg (2008) suggested expanding task-to-concept sorting and have students sort larger language chunks or even sentences into categories that relate to the concept they are studying. Using SMART Board technology gives a high-tech twist to tactile learning, although sorting words that are written on index cards or placed in a T-chart will also do. Students may contribute to a shared wiki page (i.e., wikispaces.com) to document the outcomes of their word or concept sorts. Since word relationships may range from synonyms and antonyms to whole and part, from parts of speech to idioms, each of these relationships may lend themselves to sorting activities across the curriculum.

Anchor Performance 6: Acquire and Use Accurately a Range of General Academic and Domain-Specific Words and Phrases

To be on the path to college and career readiness, students in all grades need to build and accurately use a range of general academic and content-based words and phrases. However, Goldenberg and Coleman (2010) noted that learning content-area matter would require students to acquire and use the specific register (language for a particular purpose) associated with that subject, going beyond the vocabulary unique to the content taught. In another publication, Coleman and Goldenberg (2010) emphasized that "students may know the meanings of individual content-specific words, yet still not be able to understand the larger meaning when reading them in a sentence or be able to combine them to write a sentence" (p. 62) or produce even longer, more complex oral or written responses to content-based prompts. If students have the opportunity to use the language beyond giving single-word or short-phrase answers, they are more likely to develop ownership of it.

Essential Strategy to Support Anchor Performance 6: Deconstructing and Reconstructing Academic Language

In-depth understanding is needed of not only word-level but also sentence- and text-level complexities that characterize general academic language use as well as content-specific language use. Linguistically and academically diverse students need explicit guidance in examining language as it works in the various content areas, taking language apart to see how the micro- and macrolevel pieces fit together, and then also have the opportunity to use the language in appropriate contexts.

Vocabulary Self-Assessment. The acquisition of new vocabulary occurs gradually, and students often have varying degrees of understanding with certain words. Raising awareness about word knowledge is a complex task, but it can be made accessible to all learners with this strategy. This self-assessment tool can help focus students' attention on the target vocabulary necessary for understanding the general concept of a text. You can

Figure 2.5 Vocabulary Self-Assessment Tool

Vocabulary	My Knowledge of Key Words			
	I have never heard of it	I have heard of it, I think I know what it means	I know it very well	I can tell or write a sentence with it

start by sharing and regularly using the Vocabulary Self-Assessment Tool in Figure 2.5, which is a simplified version of a classic by Isabel Beck and colleagues (Beck, McKeown, & Kucan, 2008).

Tiered Vocabulary Instruction. Since the work of Beck and her colleagues' (2002, 2008), a conceptualization of vocabulary that became fairly well-known is the following three-tier model:

Tier 1: Basic words that are often recognized and used with ease by most native speakers of English (e.g., *book, girl, happy, he,* etc.). ELLs may face a special challenge and need strategic vocabulary instruction also targeting these words.

Tier 2: General academic words that tend to be more complex and polysemous (having multiple meanings). Some of these words travel across content areas (e.g., *origin, system, table*) and have different meanings, whereas others perform similar textual or discourse level functions regardless of the content (e.g., *therefore, albeit, nevertheless*).

Tier 3: Domain-specific words and less commonly used words that are critical for understanding the subject matter of the instruction (e.g., *photosynthesis, circumference, polytheistic*). New content can be acquired only if these Tier 3 words are clearly understood and internalized by the students.

The ultimate purpose of this type of categorization goes beyond merely identifying the level of complexity or challenge certain words will pose. Instead, teachers can make important instructional decisions based on this categorization and commit to building students' Tier 2 vocabulary across the content areas to offer the most access to critical words that afford students the opportunity to comprehend a wide range of texts.

Frontload, Embed, and Blend. Carr, Sexton, and Lagunoff (2006) suggested a different way of grouping target vocabulary words. They recommend that teachers first frontload strategically selected words that are appropriate to engage students but may be successfully taught without the context of the lesson. Next, teachers should introduce lesson-embedded words while students are involved in reading a target text such as a textbook, participating in a hands-on learning activity such as conducting an experiment, or listening to the teacher presenting a minilecture. And finally, they also encourage teachers to blend vocabulary instruction by introducing new words "during front-loading, when common definitions and examples from students' prior knowledge are addressed; then during content instruction, they are revisited and refined with scientific definitions" (pp. 47–48).

Chunk It! Teaching and practicing language chunks rather than isolated words helps students see how collocations are formed in English (i.e., how certain words go together to create a larger unit of meaning). When teaching the word *according*, it makes much more sense to present examples of language chunks such as *according to the author, according to the first paragraph*, and *according to the title* in context. Phrasal verbs (e.g., *get in, get over, get back, get ahead,*) pose a challenge for linguistically diverse students, so special attention to contextualizing and offering a sentence chunk where and how these words are used can be especially helpful. Consider keeping a Chunk It! chart displayed in class that keeps a record of language chunks discussed in class and is available for students to add language chunks they find in their reading.

Modal Magic. A modal is an auxiliary verb (e.g., *can, could, may, might, should, must*) that subtly changes the meaning of phrases, sentences, or the entire text. For this strategy, select a sentence from students' reading that contains a modal auxiliary verb. Consider the following example from American President Lyndon B. Johnson's address on the issue of civil rights to a joint session of Congress delivered in Washington, DC, on March 15, 1965 (www.americanrhetoric.com):

Every American citizen **must** *have an equal right to vote.*

Display the sentence and discuss with students what it means considering the context of the speech. Next, hand out different modal auxiliary words on index cards to pairs of students (see Box 2.5). Ask them to rewrite the selected sentence with the new auxiliary word and discuss with their partners if and how the meaning of the sentence had changed. Have students report out their findings to the class. Further discuss with the whole class what the impact on civil rights movement might have been had President Johnson chosen to use a different modal auxiliary verb in his speech.

Box 2.5 Modal Auxiliary Verbs

can   could   may   might   shall   should   will   would   need to

ought to   has to   have to   got to   used to   had better

be supposed to   be allowed to   be able to

Make Me Passive. This strategy helps students to understand the derivation and meaning of information expressed in the passive voice. Begin with a piece of text the students are reading, and model for students how sentences may be changed into the passive voice. After guided and collaborative practice, have students try it on their own. Figure 2.6 is an example of a completed *Make Me Passive* activity.

Figure 2.6 *Make Me Passive Sample*

Original Text	Passive Voice
Nevada, Florida, and California all passed laws allowing self-driving cars on their roads.	Laws *were passed* by Nevada, Florida, and California allowing self-driving cars on their roads.
Scientists discovered a "carbon-rich" exoplanet in October—which turns out to be very hot, perfect for turning carbon into diamonds.	A "carbon-rich" exoplanet *was discovered* in October—which turns out to be very hot, perfect for turning carbon into diamonds.
After years of false starts and delays, Austrian skydiver, Felix Baumgartner, broke the 50-year-old skydiving record when he jumped from a capsule more than 24 miles above Earth's surface.	After years of false starts and delays, the 50-year-old skydiving record *was broken* by an Austrian skydiver, Felix Baumgartner, when he jumped from a capsule more than 24 miles above Earth's surface.

Source: Koebler, J. (2012, December 28). 10 important scientific discoveries and achievements of 2012. *US News.* Retrieved from http://www.usnews.com/news/articles/2012/12/28/10-important-scientific-discoveries-and-achievements-of-2012

Author's Phrase Palette (Anderson, 2005). For this strategy, students develop a section in their notebook to collect phrases and sentences from their assigned or independent reading. Students identify combinations of words that grab their attention, are unusually interesting, or invariably unique. According to Anderson (2005),

> I ask students to look for something fresh, not stale like "faster than a speeding bullet," but new, original, and something to aspire to as a writer: *[This cake] tastes like vacuum cleaner fuzz* (Korman, 2000, p. 2) or *Her open eye was like nearly black balsamic vinegar beading on white china* (Franzen, 2001, p. 31). (p. 39)

With this activity, students can develop an appreciation for the power of language use. In turn, they can use their collections as mentor texts to create their own piece of writing.

In sum, academic words alone will not ensure that students will use the correct vocabulary in standard English sentence structures for a specific audience. We must give multiple meaningful opportunities for students to use target words in grammatically correct sentences, in extended forms of communication, and to understand the language functions to fulfill a purpose (Fisher & Frey, 2010).

ANTICIPATED OUTCOMES

It is anticipated that academically and linguistically diverse learners' language development will be accelerated when (a) they are exposed to complex language forms of academic English, (b) they are engaged in tasks that expect them to use such language, and (c) these expectations are strategically well supported with instructional scaffolds. Further, if students are given the tools to manage more challenging academic texts in the secondary content-area classes, as well as offered ample opportunities to practice language skills in and outside of the ELA classroom, they learn to tolerate ambiguity and will handle more complex texts with less frustration and more success.

We believe that teaching and learning academic language in its complexity are critical to student success in all content areas. Exposure to complex language enhances students' ability to make progress in all four skill areas—reading, writing, speaking, and listening. Without fluency and facility with academic language, students will not be able to meet the CCSS.

INSTRUCTIONAL CHALLENGES

Academic language instruction must embrace word-, sentence-, and text-level work. Even with a strong commitment from individual teachers to implement a variety of successful, research-based strategies for vocabulary and language instruction that are aligned to the Common Core standards, schools need a schoolwide approach to language instruction that is comprehensive and integrated. We concur with Blachowicz, Fisher, Ogle, and Watts-Taffe (2006), who—based on their own and others' research—summarized the characteristics of good vocabulary instruction as follows:

- It takes place in a language- and word-rich environment that fosters . . . "word consciousness."
- It includes intentional teaching of selected words, providing multiple types of information about each new word as well as opportunities for repeated exposure, use, and practice.
- It includes teaching generative elements of words and word-learning strategies in ways that give students the ability to learn new words independently. (p. 527)

As Halliday (1996) so aptly stated, "Language is powered by grammatical energy" (p. 4). Learners whose language use—whether in writing or speech—lacks the necessary grammatical structures or *grammatical energy* will not be able to go far, with their speech halting or writing faltering. Thus, when teaching the conventions of English grammar and language use, we need to move beyond incidental learning, in which grammar and academic language acquisition is left to chance. Rather, teachers must offer all students daily opportunities to use standard American English in varied contexts and through a variety of authentic experiences. To be able to do so, we urge all teachers to commit to developing their own knowledge of the grade-appropriate formal grammar points to be taught. Through collaborative planning sessions, consider discussing the following questions:

- What grammar points should be targeted?
- Why should these points be targeted?
- Do I understand the grammar point?
- Have I based my explanation on reliable sources?
- Do I have grammar resources on hand at home and in the classroom?
- What do I want my students to do with the target form/structure?

Academic language cannot be taught in isolation from content or as a collection of distinct skills. Additionally, we must embrace that academic language learning is a complex phenomenon that takes place in the context of human interaction. "Learning is a social process that requires teachers to intentionally design learning opportunities that integrate reading, writing, speaking, and listening with the practices of each discipline" (Understanding Language, 2013, para. 2). Thus, we believe that every teacher in the secondary school context plays a critical role in the language development of all learners.

Finally, the most effective academic language instruction in a school or district must be based on a common philosophy and shared practices among teachers to ensure greater continuity and instructional intensity. At the same time, we must recognize that students come to school with a vast range of prior knowledge, background experiences, active and passive vocabulary, and language skills; thus differentiated instruction must also be considered.

PROMISING CLASSROOM PRACTICES

Wicked Word Wall in New York

One method of focusing on unusual, discipline-specific vocabulary is to establish a Wicked Word Wall, a strategy we learned from Sachem, New York, social studies teacher, Jonathan Chiaramonte. He noticed that some ELLs and other struggling learners would be uncomfortable in class revealing that they did not understand a word. Therefore, students were encouraged to self-identify words that they thought were important and did not know in an unusual way. Instead of saying, "Mr. Chiaramonte, I don't know this word," they asked, "Is this a *wicked* word?" In this way, word learning was turned into a game using a code (*wicked* word) for revealing unknown words without losing face. The Wicked Word Wall was created by students as they drew and cut out the target words in graffiti style. They not only would feel honored to cut the words out and have the chance to attach their "word art" to the wall, but they also took ownership of the words they added to the collection. Mr. Chiaramonte found that students who chose words for the Wicked Word Wall ended up being better able to comprehend the new vocabulary and used these words more frequently in class.

A Graveyard of Dead Words in Kentucky

Victoria Klaassen-Chew teaches at Bourbon County High School in Paris, Kentucky. She has noticed a recurring pattern in her students' writing:

They tend to use words that are not descriptive or specific enough. For example, students will identify the tone of a story as being *bad* or *good*. To make all students (ESL and non-ESL) more aware of word choice, she has created a Dead Word Graveyard on the bulletin board. The class first identified old, tired words such as *good, fun, bad, happy, sad,* and so on and in their place tried to think of better word choices. Each student cut a gravestone out of paper, wrote RIP (rest in peace) on it, and wrote his or her *dead* word. They then wrote better word choices on the tombstone. For example, instead of writing *good*, students would write *excellent, superb, pleasant,* and *favorable.* By posting these gravestones on the bulletin board in front of the room, students were able to refer to them when they wrote in class and were reminded to use more complex or specific words. Victoria noticed that her students really connected with replacing words such as *stuff, cool,* and *it* with words that provided more meaning and academic precision.

Connecting Literary Analysis, Grammar, Discussion, and Writing in Maryland

Let's visit Young Pahk's class at the Walter Johnson High School in the Montgomery County Public Schools in Maryland. In a CCSS-aligned unit, her high-intermediate ESOL (English for speakers of other languages) learners read and discussed two texts for the purpose of comparing parent-child relationships: "La Peseta" (a poem by Piri Thomas) and "Four Directions" (a short story by Amy Tan). Both selections were from the anthology *Voices in Literature: Gold* (McCloskey & Stack, 1996). In a previous lesson, students also were introduced to the target grammar point of the past unreal conditional/advisability.

Students were asked to examine the parent-child relationships apparent in each text. In small groups, they described, discussed, and created summary charts about the details that contributed to the particular parent-child relationships they found. The whole class met, and groups presented their charts, accepting questions and critiques from the others.

- Some sample entries included the following:

  Heading: Adversarial Parent-Child Relationship

  Detail: The daughter says her mother takes all the credit for her success at chess tournaments ("Four Directions")

  Heading: Not-Trusting Parent-Child Relationship

  Detail: The boy takes the money without asking his parents ("La Peseta")

The next day, students turned each statement that survived the previous day's scrutiny into a past unreal conditional sentence or advisability in the past.

- Some sample entries included the following:

  Heading: Adversarial Parent-Child Relationship ("Four Directions")

  Detail: The daughter says her mother takes all the credit for her success at chess tournaments.

  Past unreal: If the mother had not taken all the credit, the girl would not have misbehaved.

  Opposing argument: The girl should not have yelled at and embarrassed her mother publicly on the street.

  Heading: Not-Trusting Parent-Child Relationship ("La Peseta")

  Detail: The boy takes the money without asking his parents

  Past unreal: If the son had trusted his father, he might have asked for money instead of stealing it.

  Supporting statement: Yes, it (asking for money) would have been possible only if his father had not been too threatening.

As students presented rephrased details in the conditional form, the class agreed with, argued with, and/or helped correct grammatical conversions. They also were invited to accept or debate any of the advisability statements from other groups. As an outcome of this unit, students were expected to use past unreal conditional/advisability sentences in their writing assignments, such as when discussing facing a dilemma.

Tying Grammar, Vocabulary, and Writing Together in New Hampshire

Karen Goyette is the Director of ESOL Programs in a low-incidence school district in New Hampshire. She tries to ensure that her Grades 9–12 students are successful by creating ongoing activities for them that connect content-area vocabulary, grammar, and writing. Considering that the Hudson School District has a low-incidence of English language learners, all ELLs in Grades 9–12 are grouped together.

Karen's approach to vocabulary, grammar, and writing ties in with many Common Core standards. At the beginning of each week, Karen provides explicit vocabulary instruction through a vocabulary lesson consisting of ten words. To complement the vocabulary lesson, Karen prepares three weekly journal entries for students, each entry consisting of three choices for students. So, for example, on Tuesday the students receive three prompts (all involving vocabulary words) and the students need to choose one prompt to write about (each student can choose a different prompt). Karen ensures that the grammar used in the prompts connects with what the students have already learned or what they are in progress of learning. The class has a discussion about each journal prompt before they begin to write.

Periodically, as a review and to ensure that students notice grammatical features in texts outside the ESOL classroom (Schmidt's, 2001, Noticing Hypothesis), Karen sends her students on a Grammar Hunt. She brings in a variety of nonfiction resources (e.g., newspapers) that students can cut up. She gives students a list of grammar and vocabulary that they need to find, along with scissors, glue, and construction paper. Students can choose to work together in pairs or as a class. Their task is to find examples of each grammatical feature in their nonfiction source. The students love to read different articles and pieces and brag about how many grammatical features they can find in a sentence. They look for articles and pieces about each other's home countries. They also love to shout out when they find target vocabulary words. The Grammar Hunt activity has the students listening, speaking, and reading, and best of all, they are entirely *engaged*.

COMMON CORE LANGUAGE STANDARDS— (UN)COMMON REFLECTION QUESTIONS

1. Regardless of subject matter expertise or content-area specialization, how can we persuade all teachers that they are teachers of academic English?

2. How can all teachers' knowledge-base and skill sets regarding grammar instruction be enhanced?

3. How do the Common Core language standards translate into successful instruction for beginner English learners? How about students with language disorders? Or students who speak vernacular dialects of English?

4. Which of the ideas presented in this chapter will be the first one(s) you try in your classroom and why? What improvements/growth do you hope to see in your students by engaging in these activities?

KEY RESOURCES

Professional Books

Casagrande, J. (2006). *Grammar snobs are great big meanies: A guide to language for fun and spite.* New York, NY: Penguin Books.

Hale, C. (2001). *Sin and syntax: How to craft wickedly effective prose.* New York, NY: Broadway Books.

Lederer, R., & Shore, J. (2005). *Comma sense: A fundamental guide to punctuation.* New York, NY: St. Martin's Press.

Lukeman, N. (2006). *A dash of style: The art and mastery of punctuation.* New York, NY: W.W. Norton.

Noden, H. R. (1999). *Image grammar: Using grammatical structures to teach writing.* Portsmouth, NH: Heinemann.

Truss, L. (2004). *Eats, shoots & leaves: The zero tolerance approach to punctuation.* New York, NY: Gotham Books.

Highly Recommended, Specialized Resources to Help Develop the Grammarian in Every Teacher

Anderson, J. (2005). *Mechanically inclined: Building grammar, usage, and style into writer's workshop.* Portland, ME: Stenhouse.

Seely, J. (2012). *Grammar for teachers: Unlock your knowledge of English.* Cheltenham, UK: Oxpecker.

Online Resources

Grammar Practice
http://www.roadtogrammar.com
http://ell.stanford.edu/content/six-key-principles-ell-instruction

Guide for Using the Frayer Model
http://tinyurl.com/ch7ybkj

Office of English Language Acquisition, Language Enhancement, and Academic Achievement for Limited English Proficient Students (OELA)
www.ed.gov/about/offices/list/oela/index.html

Teaching Diverse Learners
www.alliance.brown.edu/tdl

The U.S. Department of Education's National Clearinghouse for English
Language Acquisition
   www.ncela.gwu.edu

Vocabulary and Style
   http://www.vocabulary.com
   http://grammar.yourdictionary.com/slang.dictionary

Vocabulary Development Using Digital Tools
   http://techteachers.com/vocabulary.htm
   www.wordsmyth.net
   www.wordsift.com
   www.visualthesaurus.com

3 Reading Strategies for Literature

"I really had a lot of dreams when I was a kid, and I think a great deal of that grew out of the fact that I had a chance to read a lot."

—Bill Gates

OVERVIEW

The development of sustained reading practices with the adolescent learner has a great deal of competition in the 21st century. Although it is quite possible that as a nation we read more than ever before, the use of technology and the ease with which we obtain information from the Internet as well as other sources has made many of us part of a nation of 30-second readers. We tend to read an abundance of short excerpts of text obtained from weblog posts, Twitter tweets, Facebook status updates, and text messages; yet many of us have little time to read a daily newspaper, a magazine article, a short story, or a novel as frequently as we may like. Our attention spans have thus become more accustomed to reading in shorter intervals, and this may be even more so for the adolescent learner who has grown up in the Digital Age (Prensky, 2001).

The challenge, however, may be amplified as well as somewhat altered with teaching culturally, academically, and linguistically diverse learners. On the one hand, some of these students coming from low socioeconomic backgrounds may not have easy access to digitally produced information available on technological devices such as laptop computers; handheld, touch-screen tablets; and smartphones. The lack of easy access to information places some students at a disadvantage. For others, teachers may also have to bridge the digital divide to determine how best to engage these students in the classroom.

One way to engage diverse middle and high schoolers in the reading process is to incorporate their varied lived experiences, cultural and linguistic backgrounds, and out-of-school literacies into English language arts lessons. Cummins (2001) identified the underlying predicament of diverse learners with regard to teaching practices,

> When students' language, culture and experience are ignored or excluded in classroom interactions, students are immediately starting from a disadvantage. Everything they have learned about life and the world up to this point is being dismissed as irrelevant to school learning . . . so students are expected to learn in an experiential vacuum. (pp. 2–3)

Delpit (2002) expressed a similar notion when she said, "Since language is one of the most intimate expressions of identity, indeed, 'the skin that we speak,' then to reject a person's language can only feel as if we are rejecting him" (p. 47). It is critical for teachers to strengthen and support the learning of diverse students with a variety of teaching strategies and those approaches in particular that validate the richness of students' cultural heritage, their ethnic and language diversity, and their challenges and efforts to achieve academically.

WHY TEACHING DIVERSE ADOLESCENT LEARNERS READING STRATEGIES PROMOTES COMPREHENSION OF LITERARY TEXTS

More than ever before, careful attention is being focused on the adolescent reader. Yet a common misconception among middle and high school teachers is that reading instruction beyond the elementary grades is remedial. This notion is detrimental to some culturally and linguistically diverse students as well as other struggling learners who continue to have reading difficulty and thus far have received little or no reading instruction in English language arts or other content classes even though they are faced with more increasingly difficult and complex texts to comprehend.

The positive impact of reading strategy instruction on student comprehension and assessment achievement is well documented (Fang & Wei, 2010; Griffin, Simmons, & Kameenui, 1991; McNamara, 2007). For the adolescent learner in particular, several evidenced-based recommendations for strategy instruction to improve literacy achievement have been cited as most effective (Kamil et al., 2008). These broad-based recommendations are as follows:

1. Provide explicit vocabulary instruction.

2. Provide direct and explicit comprehension strategy instruction.

3. Provide opportunities for extended discussion of text meaning and interpretation.

4. Increase student motivation and engagement in literacy learning. (p. 7)

It is important to note that these suggested strategies be employed during regular classroom instruction. However, some students may need more intensive instruction; therefore, a fifth recommendation is identified to "make available intensive and individualized interventions for struggling readers that can be provided by trained specialists" (Kamil et al., 2008, p. 7).

CORE READING STRATEGIES

This chapter contains strategies that are aligned to the ten College and Career Readiness Anchor Standards (CCRAS) for Reading with detailed application to the strand for literature. They follow the CCRAS that are divided according to *Key Ideas and Details, Craft and Structure, Integration of Knowledge and Ideas, and Range of Reading and Text Complexity.* A series of related *Anchor Performances* are derived for each of the ten standards and accompanied by applicable strategies to help diverse learners. We invite our readers to review each strategy and adapt it according to the grade-level and academic or language abilities of their students.

Box 3.1 College and Career Readiness Anchor Standards for Reading for Literature

Key Ideas and Details

1. Read closely to determine what the text says explicitly and to make logical inferences from it; cite specific contextual evidence when writing or speaking to support conclusions drawn from the text.

2. Determine central ideas or themes of a text and analyze their development; summarize the key supporting details and ideas.

3. Analyze how and why individuals, events, and ideas develop and interact over the course of a text.

Craft and Structure

4. Interpret words and phrases as they are used in a text, including determining technical, connotative, and figurative meanings, and analyze how specific word choices shape meaning or tone.

5. Analyze the structure of texts, including how specific sentences, paragraphs, and larger portions of the text (e.g., a section, chapter, scene, or stanza) relate to each other and the whole.

6. Assess how point of view or purpose shapes the content and style of a text.

Integration of Knowledge and Ideas

7. Integrate and evaluate content presented in diverse media and formats, including visually and quantitatively, as well as in words.

8. Delineate and evaluate the argument and specific claims in the text, including the validity of the reasoning as well as the relevance and sufficiency of the evidence (not applicable to literature; see Chapter 4).

9. Analyze how two or more texts address similar themes or topics in order to build knowledge or to compare the approaches the authors take.

Range of Reading and Level of Text Complexity

10. Read and comprehend complex literary and informational texts independently and proficiently.

Key Ideas and Details

Anchor Performance 1: Cite Textual Evidence to Support Analysis and Inferencing

Individual grade-level standards for this anchor performance vary in their expectations concerning the degree to which students should be able to support their analysis of text with evidence. In Grade 6, students are required to generally identify textual evidence to support their conclusions and inferences; however in Grade 7, they are asked to cite multiple pieces of textual evidence. In Grade 8, students must discern between textual evidence that strongly supports their conclusions compared with text that generally does. In Grades 9–10, students are required to cite both strong and thorough evidence for their textual understandings and inferences, and additionally in Grades 11–12, must determine to what extent the text information leaves the subject at hand uncertain.

Essential Strategy to Support Anchor Performance 1: Explicit Reading Strategy Instruction to Enhance Student Text-Based Responses

To read critically, students must develop the ability to ask their own questions while reading and be able to distinguish between critical information from subordinate details. Teacher modeling of "higher-order reading" (Schmoker, 2011, p. 79) can enhance students' application of strategies to better comprehend text. Additionally, asking questions to set a purpose for reading can further focus students' attention on critical information.

Read alouds or shared readings are often viewed as ideal activities for elementary teachers to employ with their students; however, it is often abandoned by the upper elementary grades due to the increasing demands of the core curriculum and standardized test preparation. Nevertheless, it is also a valuable activity in the secondary classroom for teachers to model fluent, expressive reading, to showcase their own generation of ideas and questions about text, and to demonstrate how to directly apply such strategies. With the onset of the Common Core State Standards (CCSS) and the increase in diversity in the mainstream, secondary educators can no longer afford to relegate reading instruction to the elementary school. It is essential to build on and enhance all students' reading abilities throughout their school careers.

Framework for Strategy Instruction. Reading strategies need to be explicitly taught to students who are struggling readers, particularly to those who have not experienced much reading success. Students benefit from the teaching of one precise strategy at a time and the opportunity to practice the targeted strategy in a number of ways. The selected strategy must be the specific focus of direct instruction, modeled with multiple texts, reinforced through guided practice, incorporated into cooperative learning tasks, and practiced individually. Figure 3.1 identifies a framework for strategy instruction with adolescent learners.

Asking Higher-Order Questions (Hill & Flynn, 2008). This approach to questioning—developed for English learners yet valuable for the questioning of all students—incorporates the stages of second-language acquisition

Figure 3.1 A Framework for Teaching Reading Strategies

1. **Select a strategy to introduce.** Plan how to incorporate strategy instruction into the overall lesson objective. Consider how to best explain to students the strategy to be used. Clearly identify the strategy and its purpose. Some examples of general reading strategies are as follows:

   - Activating prior knowledge about the topic
   - Previewing the text by skimming and scanning
   - Jotting down questions while reading
   - Monitoring comprehension through reflection
   - Visualizing the text
   - Making personal connections to what is read
   - Summarizing the story's main idea
   - Evaluating and forming opinions about the text

2. **Model the strategy.** Demonstrate for students how the selected strategy may be applied to their reading. Model one's step-by-step thinking out loud so students may better understand the cognitive processes that the strategy entails. Be as explicit as possible.

3. **Plan time for guided practice.** Guide students to try the strategy with the teacher's support. Select a short piece of text, and walk the students through the use of the selected strategy. Encourage students to share their own thoughts as they apply the strategy to their reading.

4. **Allow for collaborative application.** Offer students the time to work in pairs or teams to apply the same strategy. This step will help some students refine their use of the new skill and allow for peer support.

5. **Support individual practice.** Provide students the opportunity to try the strategy independently. Rotate the class and spot-check students' understanding and application of the selected strategy. If possible, supply students with some type of task to document the use of the strategy such as a checklist, comment card, response sheet, or graphic organizer.

6. **Monitor and reteach.** Identify students who will benefit from further instruction, guidance, and review to use the strategy.

Source: Framework inspired by Fisher, D., & Frey, N. (2008). *Better learning through structured teaching: A framework for the gradual release of responsibility.* Alexandria, VA: ASCD.

with the fundamentals of Bloom's Taxonomy to construct a framework for asking higher-order thinking questions to students at different levels of language proficiency. According to Hill and Flynn (2008),

> The beauty of this strategy, which focuses on questions in the classroom, is that it helps teachers specifically address the needs of ELLs while also meeting the needs of every student in the classroom. It allows teachers to integrate learning for ELLs in

mainstream classrooms and to help these students achieve academic success at the same levels as their native English-speaking peers. (p. 47)

To ensure rigorous text analysis and students discourse, it is vital for teachers to carefully construct their questions about a selected piece of text as part of the lesson-planning process rather than coming up with questions *on the spot.* Table 3.1 is designed as a planning guide both to write a series of higher-order questions about the same story topic and also to develop a framework that makes questions understandable and answerable for students at all levels of English language fluency. More specifically, Table 3.1 identifies how questions might be created for emergent bilingual adolescents—at the preproduction, early production, and speech emergence levels—using the story *Stardust* by Neil Gaiman (2009).

For the questions to be meaningful—such as when students speak little or no English (preproduction) or have other issues that prevent them from speaking fluently—visual representations of story elements are necessary for students to answer questions. It is beneficial at times to choose literature that is also depicted on film. This allows students to watch representative parts of the film to obtain a greater sense of the written text. Thereafter, selected excerpts from the text may be analyzed more carefully and in depth, giving students the opportunity to support what they recall or state about the story by citing textual evidence and making inferences. Not all questions in the grid will be conducive to one small piece of text. The general goal of this strategy is to be mindful of asking higher-order questions to all students, even those who are viewed—sometimes mistakenly—as less able because of their limited literacy skills in standard American English.

QAR: Question–Answer Relationship (Rafael, 1986). This approach to questioning assists students to better understand how questions are developed and subsequently promotes their ability to answer them. This skill is also related to students' facility with citing textual evidence. Question types are divided into the following two categories:

- *In the Book.* Students will either find answers to these questions in a specific place in the text (*Right There*), or they will have to look in several places (*Think and Search*) to find the answers.
- *In My Head.* These types questions fall into the categories of *Author and You,* which refers to the use of a combination of textual information, students' background knowledge, and personal experiences to arrive at an answer as well as *On My Own,* in which students rely merely on their own background experiences and knowledge to come up with the answer.

Table 3.1 Asking Higher-Order Questions

Story: *Stardust* by Neil Gaiman (2009)

Bloom's Taxonomy Concepts	Sample Stages of Language Proficiency		
	Preproduction: No English Is Spoken	Early Production: One- or Two-Word Answers	Speech Emergence: Phrases or Short Sentences
Knowledge	Show me the name of the town.	What is the name of the town in the story?	Describe the town where Tristan lived.
Comprehension	Show me why the town was named "Wall."	Tell me why Tristan left the town of Wall	What happened after Tristan left the town of Wall?
Application	Show me where someone might travel on the road from Wall.	Tell me what would happen if Tristan traveled in another direction.	How might Tristan find his way to a fallen star?
Analysis	Show me someone you think loves Tristan and someone who you think does not love Tristan.	Tell me why Victoria may not love Tristan.	Compare Victoria's and Yvaine's feelings for Tristan.
Synthesis	Point to the reasons why Tristan walked through the gap in the wall.	Tell me why Tristan walked through the gap in the wall.	How might the story change if Tristan never left the town of Wall?
Evaluation	Show me why Tristan is brave.	Tell me why Tristan is brave.	What else might Tristan do to show that he is brave?

Even though the CCSS emphasize text-based answers, it is important for students to develop an understanding of the difference in the accuracy and relevance of all reactions to questions, text-based or not. For this reason, generating *On My Own* answers may be an important exercise for students to be able to compare and contrast the validity and necessity of text-based answers. The following is an excerpt from *Stardust* by Neil Gaiman (2009) accompanied by sample questions that follow the QAR scheme.

The star had been soaked to the skin when she arrived at the pass, sad and shivering. She was worried about the unicorn; they had found no food for it on the last day's journey, as the grasses and ferns of the forest had been replaced by grey rocks and stunted thorn bushes. The unicorn's unshod hooves were not meant for a rocky road, nor was its back meant to carry riders, and its pace became slower and slower.

Right There: What was the star (Yvaine) worried about?

Think and Search: What was the overall problem with the unicorn?

Author and You: What might you advise Yvaine to do and why?

On My Own: Why is making a decision sometimes difficult to do?

For more information about the *QAR* strategy, see Chapter 5. Other strategies to help students to cite textual evidence and make inferences are *Paired Reading, Two-Column Notes, Where's the Evidence, Anticipation Guides, Inferencing Questions,* and more may be found in Chapter 4 under Anchor Performance 1.

Anchor Performance 2: Identify Central Themes and Summarize Supporting Details

Students who are able to summarize text are clearly much better able to comprehend text. However, the ability to summarize complex ideas and include objective supporting details is a skill many students, particularly those who are struggling learners, have difficulty mastering. Some students may not understand how to fully develop a summary; they may have difficulty identifying pertinent information and supporting details in chronological order.

The aim is to direct students' focus away from accounting superfluous details and toward paying more careful attention to the main story line and emerging central themes. In this way, diverse learners will be better able to produce oral and written summary accounts. These retelling skills can be supported through a variety of scaffolded teaching techniques.

For Standard 2, the grade-level expectations vary from determining central themes or ideas in a text void of personal opinions in Grades 6–7; including the relationship of characters, setting, and plot to central themes in Grade 8; further analyzing how central themes emerge, are shaped, and refined by specific details in Grades 9–10; and determining two or more central themes and how they interact and build on one another in Grades 11–12.

Essential Strategy to Support Anchor Performance 2: Frameworks for Students to Focus on Central Themes as Well as Retell and Summarize Literature.

Often, diverse learners are engaged more readily in literacy tasks when they are supported by structured frameworks and step-by-step strategies that guide them. Supportive frameworks promote and sustain students' abilities to analyze and synthesize pieces of text to create summaries as well as discover overall themes by organizing critical information. The following strategies function as overall supports and guidance for diverse learners.

I Witness. This exercise serves as a valuable introduction to central story themes. With this approach, students are better able to understand the general nature of themes and how multiple themes may be present in a single text. Instead of having students uncover the story themes on their own, they select from possible themes and *bear witness to* or find evidence in the text to support their theme of choice.

To begin, select a piece of text and identify three possible themes that students might consider. Give students a clear explanation of story themes and how authors reveal them, often in subtle ways. Next, have the students read the text in a manner that makes it most accessible to them; for example, more capable students might read silently, whereas small groups of diverse learners often benefit from a shared reading. Finally, ask students to select one of the prechosen themes and support their choice with information from the text. Have students use a graphic organizer such as the one in Table 3.2 to document their findings. With this organizer, students are able to identify phrases and sentences—characters' thoughts, deeds, and reactions—from the text (clues from the text), interpret what each means (what it reveals), and then state how it connects with their choice (why it supports the theme).

Table 3.2 I Witness Graphic Organizer

I Witness		
Story Title:		
Selected Theme:		
Clues From the Text	**What It Reveals**	**Why It Supports the Theme**

To support this process, Figure 3.2 identifies common story themes.

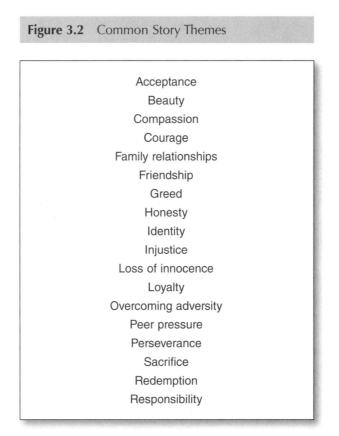

Figure 3.2 Common Story Themes

Acceptance
Beauty
Compassion
Courage
Family relationships
Friendship
Greed
Honesty
Identity
Injustice
Loss of innocence
Loyalty
Overcoming adversity
Peer pressure
Perseverance
Sacrifice
Redemption
Responsibility

To scaffold this strategy—especially when first teaching about themes—use text with clear and obvious themes that relate directly to the lived experiences of your students.

Theme Search (Shanahan, 2013). With this strategy, students discover story themes by examining the changes that take place in the main character due to some type of adversity. As a prerequisite for using this strategy, students must be able to identify character traits. For this approach, select a text in which some aspect of a character changes within the course of the story. Have students complete the reading in a way that best suits their abilities (alone, in pairs, in supportive peer groups, or with the teacher). Ask students to complete the graphic organizer (Table 3.3) with partners or in teams. Students then select a spokesperson to report their completed organizers.

Stop-and-Jot. A simple way to develop a summary is to have students pause at different intervals in their reading and synthesize or "jot down"

Table 3.3 Theme Search

Theme Search	
Title of Text:	
Describe the main character at the beginning of the story.	
Describe the main character at the end of the story.	
Identify the crisis revealed in the story.	
Identify the story theme as a result of the change in character.	

the part of the selection that was read in one sentence. Students are directed to read one paragraph or one page at a time and then pause to write down the main idea of what they just read. If students cannot complete the task, they are asked to reread the same section of the text or work with a partner. Finally, students use their summary sentences to complete a summary of the entire selection.

Anchor Performance 3: Identify How Particular Story Elements Unfold and Analyze Their Relationship to Story Events

For students to better comprehend the literature they read, they must become more familiar with the structure of narrative texts as well as the way a range of literary genres are written, which includes the knowledge of story elements such as character, plot, setting, and point of view. These structural elements provide students with a framework to recall text information more completely and a foundation to investigate and interpret the relationships between and among the story elements in the text.

The progression is clear for Standard 3. Students in Grade 6 are expected to describe story plots and characters, but in Grades 7 and up, it is anticipated that all students will be able to offer a much more detailed analysis of how story elements interact. In combination with skills acquired from earlier grades, students in Grade 8 analyze dialogues or specific details of action, students in Grades 9–10 offer an analysis of the story characters, and students in Grades 11–12 "analyze the impact of the author's choices regarding how to develop and relate elements of a story or drama (e.g., where a story is set, how the action is ordered, how the characters are introduced and developed)" (*Common Core State Standards*, 2010a, p. 38).

Essential Strategy to Support Anchor Performance 3: Use Graphic Organizers to Identify and Examine Story Elements

Graphic organizers are valuable tools that can present clear visual structures for students as well as reveal categorized information contained in story text. Their organizational schemes can promote the review and analysis of information that is classified into specific categories—namely, the elements of fiction. The arrangement of an organizer can facilitate students' becoming more strategic learners by encouraging them to connect story ideas in different ways.

Storyboarding (Illinois State Board of Education, 2012). A way of sketching out the scene-by-scene action in a story, *storyboarding* allows students to visualize the story plot as it unfolds. Generally completed during the reading of a story, this type of organizer can be modified to incorporate spaces for students to reflect on character traits or the order in which the plot develops for an additional after-reading task.

Initiate this activity by preparing a storyboard for each student and selecting a story to be read. Guide students to read part of the text, and then have them pause to sketch and write a summary of what just occurred in the story. After completing the storyboards, students may compare them with a partner, share them with other members of a literature circle they may be participating in, or present them to the whole class; alternatively, they may further analyze the plot or character traits. Figure 3.3 is one possible configuration for a storyboard.

Figure 3.3 Storyboarding

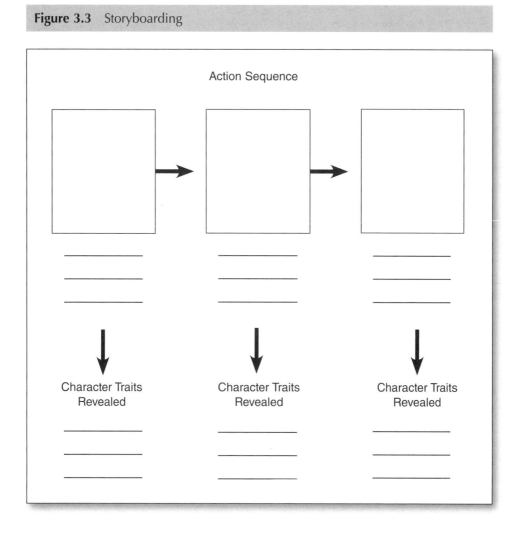

Character Perspective Chart (Burns, 1999; Shanahan & Shanahan, 1997). This strategy asks students to consider how different story elements— setting, conflict, solution, plot, and theme—relate to separate characters, and requires students to examine each of these elements from diverse perspectives. Using this graphic organizer, students uncover and compare story elements from each character's perspective, resulting in a more complete understanding about how the story elements interact and a more thorough overall analysis of the text. See Table 3.4 for a chart that accompanies this strategy and scaffolds task completion.

Table 3.4 Character Perspectives Chart

<table>
<tr>
<td colspan="2" align="center">Character Perspective Chart

Title: _____</td>
</tr>
<tr>
<td>Name: Character 1</td>
<td>Name: Character 2</td>
</tr>
<tr>
<td>Setting: Where and when does the story take place?</td>
<td>Setting: Where and when does the story take place?</td>
</tr>
<tr>
<td>Conflict: What conflict or problem does this character face?</td>
<td>Conflict: What conflict or problem does this character face?</td>
</tr>
<tr>
<td>Solutions: What possible outcomes or solutions does the character hope for? What was the actual outcome?</td>
<td>Solutions: What possible outcomes or solutions does the character hope for? What was the actual outcome?</td>
</tr>
<tr>
<td>Plot: How is the story plot affected by this character's actions/reactions?</td>
<td>Plot: How is the story plot affected by this character's actions/reactions?</td>
</tr>
<tr>
<td>Theme: What point did the author want to make through this character's actions?</td>
<td>Theme: What point did the author want to make through this character's actions?</td>
</tr>
</table>

Source: Adapted from Shanahan, T., & Shanahan, S. (1997). Character perspectives charting: Helping children to develop a more complete conception of the story. *The Reading Teacher, 50*(8), p. 670.

Story Element Analysis. With this strategy, students have the opportunity to examine the story elements contained in a recently shared piece of fiction. By using a familiar story line, students should be better able not only to identify story elements but also to more readily analyze how story elements interact and influence the story as a whole.

Begin the lesson by brainstorming what students liked about the story. Discuss the elements that make a great story. Suggest that if one or more story elements were altered in some way, the story itself might have a different impact on its audience. Next, have students consider and identify each of the following story elements: theme, conflict, characters, setting, plot, and point of view. Finally, ask students to consider the overall impact if each story element was altered in any way. The graphic organizer depicted in Table 3.5 can assist students to complete the identified tasks.

As an alternative to students' considering the impact of each story element on other aspects of the story, one story element might be selected to examine such as the *setting*. In this way, students would consider how a variation in that one element (the setting) affects each of the other story elements listed.

Table 3.5 Story Elements Analysis

Title:		
Story Elements	**Description**	**What impact would an alteration of this element have on other aspects of the story?**
Theme		
Conflict		
Characters		
Setting		
Plot		
Point of View		

Craft and Structure

Anchor Performance 4: Determine the Meaning of Words and Phrases, Including Figurative Language and Analyze How They Are Used in Text

Figurative language is one essential component of literary expression; its usage accentuates an author's tone, expressing his or her attitude toward the topic, characters, or other aspects of a story. Gordon-Thaxter (n.d.) identified the various ways figurative language expresses tone in literature:

- Simile: directly compares two images and imparts an author's meaning or tone directly
- Metaphor: implies an evocative tone; it suggests a comparison without stating it outright
- Irony: indicates a caustic tone; the use of irony signifies the author means the opposite of what was stated
- Personification: establishes a distinct or dramatic tone, giving human qualities to inanimate objects
- Hyperbole: generates a humorous tone; it is purposeful exaggeration to highlight a point or to amuse the reader

In addition to identifying an author's attitude, figurative language can enhance story ideas, create visual images, shape the mood or overall feeling for the work, and make the reading more enjoyable. Yet for the most part, the use of figurative language creates confusion for struggling readers.

In fact, different types of metaphorical language coupled with low-frequency vocabulary can often make reading a challenging task for many linguistically and academically diverse learners. Therefore, the focus of this anchor performance is to engage students in determining word meanings, with an emphasis on figurative language.

The increasing demands to meet this standard are apparent in each grade-level expectation. In Grade 6, students are asked to analyze the general impact of specific word choices on text meaning and tone; however, in Grade 7, there is an additional reference to word usage in poetry and its impact on rhyme as well as specific verses or stanzas. In Grade 8, the expectation is expanded to the impact of word choices on meaning and tone, including analogies or allusions to other texts. In Grades 9–10, students must be able to analyze the cumulative impact of word choice as it affects a sense of time and place as well as formal and informal tone. Last, in Grades 11–12, the impact of words focuses on multiple meanings or "language that is particularly fresh, engaging, or beautiful" (*Common Core State Standards*, 2010a, p. 38).

Essential Strategy to Support Anchor Performance 4: Analyze Word Meanings and Relationships

A most valuable practice is teaching vocabulary in context as "most vocabulary is learned through reading" (Burns, 1999, p. 185). Beck, McKeown, and Kucan (2002) advocated for robust vocabulary teaching "that offers rich information about words and their uses, provides frequent and varied opportunities for students to think about and use words, and enhances students' language comprehension and production" (p. 2). They suggested that the majority of vocabulary teaching and learning should occur with words in context. Accordingly, we offer several strategies for teaching robust vocabulary, most of which help students understand words in context.

Team Trackers (Lorcher, 2011). *Team Trackers* is a strategy that involves students working in teams of three or four to create definitions for unknown or difficult words and phrases in context without the use of dictionaries, glossaries, thesauri, or the Internet. Begin by assigning teams of students up to five words found in the literature, or students may be given handouts of a short piece of text in which the words are already highlighted. Distribute one organizer such as a semantic web (see Figure 3.4) for each word assigned to the group or have students create their own semantic webs. Next, students attend to the following process:

- Read the short text that contains the target word or phrase and discuss its meaning.
- Write one target word or phrase in the center of each semantic web.
- Identify and write synonyms that may mean the same as the target word or phrase and that make sense when substituted in the text.
- Student groups report their answers to the whole class.

Figure 3.4   Semantic Web

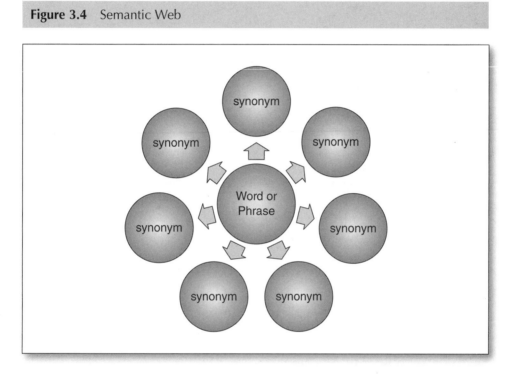

Throughout this activity, assist student groups that are having difficulty with the text. At the end of task, share correct definitions of each of the words or phrases in student-friendly terms while also connecting the word to the literary text. Have students indicate the synonyms in each of their semantic webs that most closely relate to the shared definitions. This activity may also be accomplished with students working alone, in pairs, or in teacher-guided groups.

Word Relationships (Beck et al., 2002). This strategy has students consider the meaning of pairs of words within a question and from their understandings of both words respond to the question and justify their answers. Target words are chosen from a text students are reading. Beck et al. (2002) offered the following examples:

- Would you pay *homage* to something *tolerable?*
- Would you have *compassion* for someone *imperious?*
- Would you *suppress* a *profound* thought?
- Would *blurting out* your thoughts be an example of *indecorum?* (p. 89)

In an extension of this activity, students work in pairs to create their own challenging questions for each other. Another variation of this strategy is to have students consider the meaning of two words in relationship to a story character such as the following:

- Would you abhor or revere Gandalf (*Lord of the Rings*) (Tolkien, 1954)?
- Do you think Katniss (*The Hunger Games*) (Collins, 2010) is credible or reprehensible?
- Would you consider Voldemort (*The Harry Potter Series*) (Rowling, 2009) to be noxious or placid?

Beck et al. (2002) further suggested that target vocabulary be incorporated into class discussions about a piece of writing so that academic language is used for discussion and thereby relating the meaning of words to actual points in the text. They offer the following examples from *Prince and the Pauper* by Mark Twain (2007):

- What might Tom have considered to be *compensations* for his present state?
- *Imperious* is often appropriate for describing a king. How appropriate is it to Tom?
- How do Tom's *blurting* out and *suppressing* his words relate to a judgment of him as *imperious?* (p. 89)

SIFT Method (College Entrance Examination Board, 2002). To investigate an author's choice of words, expressions, and stylistic techniques, introduce the *SIFT Method* for literary analysis. It helps students analyze different parts of a piece of literature in order to come to a deeper understanding of the text as a whole. *SIFT* stands for the following:

- **S**ymbol: examine the title and text for symbolism
- **I**mages: identify images and sensory details
- **F**igures of Speech: analyze figurative language and other devices
- **T**one and Theme: discuss how all devices reveal tone and theme (p.17)

Figure 3.5 describes each component and illustrates some examples of this method's application.

Figure 3.5 SIFT Literary Analysis Method

SIFT Literary Analysis Method		
S-I-F-T	**Description**	**Examples**
Symbol	*In literature, symbols represent an abstract idea; events, people, animals, places, and objects can all have on a symbolic meaning. Symbols often are related to the story theme.*	• *In* A Raisin in the Sun, *sunlight is a symbol for hope* • *In* Of Mice and Men, *the farm is a symbol of the American dream* • *In* The Great Gatsby, *the color white is a symbol of false purity*
Images	*Select language use can create sensory images that elicit reactions from the reader to characters, objects, or events in the writing. Imagery can function as symbolism and create mood and tone.*	• *In* Jane Eyre, *bird imagery is used to depict Jane as an unhappy child (dove and sparrows) and Mr. Rochester as strong (eagle)* • *In* Macbeth, *constant images of blood and water symbolize treason or murder*
Figures of Speech	*Authors employ figurative language such as similes, metaphors, hyperbole, and personification to convey effect and meaning.*	• *"Kate inched over her own thoughts like a measuring worm."—East of Eden* • *"The very mystery of him excited her curiosity like a door that had neither lock nor key."—Gone With the Wind*
Tone and Theme	*Tone: symbolism, imagery, and figurative language reveal the author's attitude or tone*	• *"There was a steaming mist in all the hollows, and it had roamed in its forlornness up the hill, like an evil spirit, seeking rest and finding none"—A Tale of Two Cities (ominous tone)*
	Theme: Often revealed through the examination of a character's life lessons, symbolism present in the writing, or a story summary	Major themes in *Catcher in the Rye:* • Alienation • Loneliness • Deception

Word Analysis Framework. Challenging new words, especially when embedded in figurative language, are more easily acquired when students connect them with words they already know, attach them to visual representations of the same concepts, and have the opportunity to use them frequently (Elley, 1996). The *Word Analysis Framework* is a strategy that capitalizes on how new vocabulary is learned. It requires students to complete a series of tasks for each new word in which they write a definition, identify synonyms and antonyms, provide real-life examples, find or sketch an illustration, and write a sentence with the new word. Figure 3.6 is an example of this strategy.

Figure 3.6 Word Analysis Framework

Word: apotheosis		
Synonyms: ideal, epitome, quintessence, exemplar, perfection	**Definition:** *the best and most perfect; an ideal example*	**Illustration**
Antonyms: imperfection, incompleteness, worthlessness	**Examples:** MacBook computer Häagen-Dazs chocolate chocolate chip ice cream	

Sentence: Among all the beaches I have visited in the world, the beach at Half Moon Cay in the Caribbean is the *apotheosis.*

Anchor Performance 5: Compare and Contrast Different Types and Structure of Texts (Poetry, Fiction, and Drama), and Analyze How Authors' Choices Create Effects

The level of text complexity is often a challenge for academically and linguistically diverse learners when they must complete tasks such as comparing different pieces of literature. For this reason, scaffolding instruction of complex texts and breaking down tasks into assignments that can be completed more readily "help learners bridge the gap between what they know and can do and the intended goal" (Graves, Graves, & Braaten, 1996, p. 14).

In Grade 6, students are asked to analyze a short length of text and determine how it relates to the overall structure of the piece. In Grade 7, the analysis of poetry as well as drama forms and structure are emphasized. In Grade 8, students are expected to compare and contrast the structure of two or more texts and determine how the structure of each contributes to understanding. In Grades 9–10, the focus shifts to examining the author's choice of text structure or order of events to shape time and develop literary effects such as tension or mystery. In addition to the previous grade bands' expectations, students in Grades 11–12 are asked to analyze the overall effect an author's choice plays in determining comedic or tragic outcomes as well as its aesthetic impact.

Essential Strategy to Support Anchor Performance 5: Organizers to Compare and Contrast Text Types and Analyze Authors' Choices

The use of organizational strategies supports students' ability to analyze, compare, and contrast different text types and their structures. Various configurations of graphic organizers can offer visual support so students can more closely examine a variety of literary texts. They can also assist students to order story events to determine the overall impact of an author's choice of structure.

Episodic Notes (Burke, 2002). The purpose of this strategy is to help students identify the defining moments of a text—distinct scenes or events that occur during the course of a story—and analyze how each of them relates to the overall structure of the text in terms of the story theme, setting, and plot. Using a graphic organizer (see Table 3.6) to complete the task, invite students to do the following:

1. Select the three most important scenes or events in the story and carefully reread each scene.

2. After each reading, visualize the scene; sketch in detail images that are brought to mind. Do not be concerned with the quality of the drawings. The main idea is to complete a quick sketch with as many details as possible.

3. Write a description of what occurred in each scene; explain why the scene is important.

4. Identify how each of these pieces of text relates to the overall structure of the work; consider the story theme, setting, and plot.

Table 3.6 Episodic Notes

Episodic Notes			
Scene	Sketch	Description	Relation to Overall Text: Theme, Setting, Plot
Scene 1			
Scene 2			
Scene 3			

To scaffold this activity, have students brainstorm in pairs or small groups to determine the most important scenes. Have some students work in trios in which they must only complete the task for one of the three scenes. The writing about each scene may be further scaffolded using sentence starters. This strategy is most effective after sufficient modeling and guided practice have taken place.

Poetry Analysis Outline. By the end of Grade 7, students are expected to analyze how a poem's structure contributes to its meaning. However, poetry analysis is not exclusive to Grade 7 instruction, and its related skills should be supported upward through the grade levels. To help students break down the process of poetry study, have them investigate different poetry elements in a meaningful way. Begin by explaining and jointly examining with students the type of poem they will analyze. Some poetry forms are as follows (www.poets.org):

- *Ballad.* This form of poetry generally tells a plot-driven tale about love, crime, religious ideas, and adversity. One example of a ballad is *Rime of the Ancient Mariner* by Samuel Taylor Coleridge (2008).
- *Dramatic Monologue.* Also known as a persona poem, with this form, the author assumes a fictional identity and speaks through that character's voice. "Lady Lazurus" by Sylvia Plath (2004) is an example of this form.
- *Ode.* Originally accompanied by music, the ode conveys strong convictions and sentiments addressed to a person, event, or object. An example of this form of poetry is *Ode to a Grecian Urn* by John Keats (1963).
- *Sonnet.* Generally speaking, this form of poetry contains fourteen lines, is tightly structured, and is written in iambic pentameter. Shakespeare's sonnets are a well-known collection of this type of poetry.

After reading and discussing students' general impressions of the poem, assist them in conducting a deeper analysis using the organizer shown in Table 3.7. For this tool to be effective, students must have a clear understanding of the basic elements of poetry, including literary devices, theme, mood, and figurative language; supports for each of these elements should be made accessible to students in the form of descriptive lists available through websites, word wall displays, or printed checklists.

As always, consider the needs of individual learners and decide whether or not they may better perform the task working alone, in pairs, in teams, or directly with the teacher. This activity may be divided among several days for a thorough analysis to occur or completed as a jigsaw activity in which certain groups of students investigate only one of the four elements—literary devices, theme, mood, figurative language—and report back information for students to accomplish their written interpretations.

Text Sequence Analysis (Dickson, Simmons, & Kameenui, 1995). This strategy helps students analyze how an author creates certain effects such as mystery, tension, and surprise by the way the text is structured, events

Table 3.7 Poetry Analysis Outline

<table>
<tr><th colspan="3">Poetry Analysis Outline</th></tr>
<tr><td colspan="3">Title of Poem:</td></tr>
<tr><td colspan="3">Author:</td></tr>
<tr><td colspan="3">Brief Summary:</td></tr>
<tr><td colspan="3">Directions: Identify each of the following points of analysis, cite examples from the poem, and use your findings to write an interpretation of the poem.</td></tr>
<tr><td>Points of Analysis</td><td>Type/Description</td><td>Examples</td></tr>
<tr><td rowspan="2">Literary Devices (allegory, allusion, anastrophe, antithesis, etc.) http://literary-devices.com</td><td></td><td></td></tr>
<tr><td></td><td></td></tr>
<tr><td>Theme (friendship, family, love, honor, loss, etc.)</td><td></td><td></td></tr>
<tr><td>Mood (an atmosphere of peace, chaos, love, fear, etc.)</td><td></td><td></td></tr>
<tr><td rowspan="2">Figurative Language (alliteration, imagery, simile, metaphor, hyperbole, etc.)</td><td></td><td></td></tr>
<tr><td></td><td></td></tr>
<tr><td colspan="3">Interpretation—Explain how literary devices, theme, mood, and figurative language contribute to the overall meaning.</td></tr>
</table>

are ordered, and time is manipulated and by the use of literary devices. Have students complete a reading of a piece of fiction and subsequently brainstorm a list of ten key events that occurred. With students' input, complete the following activities:

- Order the list of events according to the way they occurred in the story.
- Examine the list and identify how the order of events helped to create suspense, conflict, foreshadowing, irony, or other appropriate literary device.
- Next, organize students into small groups.
- Have them reorder the story events in different ways in an attempt to create, intensify, or eliminate mystery, tension, and surprise.
- Direct students to discuss their manipulated sequence of events and its overall impact on the story as well as any alteration in literary devices, such as an increase or decrease in suspense, conflict, and so on.
- Ask one student from each group to report.

Invite students to use the chart illustrated in Table 3.8 to guide them in completing this activity. Students can use information from their completed charts to compose a summary of the change in the story that occurred after the order of events was manipulated.

Table 3.8 Text Sequence Analysis

Text Sequence Analysis		
Original Order of Text Events	**Reorder of Text Events**	
1. 2. 3. 4. 5. 6. 7. 8. 9. 10.	1. 2. 3. 4. 5. 6. 7. 8. 9. 10.	
Identify how the order of events helped to create suspense, conflict, foreshadowing, and so on.	**Original**	**Reordered**
Overall impact of story order on the text—*Does it create, intensify, or eliminate mystery, tension, and surprise?*	**Original**	**Reordered**

Anchor Performance 6: Distinguish the Point of View of Various Characters as Well as Their Own and How It Shapes the Content and Style of Text

Understanding point of view is a challenge for many diverse adolescent learners. Although an author generally expresses a single point of view, most often "that voice is only one voice of many, including the reader's that may speak in the writing . . . A writer can use other people's voices directly through quotation, paraphrase, or summary" (Angelillo, 2003, p. 88). In other words, in spite of the many voices apparent in a written piece, one strong voice generally emerges, which is the author's point of view. Yet discerning which one is the author's can be a complicated task for those who are not fluent readers. Students need to understand the structure of the multiple voices an author creates in order uncover the author's genuine point of view.

In examining the 6–12 grade-level standards associated with this anchor performance, we found distinct variations in expectations for student skills. In Grade 6, students are required to explain how an author establishes the narrator or speaker's point of view, whereas in Grade 7, students are required to analyze how the author contrasts the points of view of text characters or narrators. By Grade 8, students are expected to analyze how different points of view produce effects such as suspense or humor. However, in Grades 9–10, there is a shift in focus to analyze points of view drawn from international literature and the cultural experiences they reflect. Finally, in Grades 11–12, students are asked to discern what is directly and indirectly stated by points of view with consideration for techniques such as satire, sarcasm, and irony.

Essential Strategy to Support Anchor Performance 6: Activities That Draw Students' Attention to Story Point of View

Students who are attempting to uncover an author's point of view in their reading might meet with some confusion. According to Murray (2011), many people use the terms *perspective, opinion,* and *point of view* interchangeably. Understanding point of view begins with knowing the distinction between all three of these terms, as Murray defined them as follows:

Perspective: Perspective is the mental state that combines available facts and personal ideas to shape a meaningful whole to the individual.

Opinion: Opinion is a belief, often firmly expressed as a judgment, but which does not rise to the level of fact. Opinions can be changed as new facts and ideas are presented to the individual.

Point Of View—Point of view or POV can be used to describe one's physical or mental relationship to an object or event. (para. 3)

To understand point of view more clearly, Murray suggested visualizing walking outside the front door of your home. If you look to the left, what you see is your point of view. However, if by some chance you were lifted off the ground and were standing atop a tall tree or the roof of your home, your point of view of the same place would be altered. We offer the following activities to assist students in recognizing an author's point of view.

Point of View: A Preteaching Activity (Illinois State Board of Education, 2012). For this strategy, students come to an understanding of point of view through a hypothetical situation that is relevant to their age/grade level. Ultimately, students must retell the story from a diverse point of view. To begin, select a scenario to present to students—that is, an incident of bullying, a team sport in which someone was accused of cheating, or two students arguing in the cafeteria. Continue with the following steps:

- Tell the chosen scenario with as much detail and description as possible. Have the scenario available for students in writing either in its entirety or as an outline that includes its major points so students can refer to it.
- Ask students to take on different roles in the chosen scenario be it the teacher; an administrator; one of the students involved in the incident; friends, classmates, teammates of the students involved; an onlooker.
- Direct students to retell the story from the point of view of their assigned role by rewriting the scenario.
- Invite them to share their writing with the class. Use students' work as an opportunity to further discuss how and why an author's point of view can change.

Differentiate this activity for certain groups of diverse learners by assigning pairs of students the same role and having them discuss how to retell the story before they write.

Character Exploration. In many fictional tales, different characters can be involved in the same story scene or event, but not experience it in the same way. An example of a novel in which the author expresses multiple points of view through his characters is *The Grapes of Wrath* by John Steinbeck (1993). Within some chapters,

> The narrator assumes the voice of a typical individual, such as a displaced farmer or a crooked used-car salesman, expressing that person's individual concerns. . . . The chapters focusing on the Joad family are narrated primarily from an objective point of view. . . . At certain points, however, the narrator shifts and presents the Joads from an omniscient point of view, explaining their psychologies, characters, and motivations in intimate detail. (Sparknotes, 2013, para. 2)

With this strategy, students explore the multiple points of view that authors' directly express or imply through their characters. To begin, divide students into groups that contain the same number of characters involved in a single story event you want your students to explore. Next, assign each student in the group one of the characters from that scene.

Direct students to write a brief summary of their assigned character's point of view. Have students share their ideas in their group. Ask one student from each group to report their group's findings. Chart students' shared information and have them come to consensus about each character's point of view.

Freeze Frame. Writers of literary fiction can focus their readers' attention on certain story details that lead them to understand the author's points of view. To explore the multiple views of different characters, engage students in an activity that asks them to use inference and to draw conclusions about what a character can see, hear, touch, taste, and smell. Select a piece of text that has multiple story characters present and ask students to visually *freeze the frame* of the scene in their minds. If available, choose a photograph, a piece of film, or video depiction of the scene and have it available for students to view. Direct students to complete a sensory inventory of each character in the scene (e.g., *What does the character see? Hear? Touch?*). Ask students to draw conclusions about each character's point of view from their completed inventories. (See Chapter 5 for a similar strategy, *Sensory Chart,* Table 5.3.)

The Role on the Wall. Based on a classic drama strategy to help actors fully understand the role of a particular character, it has been adapted here to help students investigate characters' points of view. It can also be used to conduct an in-depth character study as well as examine characters' perspectives, motivations, and opinions. With this strategy, students work in groups each with an outline drawing of one or more of the characters depicted on chart paper placed "on the wall" around the classroom. Students are then invited to brainstorm the character's thoughts, words, feelings, observations, reactions, interactions, and so on, and write the information on the appropriate character chart. Students then use the information they gathered to draw their own conclusions about characters' points of view.

Integration of Knowledge and Ideas

Anchor Performance 7: Evaluate Story Content as It Is Presented in Multimedia Formats

To develop this anchor performance, students need to have increased opportunities to compare grade-appropriate story text with variations of the same story represented through mixed forms of media to be better able to analyze the multiple elements a given piece of fiction. The analysis of combined media should increase students' ability to compare and contrast different representations of the same story in terms of outcomes and fidelity as well as examine what and how information is dramatized or eliminated from the original story.

To meet the expectations for this standard, students in Grade 6 will compare and contrast the experience of reading a piece of literature with an audio, video, or staged drama of the text. In conjunction with Grade 6 expectations, students in Grade 7 will be asked to analyze the outcomes of the elements particular to each medium. In Grade 8, students are asked to compare and contrast to what extent a multimedia version of the text has remained faithful to the original story line. In Grades 9–10, students will identify to what extent key scenes from different mediums are either emphasized or minimized. Finally, in Grades 11–12, students will analyze multiple interpretations of text presented through different mediums and determine how each medium represents the original text.

Essential Strategy to Support Anchor Performance 7: Create Opportunities for Students to Work With Visual, Oral, and Multimedia Representations of Literature

Providing students with multimedia representations of the same story is often beneficial for academically and linguistically diverse learners. Obtaining information from multimedia sources can support students' overall comprehension and reduce their anxiety due to lack of understanding. By integrating multiple story accounts, students should be better able to construct meaning in spite of the difficulties they may have with the written text.

Summarize-Compare-Contrast-Reflect. With this strategy, students have the opportunity to compare and contrast two different representations of the same story as well as reflect on the particular outcomes of each of them. To begin, direct students to perform the following tasks:

- Read, listen to, and/or view two different representations of the same piece of story.
- Summarize or give a short synopsis of the work (ask students to concentrate on the *big idea* of the story that is contained in both representations).
- Compare and contrast the two forms of media; identify key points they have in common and indicate their main differences.
- Reflect on the story changes due to the different types of media used.

A graphic organizer for this task is represented in Table 3.9. This strategy can be adapted for students to compare multiple representations of the same story. Additionally, it can be used across other literary genres.

Table 3.9 Summarize-Compare-Contrast-Reflect

Story Title:				
Brief Summary of the Story:				
Contrast What ideas are unique to Medium 1?		Compare What ideas are the same?		Contrast What ideas are unique to Medium 2?
	Medium 1		Medium 2	
Reflect: How did each medium impact the story outcome?				
Medium 1		**Medium 2**		
Which media version did you prefer? Explain why.				

Movie Adaptations: Altered Elements. With this strategy, students compare carefully selected essential scenes that they will watch (five- to seven-minute segments). They then read the corresponding narrative of the original or adapter version of the literary fiction. This allows for deep reading and deep viewing. Ask students to brainstorm a list of story events that were altered or eliminated in the film adaptation of the text. Next, direct them to select those events they thought were most significant in changing the story in some way. Have students analyze the movie adaptations' effect on the literary elements of the original text. Ask students to share their preferred elements or story outcomes. An example of this strategy, comparing the novel and movie adaptation of *The Color Purple* by Alice Walker (2011) can be found in Figure 3.7.

Figure 3.7 Movie Adaptations: Altered Elements

Story: The Color Purple		
Movie Adaptation	**Why This Change Is Significant**	**Literary Elements Altered**
When Nettie returns from Africa, Celie has not spoken to Mister in quite some time. They have been completely estranged up until that moment.	In the text, Celie no longer hates Mister. She has already forgiven him before Nettie's return, and together they have been able to enjoy conversations, family, and friends.	Although the plot is altered slightly in the movie version, the theme of redemption is more apparent in the movie even though his character was much altered at the end of the novel.
Personal Preference		
I preferred the strong elements of redemption expressed in the movie adaptation.		

Two additional strategies that address this anchor performance, *Media Mash* and *SIGHT,* can be found in Chapter 4.

Note: Anchor Standard 8 is not applicable to the Reading for Literature section of the CCSS, thus no Anchor Performance 8 is presented here. See Chapter 4, which addresses this standard in Reading for Informational Texts.

Anchor Performance 9: Compare and Contrast Different Genres With Similar Story Themes

The CCSS grade-level benchmarks for a number of standards identify the skill of making logical comparisons between and among pieces of writing for various purposes. This standard along with its identified anchor performance expects students to be able to compare different genres that contain similar themes or topics. According to Smith (1994),

The analysis of different types of literature promotes cognitive development because it gives students an opportunity to apply similar skills and strategies, such as identifying themes discussed in one genre—fiction, for example—to other genres like poetry, reports, descriptive pieces, and plays. (para. 2)

As a result, students will be better able to comprehend information as it is expressed in different forms of literary text.

Individual grade-level expectations for this anchor performance vary from grade to grade. In Grade 6, students are required to compare and contrast different genres in terms of their representation of similar themes or topics, whereas in Grade 7, they are asked to examine both a fictional and a historical account of the same time period in order to compare and contrast texts. In Grade 8, students investigate how current works of fiction draw on themes from traditional stories. However, in Grades 9–10, students analyze more deeply how authors drawn on specific works to develop that information into a new piece of writing. Last, in Grades 11–12, students must demonstrate their understanding of past works of American literature and how these works exemplify similar themes and topics.

Essential Strategy to Support Anchor Performance 9: Contrast Different Literary Forms With Similar Themes or Topics

It is necessary for students to establish the various schemata for the content, structure, and devices of various literary genres so that they may become active readers—make predictions, inferences, and comparisons as well as draw conclusions. Through individual text analysis, students learn much about the overall makeup of one particular genre, yet they may not be able to apply the same analytical thinking to another (Smith, 1991). For this reason, students must have the opportunity to compare different genres and explore the uniqueness of each literary form. Here, we offer several strategies to assist students in the task of comparing different forms of literature.

Comparison Chart (Marzano, Pickering, & Pollock, 2001). This strategy takes a broad-based approach for comparing two different genres. Students identify the similarities and differences of each text and incorporate supporting evidence for their claims. Table 3.10 is an example of one way to organize a chart for this purpose.

Theme Studies. This type of study allows students to delve more deeply into a particular topic and compare how the same subject is treated by different authors and in different genres. A theme study provides a framework for in-depth learning. It can help students to think more critically about what they read and support efforts to develop their research skills. A theme study might involve a broad topic such as perseverance; students read a wide selection of literature and nonfiction texts (Maya Angelou's *I Know Why the Caged Bird Sings*, Yann Martel's *Life of Pi*, and Greg Mortenson's *Three Cups of Tea*) as well as examine nontext items such as photographs and other

Table 3.10 Comparison Chart

Text 1	Text 2
How they are similar?	
Evidence of Similarities: Text 1	Evidence of Similarities: Text 2
How are they different?	
Evidence of Differences: Text 1	Evidence of Differences: Text 2

images. Questions for students to consider in this comparative study are as follows:

- What was the main goal of each main character?
- What difficulty or conflict did each character face?
- How did each main character respond to his or her difficulties?
- How was the conflict or problem in each story resolved?
- How was the same theme in each story made evident by the author?

Students might also have the opportunity to read and compare information about the concept of perseverance from the perspective of science/ nature, art, music, and social studies.

Comparing Multiple Genres. Similar to *Theme Studies*, this strategy also has students read several types of literary texts (i.e., short story, poetry, historical fiction) that focus around a similar theme or topic. The difference is this activity asks students to go beyond the analysis of basic story elements to examine a variety of literary components. Table 3.11 contains examples of some of the points students may compare.

For additional organizational strategies for comparing and contrasting different genres, see Venn Diagrams in Chapter 4.

Table 3.11 Comparing Multiple Genres

Common Theme:			
	Text 1	**Text 2**	**Text 3**
Basic story plot			
Point of view of the author			
Overall tone			
Major conflict			
Additional story themes			
Use of symbols			
Literary devices (irony, satire, paradox)			

Range of Reading and Level of Text Complexity

Anchor Performance 10: Read and Comprehend Literature, Including Stories, Drama, and Poetry at Grade Level

At the end of the school year, the expectation is that all students will be reading and comprehending literature on grade level. Of course, this anchor performance is most challenging for diverse learners. Although goals and expectations must remain high for all students, teachers, and administrators must also be realistic about goal setting for adolescents who have learning difficulties, have had inadequate schooling, or are English learners. Goals should be attainable and achievable, and when students are reading well below their grade levels, students must be given adequate time and support to develop their skills.

Educators should review students' overall progress toward meeting targeted goals as specified by the standards. For this reason, a portfolio assessment apart from standardized testing is most helpful in ascertaining the amount of progress diverse learners have made. With a portfolio, teachers collect and assess sample pieces of students' best work or efforts over a period of time (a quarter, semester, or year); the work in the portfolio is used to document the students' growth and development (Paulson, Paulson, & Meyer, 1991). In this way, students, overall progress can become far more apparent compared with the results of annual grade-level testing that may be well above their ability to perform. In the long run, the overarching goal for all students should be direct and sustained progress toward meeting grade-level literacy. To this end, documented evidence that students have increased not only their reading and writing skills but also their speaking and listening abilities can support this overarching goal.

Essential Strategy to Support Anchor Performance 10: Multiple Opportunities for Exposure, Adequate Time to Learn, and Quality Interventions

The problems associated with adolescent literacy involve a wide range of reading difficulties among middle and high school students, "from those with the most basic skill needs to those who have developed general comprehension strategies, but not the specialized strategies, vocabulary and knowledge base required for understanding complex discipline specific texts" (Lee & Spratley, 2010, p. 2). Apart from the general approaches teachers apply in the classroom to foster student literacy development—multiple opportunities to learn new and difficult information; use of auditory, visual, tactual, and kinesthetic activities; learning environments that support students' persistence, perseverance, and self-confidence—some students need specific interventions to become college- and career-ready readers and writers. To this end, Moore and Hinchman (2003) identified the dimensions of responsive interventions:

- *Positive relationships.* Teachers learn as much as they can about their students and foster the development of mutual respect and caring.
- *Shared agenda.* Forming partnerships with students, teachers collaboratively plan with them to determine effective interventions.
- *Existing literacies.* Students bring with them existing literacies and interests that teachers need to capitalize on in order for them to develop school literacies.
- *Models of proficient performance.* Using a model for the gradual release of responsibility (Gallagher & Pearson, 1983), teachers model and provide guided practice before having their students try new strategies independently.
- *Engaged, extended reading and writing.* Even struggling readers must have the opportunity to engage in "extended school-assigned reading" (Moore & Hinchman, 2003, p. 112) in order to construct meaning by applying strategies taught explicitly to them for independent reading tasks.

- *Planning interventions with balance and breadth.* Frameworks for teaching preadolescent youngsters that incorporate reading, writing, and skill work on a daily basis can be incorporated into the literacy development of adolescent learners. These program models include Clay's (1993) Reading Recovery and Cunningham's Four Blocks (Cunningham & Allington, 1999). More specific to the needs of some adolescent learners, Luke and Freebody define literacy in terms of multiple capabilities in their Four Resource Model (Freebody & Luke, 1990; Luke & Freebody, 1997, 1999). (See Key Resources at the end of this chapter to obtain more information about each of these program models.)

Helping diverse learners understand a range of literary texts is a complex task. According to Lee and Spratley (2010),

It remains the case that literature teachers are more likely to ask students about the symbolism in literary texts than to model or teach how to detect the symbolic from the literal and how to re-construct the figurative inferences to be made about symbols in literature. (p. 10)

They furthered suggested that teachers plan instruction to incorporate literacy development into their instruction in the following ways:

- Emphasize that reading is a process of making meaning from the printed word.
- Offer supports that guide students while they are reading.
- Foster students' ability to independently and with peer support make sense of the texts they read.
- Scaffold reading tasks to help develop students' knowledge and skills over time.
- Plan classroom discussions about strategic learning from texts.
- Consistently offer support in order for students to achieve ongoing success.

ANTICIPATED OUTCOMES

The strategies introduced in this chapter will help all learners to have a better understanding of the complexities of different types of literature. It is anticipated that students will be better able to do the following:

- Apply various reading strategies to enhance comprehension and engage in text-dependent discussions
- Focus more readily on central story themes
- Retell and summarize literature
- Use graphic organizers to more fully examine story elements
- Understand, compare, and contrast the various points of view of different story characters
- Analyze story content as it is presented in multimedia formats

It is important to keep in mind that the CCSS "define what all students are expected to know and be able to do, not how teachers should teach" (*Common Core State Standards*, 2010a, p. 6). Therefore, teachers of diverse learners must maintain their autonomy to plan and select research-based instructional strategies that are most crucial for their students to develop literacy skills as well as to learn the complex aspects of analyzing various forms of literature.

INSTRUCTIONAL CHALLENGES

According to the National Council of Teachers of English (NCTE) (2006), more than 8 million youngsters in Grades 4–12 read below their grade-level expectations and "3,000 students with limited literacy skills drop out of high school every day" (p. 2). There is no doubt that the stakes are high, and literacy instruction is key. Therefore, secondary school teachers, particularly those who work with academically and linguistically diverse students, need to consider how best to support the development of fluent readers and writers in their classes.

One of the key advances of the CCSS for English Language Arts is to progress students' exposure to more complex texts, an ongoing challenge for teachers of diverse learners. Further compounding this challenge is the teaching of fiction that incorporates often subtle and figurative language, making meaning less obvious to struggling readers. Advanced-level literature often contains low-frequency vocabulary, metaphorical language, and elaborate sentence structures. Additionally, story events do not always unfold in a logical or linear fashion.

The NCTE (2006) identified some broad-based strategies to improve adolescent literacy, including "increased [student] motivation, comprehension, critical thinking, and classroom-based assessment" (p. 7). The council suggested that in order for teachers to be best prepared to meet the instructional needs of adolescent learners, "substantial reform, both in teaching practices and in school infrastructures" (p. 7) will be required. It further suggested that in light of teachers having the greatest affect on student learning, "professional development of teachers holds the greatest potential to improve adolescent literacy achievement" (p. 7). Therefore, with the proper amount of instructional knowledge, adolescent students may be guided to become confident and independent readers and writers.

PROMISING CLASSROOM PRACTICES

Using Literature in Content-Area Studies in Ohio

In a unit about freedom in the United States, social studies teacher at Theodore Roosevelt High School in Kent, Ohio, Mike Markulis, introduced the right to free speech to his ninth-grade class, which is composed of all students who have been identified as at-risk due to unstable home situations, struggles in the traditional classroom, or social immaturity. The class completed a deep reading of an excerpt of the Espionage and Sedition Acts of 1918 that focuses on the limitations that were placed on Americans about what they could say or write about the government, the military, and the flag. The act disallowed any criticism of the draft, taxes, and the war, and so Mike presented his students with a list of activities that would have been considered illegal, and the students had to determine which ones would have warranted arrest in 1918 based on what they read in the primary source document.

Mike then read an excerpt from Dalton Trumbo's fictional work, *Johnny Got His Gun,* which was published in 1939. The excerpt is a stream-of-conscious criticism about the American government and military. The students subsequently compared the document from 1939 to the Espionage and Sedition Acts of 1918, and they found examples of how *Johnny Got His Gun* would have violated the law 20 years earlier. The class then discussed how the right to free speech is an issue that has always been in the forefront of American culture but that the freedom has certainly evolved through time. By using literature and primary sources, Mike was able to incorporate the reading standards of the Common Core while teaching his students about important historical events.

A Literacy Project for English Language Learners From Maryland

At Richard Montgomery High School in Rockville, Maryland, Ann McCallum's class of intermediate English language learners brainstormed about what makes a good book after reading *Holes* by Louis Sachar (2000). Ann carefully recorded students' answers. Her class offered words and phrases such as *the people, interesting, understand it, suspense, emotion, funny, action, not too long,* and *happy in the end.* She then asked students to rate how well they enjoyed the book *Holes* by showing one to five fingers with five indicting the greatest enjoyment. As the majority of students indicated at least a four in terms of enjoyment level, the class consensus was that most students had enjoyed the book.

Ann went back to the brainstormed list, and under the direction of the students, she circled those words that could best relate to *Holes.* Of the eight-circled terms, the teacher asked students to choose three that most influenced their enjoyment of this book. Once voting was complete, the following words were chosen: *the people* (characters), *action* (plot), and *emotion* (conflict). The words in parentheses were the corresponding literary terms the teacher wrote to connect the student vocabulary to more formal, academic equivalents.

The essential question, the focal point for the next step, was the following: *What is most important in determining whether a book is good or not?* With this question in mind, students participated in writing a guided essay by first filling in an outline as a class and then using the detailed information to compose their own five-paragraph essay. The teacher facilitated the process by eliciting a whole-class hook-and-thesis statement and asked students to develop each of the main categories of enjoyment they had voted for previously. For instance, for "the people/ characters" section, students chose to discuss the main character of the book, Stanley Yelnats. Under details, they wrote character traits such as funny, hard-working, and unlucky. The teacher then prompted students to work independently to give specific examples as evidence to back up these claims.

Ms. McCallum reported that the project worked well for most students. For all but two of the eighteen in the class, students were able to produce a comprehensive and cohesive essay with little further intervention. For the two that struggled, the teacher worked through the first body paragraph with each of them, modeled the desired organization of the writing, and then steered them to produce their own, coherent essay. Overall, students demonstrated significant learning and, as evidenced by their level of engagement, they seemed to enjoy themselves at the same time.

Exploring Archetypes With Superheroes in California

The students in Paula Dreyfuss's class are at-risk adolescents at Chaparral High School, a continuation school in San Dimas, California.

One of her classes is a repeat English class for students who have failed previous English courses and are behind in credits. Students have reading levels from fourth to twelfth grade, with most students reading between fifth and seventh grade. Over 40% of the students are from group homes or foster homes; many others are also from low socioeconomic households.

Paula found that the concept of archetypes can be difficult for her students to understand because characters such as *Beowulf* are unfamiliar to them. However in this lesson, she used the archetype of superheroes to demonstrate its characteristics and meaning in a way that students could better understand.

Using personal whiteboards, students wrote the name of a superhero and held up their board. While a few tried to be nonconforming and chose villains, they were redirected to choose only heroes. Some selected lesser-known superheroes such as the Green Lantern, Flash, and Thor, although most students chose Superman, Batman, Wolverine, and Wonder Woman. Paula observed that only girls chose Wonder Woman.

Students were then asked to write on their whiteboards the traits that they thought were most common among all superheroes that were named, and they were successful in listing their personality types and traits. All of them came up with characteristics such as bravery, kindness, saving people without regard to their own safety, and so on. When asked how they knew this information without having to research it, the students agreed they had learned it from an early age through cartoons, movies, and books. They further drew their own conclusions about the use and appeal of superhero characters in popular culture—these characters are often written with the intent to teach right from wrong, and students concluded that this was an opportune way to teach children lessons at an early age.

The written assignment for this lesson involved students' creating their own superheroes. They had to devise a name for their characters, identify their specific powers, and determine a method in which they would deal with a nemesis. Students were very engaged and enjoyed sharing their own superheroes with the rest of the class. From this introductory lesson, students were better able to transfer their understanding of archetypes to the reading of classic literature such as *Beowulf.*

Comparing and Contrasting Literature in a New York Middle School

At Bellport Middle School in New York, Loraine K. McCray teaches students with interrupted formal education (SIFEs) and English language learners (ELLs) with individual education programs (IEPs). These students usually have an identified goal of increasing their reading comprehension and their ability to answer questions based on what they have read. Equally, the CCSS expect students to be able to cite, analyze, and make inferences from textual evidence. To that end, Loraine directed her mixed-grade-level English-as-a-second language (ESL) classes, containing general education ELLs, SIFEs, and ELL students with IEPs, to engage in collaborative discussions with classmates as well as reading and writing tasks related to the theme of *Courage in Literature.*

Loraine developed an essential question for her students to consider: *How can we judge which characters have courage?* She explained to her students that they would be reading two pieces of fiction whose characters were involved with overcoming adversity, *Holes* by Louis Sachar (2000), and *Powerful People Powerful Lives: Stories of Champions* by Joy T. Vaughan (2010). The students had the overall task of comparing and contrasting these two stories and developing an understanding about what it means to be courageous.

To support their comprehension of the texts, students used journal writing as well as completed character maps. They engaged in the discovery of the different meanings of courage and why people are often described as courageous. In reading the two pieces of literature, one fiction and the other based on real-life events, students compared and contrasted the stories and situations that the characters faced and tracked each of the character's paths to becoming courageous. There were guiding questions related to the reading to ensure that the students understood the plot and setting as well as the conflict. Loraine also had students focus on the conventions of written and spoken language as they completed each task related to the reading.

As a culminating activity, the students composed their own description of a person they know whom they considered to be courageous and revealed how that person demonstrated courage. Loraine used a sensitive approach in her evaluation of what students considered courageous and how it was displayed. Together, the students considered the different levels of courageous acts and how each can impact lives. Special emphasis was given to what might be considered quiet acts of courage, which often go unnoticed but are just as important as overt acts.

These stories were connected together to weave a tapestry of courage that was made into a booklet and shared with families at the yearly districtwide ESL Parent Celebration. In addition, Loraine believed that reading these two pieces of literature not only helped students advance their understanding of American culture but also provided students with important role models to help support their schoolwide character-building initiative.

COMMON CORE READING STANDARDS— UN(COMMON) REFLECTION QUESTIONS

1. Which of the ten anchor standards or the grade-appropriate equivalents will present the greatest departure from your previous literacy instructional practices regarding teaching fiction or narratives? Why?

2. Which of the ten anchor standards or the grade-appropriate equivalents will present the greatest challenge to your students? Why?

3. How are you planning to strategically address the difficulties your students will face with select standards?

KEY RESOURCES

Professional Books

Alber-Morgan, S. (2010). *Using RTI to teach literacy to diverse learners, K–8: Strategies for the inclusive classroom.* Thousand Oaks, CA: Corwin.

Beck, I. L., McKeown, M. G., & Kucan, L. (2002). *Bringing words to life: Robust vocabulary instruction.* New York, NY: Guilford Press.

Cloud, N., & Genesee, F. (2009). *Literacy instruction for English language learners.* Portsmouth, NH: Heinemann.

Fisher, D., & Frey, N. (2011). *Teaching students to read like detectives: Comprehending, analyzing, and discussing text.* Bloomington, IN: Solution Tree

Online Resources

Classroom Strategies
http://www.adlit.org/strategy_library
https://www.teachingchannel.org/videos/pre-reading-strategies

Compare and Contrast Graphic Organizers
http://www.greece.k12.ny.us/files/filesystem/comparecontrast.pdf

Four Blocks Literacy Model
http://www.wfu.edu/education/fourblocks/about_fourblocks.html

Four Resources Model
http://www.newliteracies.com.au/what-are-new-literacies?/116
http://www.readingonline.org/research/lukefreebody.html

List of Common Literary Devices in Poetry
   http://quizlet.com/5328743/25-common-literary-terms-used-in-
      poetry-flash-cards/

List of Literary Devices
   http://literary-devices.com

No Fear Literature (the original text side by side with an easy-to-under-
stand version.)
   http://www.sparknotes.com/nofear/lit/

Reading Recovery
   http://readingrecovery.org/reading-recovery/teaching-children/
      basic-facts

Role on the Wall Example
   http://thinkingofteaching.blogspot.com/2011/05/role-on-wall.html

Teaching Figurative Language With Commercials
   http://classroommagic.blogspot.com/2013/02/teaching-figurative-
      language-with.html

Topics in Adolescent Literacy
   http://www.adlit.org/topics/

Understanding Story Elements
   http://www.yale.edu/ynhti/curriculum/units/1983/3/83.03.02.x.html

What We Know About Adolescent Reading
   www.leadered.com/pdf/adolescent%20reading%20whitepaper.pdf

4 Reading Strategies for Informational Texts

A complex society is dependent every hour of every day upon the capacity of its people at every level to read and write, to make difficult judgments, and to act in the light of extensive information.

—John W. Gardner (1995, p. 53)

OVERVIEW

Several key advances are identified by the Common Core State Standards (CCSS) for instruction in Grades 6–12, one of which is for students to read more complex texts. Apart from learning required subject-area content, the CCSS outline a set of skills for all students to be able to think more deeply about what they read, critically analyze information from different media, evaluate the evidence and reasoning behind the work of various authors, and present detailed arguments as well as support their opinions concerning diverse issues. To foster these skills, there must be a shift from direct teaching about content to students' discovering and analyzing content through various reading and learning tasks. For this reason, students will need to spend more time engaged in close reading of texts with increasing complexity as well as answering text-dependent questions and less time listening to the teacher lecture, copying notes, and completing worksheets.

WHY TEACHING DIVERSE ADOLESCENT LEARNERS READING STRATEGIES PROMOTES COMPREHENSION OF INFORMATIONAL TEXTS

Reading and understanding grade-level informational texts is not surprisingly a challenge for many academically and linguistically diverse learners. However, not only will diverse learners find these literacy tasks challenging, but all students will be confronted with reading more complex texts that are at times above their individual reading or comprehension ability. For this reason, explicit strategy instruction will support the learning of most students to develop skills for citing textual evidence, determining central ideas, understanding subject-specific vocabulary, identifying the organization of text structure, and evaluating as well as supporting specific claims about the text.

Some frameworks for teaching diverse students focus on making lessons accessible and comprehensible (Crawford & Krashen, 2007), but they rarely emphasize direct reading instruction at the secondary level. Additionally, instruction geared for diverse learners often does not expose them to grade-level texts, let alone above-grade-level reading material. However, the CCSS require a shift in thinking for the instruction of all students, which includes academically and linguistically different youngsters. Therefore, to enhance the ability of those who are struggling to read grade-level texts, targeted literacy and explicit strategy instruction should be part of the overall instruction in content-area classes.

Competent readers apply various comprehension strategies routinely and automatically; however, the same strategies must be explicitly taught—through modeling, guided practice, and collaborative peer work—to those who are reading below grade level in standard American English. For this reason, *all* teachers must develop and embed general reading strategies into content lessons and apply techniques to scaffold learning in order to enhance the reading ability of diverse learners. Some reading strategies include carefully selecting and presenting a reduced amount of rigorous text for students to closely read, while teaching academic vocabulary explicitly and consistently (Feldman & Kinsella, 2005), and guiding students understanding through the shared reading of text. By developing improved reading skills, diverse students will be better able reach the goals identified by the CCSS, such as to fully analyze and interpret text meaning, to learn from multiple text sources, and to determine the author's point of view. Furthermore, explicit strategy instruction can help many struggling learners become independent, confident readers as well as enhance their overall understanding and use of academic language.

CORE INFORMATIONAL READING STRATEGIES

The strategies contained in this chapter follow the expectations of the ten College and Career Readiness Anchor Standards (CCRAS) for Reading with particular attention to the reading strand for informational texts and the Standards for Literacy in History/Social Studies, Science, and Technical Subjects. They are framed by the CCRAS strand-specific sets of *Key Ideas and Details, Craft and Structure, Integration of Knowledge and Ideas, and Range of Reading and Text Complexity.* From each of the ten CCRAS, we derived and aligned a series of related *Anchor Performances*—skill sets that all students need to develop—and suggest strategies to help diverse students build these skills in order to meet the standards. Some strategies may be more appropriate than others depending on the grade-level or language facility of the students. To that end, we make suggestions on how to adapt strategies to meet the needs of diverse individual learners.

Box 4.1 College and Career Readiness Anchor Standards for Reading

Key Ideas and Details

1. Read closely to determine what the text says explicitly and to make logical inferences from it; cite specific textual evidence when writing or speaking to support conclusions drawn from the text.

2. Determine central ideas or themes of a text and analyze their development; summarize the key supporting details and ideas.

3. Analyze how and why individuals, events, and ideas develop and interact over the course of a text.

Craft and Structure

4. Interpret words and phrases as they are used in a text, including determining technical, connotative, and figurative meanings, and analyze how specific word choices shape meaning or tone.

(Continued)

(Continued)

5. Analyze the structure of texts, including how specific sentences, paragraphs, and larger portions of the text (e.g., a section, chapter, scene, or stanza) relate to each other and the whole.

6. Assess how point of view or purpose shapes the content and style of a text.

Integration of Knowledge and Ideas

7. Integrate and evaluate content presented in diverse media and formats, including visually and quantitatively, as well as in words.

8. Delineate and evaluate the argument and specific claims in a text, including the validity of the reasoning as well as the relevance and sufficiency of the evidence.

9. Analyze how two or more texts address similar themes or topics in order to build knowledge or to compare the approaches the authors take.

Range of Reading and Level of Text Complexity

10. Read and comprehend complex literary and informational texts independently and proficiently.

Key Ideas and Details

Anchor Performance 1: Citing Textual Evidence and Making Logical Inferences

Citing textual evidence is an essential skill for students to develop so that they are best able to support their understandings with specific information directly from the text. Furthermore, the ability to make inferences and to draw conclusions from various pieces of information is an additional expectation for secondary students; they must be able to aptly go beyond the literal meaning of the printed words and reveal suggested meanings or make judgments.

Considering the grade-level Reading Standards for Informational Texts, Grade 6 students are generally expected to cite textual evidence to support text analysis as well as inferences; however, Grade 7 students are asked to identify several pieces of evidence from the text to defend a particular conclusion. By Grade 8, students must be able to discern between strong and weak textual evidence, and by Grades 9–10, students should able to cite both strong and thorough evidence. Finally, in conjunction with the skills specified in the previous grade levels, students in Grades 11–12 must be able to determine what matters the text leaves uncertain.

With regard to the Reading Standards for Literacy in History/Social Studies for this standard, students in Grades 6–8 are expected to cite both primary and secondary sources, whereas students in Grades 9–10 must also focus on the date and origin of information. Those students in Grades 11–12 must additionally link their understandings of text details as they relate to the text as a whole.

Considering the Reading Standards for Literacy in Science and Technical Subjects, the focus in Grades 6–8 is on citing evidence in science and technical texts. Grade 9–10 students are expected to focus on the scientific and technical details of explanations and descriptions, and students in Grades 11–12 must additionally attend to pertinent scientific and technical distinctions made by the author as well as any inconsistencies in the text.

Essential Strategies to Support Anchor Performance 1: Organize Textual Evidence and Activate Inferential Thinking

The ability to make inferences is a powerful skill that supports students' overall understanding of text—it is "the bedrock of reading" (Harvey & Goudvis, 2007, p. 23). According to Keene and Zimmermann (2007), "Proficient readers use their prior knowledge (schema) and textual information to draw conclusions, make critical judgments, and form unique interpretations from text" (p. 23). Teachers not only need to provide students with opportunities to tap into their prior knowledge to connect what they already know with the new information, but they must also explicitly teach students how to engage in inferential thinking. In some cases, students who are linguistically or culturally diverse may not have prior knowledge of a particular subject and benefit from frontloaded information to build their background knowledge on the topic (Marzano, 2004).

To meet this anchor performance, students also must be able to organize pertinent text information—both key ideas and details—from which inferences may be drawn. Not only do students need to distinguish between main ideas and supporting details, they must also determine where the evidence lies and critically interpret, evaluate, and draw conclusions from the information in the text. Here, we identify some approaches to support students' inferential thinking and strategies to assist students with organizing text information.

Paired Reading. With this strategy, students work in pairs to analyze text. They not only discover and differentiate key ideas and details, but they are able to support each other's overall understanding of the text. The steps for paired reading are as follows:

1. Each student reads silently a selected, short piece of text. It may be a sentence, a paragraph, or a page depending on the level of text complexity and the readiness of the students.

2. One student identifies the main idea by summarizing the reading in his or her own words. The other student must agree or disagree and state why.

3. Both students must come to a consensus about the main idea of the text.

4. Next, each student takes a turn to identify text details that support the main idea.

5. Students read the next selection silently. They switch their previous roles and repeat the above steps.

6. Students can keep track of main ideas and details using *Two-Column Notes*.

Text Coding. Harvey and Daniels (2009) suggested active reading strategies including text coding or text monitoring (see Box 4.2). As students read short selections appropriately assigned to them for independent reading, they use the following notations on the margins or sticky notes. Introduce text coding through modeled reading and text monitoring one or two codes at a time, gradually building up to all eight codes.

Box 4.2 Text Codes

✓ = I know this

X = This is not what I expected

* = This is important

? = I have a question about this

?? = I am really confused

! = This surprises me

L = I have learned something new here

RR = I have to reread this section

Two-Column Notes. The purpose of this strategy is for students to identify and record main ideas and corresponding details of a selected text. Students use *Two-Column Notes* while reading or listening to a text being read. After introducing, modeling, and practicing the use of this tool, provide ongoing opportunities for students to complete two-column notes in order to strengthen their ability to organize text information that can be the basis for further text analysis such as identifying pieces of data to support a conclusion or evaluating if evidence is substantial enough to support an author's claims. Figure 4.1 is an example of a two-column note organizer based on the Lincoln's historical *Gettysburg Address*.

Two-Column Notes may be differentiated by placing partial information in one or both columns to help linguistically and academically diverse learners better understand and organize the main ideas and details of challenging texts.

Figure 4.1   Two-Column Notes

Two-Column Notes	
Title: *The Gettysburg Address*	
Main Ideas	**Details**
Our founding fathers created the United States	• Conceived in liberty • Dedicated to all men being created equal
Now the United States is in a civil war	• Testing whether the nation as it was conceived can remain together (can endure)
We have come to dedicate the battlefield at Gettysburg	• The field is dedicated to those who have died in the war • It is a final resting place • It is fitting and proper to do so

Where's the Evidence? Students work alone, in pairs, or in teams to discern the best reason(s) why an event has taken place. The topics and main points of the event are either uncovered through the reading of the text or—to differentiate for some learners—are stated before the text is read. Students then must read or reread the text to gather additional evidence and draw their own conclusions. An example of this strategy is in Figure 4.2.

Figure 4.2 Where's the Evidence?

Where's the Evidence?	
Topic	9/11:United 83
Source	The 9/11 Commission Report
Question	What brought down United 83 on the morning of 9/11?
Inference	The passengers were the cause of the plane crashing in an empty field in Shanksville, PA, instead of Washington, DC.
Evidence from the document	• "At 9:57 AM, the passenger assault began." • "Several passengers had terminated phone calls with loved ones in order to join the revolt." • "The cockpit voice recorder captured the sounds of the passenger assault . . ." • " . . . the passengers were only seconds from overcoming them."
Conclusion	The passengers caused the hijackers to abort their mission to bring the airliner down in Washington, DC.

Anticipation Guides. Anticipation guides can build student interest about a subject and establish a purpose for reading, as well as tap into learners' prior knowledge that is essential for building inferencing skills. Before reading, students respond to a series of statements about the text by indicating whether they think they are true or false. Students make predictions about what the text will reveal. As the text is read, students are able to verify their predictions. Figure 4.3 is an example of an anticipation guide written for a text about photosynthesis.

Anticipation guides may also take a more complex form or shape, see Figure 4.4 for a blank template of an anticipation guide that asks students to agree or disagree with a set of statements prior to and then following the reading of target text. Although the reading of the anticipation guide might be beyond the reading readiness of some students, its additional purpose is to focus students on the important points of the reading selection and expose them to targeted content-specific vocabulary that they must know.

Through the process of using anticipation guides, diverse learners are often better able to remain focused on more difficult texts. To help struggling learners, teachers can project the image of the anticipation guide to the class and read each statement aloud. Instead of asking students to respond with a paper and pencil activity, students might be surveyed by asking them to raise their right hand if they think an answer is true or their left hand if they think it is false. Additionally, individual, hand-held whiteboards can be used to log student answers for a preassessment activity.

Figure 4.3 Anticipation Guide

Photosynthesis

Directions: Read the following sentences about what happens during the process of photosynthesis.

Write "T" if you think the sentence is true.

Write "F" if you think a sentence is false (not true).

_____ Photosynthesis is the process of converting light energy from the sun to chemical energy.

_____ It occurs in the *chloroplasts* using *chlorophyll*.

_____ Energy is converted primarily in leaves of the plant.

_____ The various parts of a leaf are the *epidermis*, the *mesophyll*, the vascular bundles, and the *stomates*.

_____ The *epidermis* has no *chloroplasts*.

_____ Photosynthesis occurs in the *mesophyll* cells.

_____ *Chlorophyll* looks green because it absorbs green light.

_____ The chemical reaction that occurs during photosynthesis creates the oxygen we breathe.

Source: http://biology.clc.uc.edu/courses/bio104/photosyn.htm

Figure 4.4 Blank Anticipation Guide Template

Check if you agree or disagree with these statements before you read the chapter and again after you read it.	Before Reading		After Reading	
	Agree	Disagree	Agree	Disagree

Inferencing Questions. Marzano (2010) identified four questions teachers can use to guide students in their discussions and to evaluate the validity of their inferences. They are as follows:

1. *What is my inference?* Students infer from their reading information that was not directly stated in the text.

2. *What information did I use to make this inference?* With this question, students identify the evidence they found to support their inferences. Students are made to understand that they have drawn conclusions based on textual evidence or generalizations made from their prior knowledge and past experience.

3. *How good was my thinking?* Students are asked to evaluate the foundation of their inferences. They must examine the basis for which they have drawn certain conclusions and identify whether or not they were justified.

4. *Do I need to change my thinking?* Here, students further consider their own thinking and decide whether or not to change their ideas. The point here is to have students reflect on their process and amend their thinking when necessary.

To support diverse learners, have them work in pairs. Students first read silently and make their own inferences or take turns reading and explore the identification of inferences together. The questions may be used to further examine their thinking.

Some additional strategies that are often helpful for diverse learners to build and activate prior knowledge to support the task of inferencing are:

- **Brainstorming**. With the teacher as facilitator, students offer their information and ideas about a particular topic or question.
- **Brainwriting.** Similar to brainstorming, students are given a set amount of time to jot down their ideas about a subject. Some students would benefit from sharing these with a partner or in small groups.
- **Visual Images**. Introduce new vocabulary, and build background knowledge using photographs, drawings, charts, and video. Some

students benefit from having exposure to the content through visual means before they are asked to uncover meaning from the text.

- **Think Alouds**. Teachers verbalize their own thinking after reading a short piece of text to model how students can make inferences from both evidence in the text and their own prior experiences.

Anchor Performance 2: Identify and Summarize Key Themes and Supporting Details

Students often need some guidance to identify and organize the main ideas and details that are evident in informational texts as well as to objectively summarize information. Moreover, diverse learners who generally find grade-level texts challenging to maneuver particularly need structured support. Consequently, these students would benefit from learning how to classify text information using different organizational schemes.

For this anchor performance as well as to meet grade-level expectations for Reading Standards for Informational Texts, Grade 6 students must identify and summarize the main idea and details of a text free from personal opinions. In Grade 7, students additionally need to determine two or more fundamental ideas in a text. In Grade 8, they must also focus on how a central theme is developed from the beginning to the end of a text. Moreover, in Grades 9–10, students need to include how ideas are fashioned and clarified by particular details. Finally, Grade 11–12 students are expected to perform all the tasks identified in the previous grade levels including providing a detailed analysis of how multiple themes influence one another.

With regard to the Reading Standards for Literacy in History/Social Studies for this anchor standard, students in Grades 6–8 are expected to cite central themes from either primary or secondary sources, whereas students in Grades 9–10 must also focus on how key ideas and details develop over the course of the text. Those students in Grades 11–12 must additionally provide an unbiased summary that clarifies the relationship among the key themes and text details.

With consideration for the Reading Standards for Literacy in Science and Technical Subjects, the focus in Grades 6–8 is determining not only key ideas but also conclusions of a text. Grade 9–10 students are expected to delineate and summarize an identified complex process or concept, and students in Grades 11–12 must additionally construct summaries that break down stated complex concepts in simpler terms.

Essential Strategy to Support Anchor Performance 2: Organize Summary Information

There are various ways of organizing summary information to help students sort and categorize main ideas and details during active reading. Some approaches create frameworks for diverse learners to identify and process pieces of text, most often with teacher guidance or peer support. Other means are through the use of graphic organizers that can be adapted to suit the needs of individual learners and completed independently, in student pairs, or in small groups. They may be differentiated to already contain some of the text information with the task remaining for students to find the details to complete the summary. The following are various ways to organize summary information.

Series-of-Events Chart (Moss & Loh, 2010). This is a visual guide that can help students identify the main ideas of a text in preparation for a summary. This type organizer works best with information that is presented in a sequence, a common expository text pattern often conveyed by words such as *first, last, after,* and *finally.* Similar to a timeline, this chart focuses students on the order of events. Figure 4.5 is an example of this strategy.

Figure 4.5 Series-of-Events Chart

Series-of-Events Chart
Initiating Event: The Launching of Sputnik I
Event 1
The Soviet Union launched Sputnik I, an artificial satellite, on October 4, 1957.
Event 2
Sputnik I was a technological accomplishment that captured the world's attention and marked the beginning of the space race between the United States and the Soviets.
Event 3
Since the Soviets had the capability to launch satellites, it was believed that they also had the technology to launch nuclear weapons.
Event 4
Shortly after the Soviets launched their first satellite, the U.S. Defense Department responded by approving funding for a U.S. satellite project.
Event 5
The success of the Sputnik launch also sparked the formation of National Aeronautics and Space Administration (NASA) in July 1958.

Source: http://history.nasa.gov/sputnik/

Coffee Klatsch. This activity helps students make decisions, gather important information, and identify the main ideas of a text in order to create a summary of events. The end result is that students create their own graphic organizers to summarize the selected text. The steps for this strategy are as follows:

Step 1: Students are divided into groups. Each group prepares index cards with the most important facts written in short phrases from the assigned text. Students within a group may read their text silently or take turns reading aloud. Index cards should be completed in consultation with one another.

Step 2: After each student prepares two or three cards, students are invited to walk around and read as many of their classmates' cards as they can within a specified frame of time. Students will take notes as they speak to their fellow students.

Step 3: Students return to their original group to discuss the information they have gathered.

Step 4: Each group must then develop a graphic organizer that shares the most important information regarding the topic, using all the information that has been gathered.

This activity works well with academically and linguistically diverse learners because all students have the opportunity to gather information as a team as well as practice all four language skills—listening, speaking, reading, and writing—to complete the task.

Retell and Write (Moss & Loh, 2010). For this activity, students are asked to recall information after reading or hearing a text read aloud to them. Students begin by working in pairs taking turns to retell the story. Teachers should consider with whom diverse learners are paired and invite the more linguistically capable student to share the text contents first. During this paired activity, students can also be encouraged to jot down information that was shared. Next, students write their informational summaries using the summary checklist in Figure 4.6 (see p. 106).

Anchor Performance 3: Analyze and Compare the Relationship of Text Elements

Prior to being able to examine the interplay between text elements, academically and linguistically diverse learners must understand the general

Figure 4.6 Checklist for Retell and Write

Checklist for Retell and Write
_____ Identified the author and title of the text
_____ Stated summary of main ideas clearly
_____ Included important details
_____ Placed summary information in the correct order
_____ Indicated facts accurately
_____ Added vocabulary from the text in summary
_____ Included all material for a complete summary
_____ Eliminated all unnecessary information

text. Providing students with a comprehensive overview of the text before they read would support their skills to make connections within the text. Additionally, explicitly teaching students the typical format of academic text structures, such as cause and effect, would support their understanding of social studies or scientific events or phenomena and their related causes.

For this anchor performance as well as to meet grade-level expectations for Reading Standards for Informational Texts, Grade 6 students must examine in great depth particular elements (individuals, ideas, or events) that are revealed in the text. Additionally, Grade 7 students will analyze how individuals, events, or ideas influence each other as they investigate the interplay between and among these elements. By Grade 8, students should be able to consider how the text reveals similarities and differences between people, events, or ideas through analogies or comparisons. In addition to these skills, students in Grades 9–10 consider how an author uncovers, orders, and develops a series of ideas as well as how these ideas are connected. Together with the previously identified skills, students in Grades 11–12 are expected to analyze how a multilevel set of ideas develops over the course of a text.

With regard to the Reading Standards for Literacy in History/Social Studies for this standard, students in Grades 6–8 are expected to distinguish the major steps of a process revealed in the text related to history/social studies, whereas students in Grades 9–10 must additionally determine whether a set of preceding events affected subsequent ones. Furthermore, students in Grades 11–12 must also evaluate different accounts of the same event and identify which interpretation best matches the textual evidence.

With consideration for the Reading Standards for Literacy in Science and Technical Subjects, students in Grades 6–8 must be able to perform multistep procedures such as when conducting experiments. Students in Grades 9–10 additionally must focus on exceptions to procedures as identified in the text, and students in Grades 11–12 must also evaluate the results of completing technical tasks based on details from the text.

Essential Strategy to Support Anchor Performance 3: Teacher- or Student-Created Structured Overviews

A structured overview scaffolds the organization of the main ideas and details from the text, thus making the information more accessible and ready for analysis. With a structured overview, students are better able to identify major concepts and be better prepared to analyze the relationships among individuals, ideas, and events revealed in the text. The following are several ways to develop structured overviews.

Pause, Process, Pen. This type of overview is student constructed during the reading of the text. Students are directed to read a small portion of the text, usually a paragraph, and then are asked to pause and critically think about what has just been read. Next, they write down something that stood out in the text—words, phrases, or sentences—and can also create illustrations to capture information. Then, they read another short piece of text and the activity is repeated until the entire text is read.

As they pause, students may be instructed to consider how the key elements (individuals, ideas, or events) in the text relate to one another. This activity might work well as a shared reading with learners who benefit from a more structured exercise. Teachers may also guide students with select questions as they stop and process information. The following questions may be used to direct students' thinking:

- What can you visualize about what you just read?
- What are you wondering about now?
- Why do you think things may be occurring this way?
- Who are the key individuals and how are they interacting with each other?
- What are the three key ideas and how are they connected?
- What are the three major events so far and how are they connected?
- How are individuals, ideas, or events interacting with one another?
- What, if anything, might be confusing or left unanswered?
- How do you feel about what you just read?
- What will happen as a result of . . . ?
- What do you find interesting? Fascinating? Frightening?

One Pager. This type of teacher-created overview identifies the main ideas and some details contained in the text in a list of complete sentences that follow the order the information is revealed in the reading. Students have the opportunity to examine and comprehend smaller amounts of text that contain important concepts and vocabulary reflective of the target text complexity that can be discussed before the full-length text is read. Teachers can project the image of the one pager and read aloud each statement, pause to discuss the more difficult vocabulary and concepts, and paraphrase the information to verbally scaffold instruction. Take a look at the sample one pager (Figure 4.7) written for an article titled *Minnesota, the Next Battleground State in the Fight to Label GMOs* (Benson, 2013).

Figure 4.7 One Pager

One Pager: Minnesota, the Next Battleground State in the Fight to Label GMOs

- Two pieces of legislation introduced in both the Minnesota House and Senate could soon require the labeling of all foods that contain genetically modified organisms (GMOs).
- Following the defeat of Proposition 37 in California last fall, more than 20 states have since introduced their own versions of GMO labeling legislation.
- This legislation does not ban genetically modified ingredients but lets consumers know about them so they can make their own choices.
- In a state heavily controlled by corporate agriculture interests such as the Minnesota Farmers Union, efforts are already being made to block the legislation from passing.
- Due to special interests having much control over Congress, the likelihood of passing similar legislation on the national level is considerably diminished.
- Polls indicate that the majority of Americans favor mandatory GMO labeling.

Structured Note Taking (Smith & Tompkins, 1988). This activity uses various graphic organizers selected according to the structure of a particular text (e.g., enumeration, compare/contrast, cause/effect) (see online resources at the end of this chapter for sample graphic organizers). This strategy helps students organize information, better understand what they are reading, and make connections among key individuals, ideas, or events. Teachers select appropriate organizers for students to complete. Organizers may be partially completed by the teacher for some students to focus their attention on pertinent information in the text. In time, help students select their own graphic organizers by making them aware of key words that signal particular text configurations. Some of these key words are as follows:

- **Enumeration**: *for instance, for example, such as, to illustrate, most important, in addition, another, furthermore*
- **Sequence (Time Order)**: *first, next, then, finally, before, after, not long after, shortly thereafter*
- **Compare/Contrast**: *same as, similar, alike, different from, the opposite of, opposed to, as well as, not only . . . but also, both, instead of, either . . . or, on the other hand*
- **Cause/Effect**: *so, because, therefore, since, as a result, consequently, for this reason, may be due to, if . . . then*

Also see Chapter 5 for a different discussion of structured note taking.

Graphic Representation. This type of teacher-prepared structured overview includes various visual depictions such as diagrams, maps, graphs, photo displays, and the like that represent ideas contained in the text arranged in some type of graphic organizer. It may be more appealing to some visual learners who are overwhelmed by a full page of text.

Craft and Structure

Anchor Performance 4: Determine Meaning of Words and Phrases

To develop students' academic vocabulary and enhance their comprehension, it is not sufficient for them to have a list of definitions for new terms as a reference. To best increase their understanding of complex texts, students need multiple opportunities to be exposed to content-specific vocabulary through reading, class discussions, and application of new words and phrases in their writing. Additionally, explicit vocabulary instruction should be incorporated into lessons in order to focus on developing students' abilities to apply strategies for learning new vocabulary independently.

For this anchor performance as well as to meet grade-level expectations for Reading Standards for Informational Texts, Grade 6 students must interpret the meaning of words and phrases in context, including figurative language, whereas in Grade 7, students also need to examine the outcomes of using particular words on the overall meaning and tone of the text. In Grade 8, students must analyze specific word choices, including analogies or allusions to other texts. In addition to these skills, students in Grades 9–10 must identify the cumulative effect on the text of specific word choices, and in Grades 11–12, students also need to determine how authors employ and refine meaning of words from the beginning to the end of a text.

With regard to the Reading Standards for Literacy in History/Social Studies for this anchor performance, students in Grades 6–8 need to determine the meaning of words that are specific to the study of history/social studies, whereas students in Grades 9–10 additionally must analyze how words are used to express various aspects of politics, economics, and other social aspects of the subject. Furthermore, students in Grades 11–12 must also examine how the author's use of words shapes the meaning of the text.

With consideration for the Reading Standards for Literacy in Science and Technical Subjects, students in Grades 6–12 must be able to develop an understanding of key symbols and terms as well as subject-specific words and phrases as they relate to scientific and technical texts and topics at each grade level.

Essential Strategy to Support Anchor Performance 4: Build Vocabulary Sense

In the previous chapter on Reading Strategies for Literary Texts (see Chapter 3), many suggested strategies for teaching vocabulary are also applicable to informational texts (also see Chapter 2 for vocabulary work). In addition to those strategies, we have compiled several approaches to learning words and phrases to better help students understand informational texts.

List-Group-Label (Taba, 1967). A combination of brainstorming and semantic mapping, *List-Group-Label* activates students' prior knowledge, increases their use of academic vocabulary, and helps students understand the relationship between groups of words. The teacher directs students to brainstorm a list of words about a topic within a particular time frame. Using critical-thinking skills, students then group the words according to categories that they recognize. Last, they devise labels or titles for each of their word groups. This strategy is often completed in student pairs, trios, or small groups and can be used before, during, or after the text is read. Lists can be generated in a whole-class setting with students partnering to complete the rest of the task. Two variations of this strategy to differentiate instruction are as follows:

- *Word Sorts.* Teachers prepare printed lists of words along with titled categories. With partners, students cut out the words and sort them according to the teacher-specified categories.
- *Photo Sort.* No words are involved with this activity. Students are given a small stack of photos (generated from Google Images) that they must group and categorize. Category labels may be teacher-specified or student-devised.

Concept Maps. To organize text information, students use a concept map (Novak & Cañas, 2006) to identify key words and phrases about a topic. This during-reading or after-reading strategy helps students make meaningful connections by identifying essential vocabulary. These organizers can be completed individually, with partners, or in full-class settings with a projected image. The concepts they contain are generally new material for students, and teacher modeling and guidance in their completion is particularly helpful with diverse learners (see Figure 4.8).

Figure 4.8 Concept Map

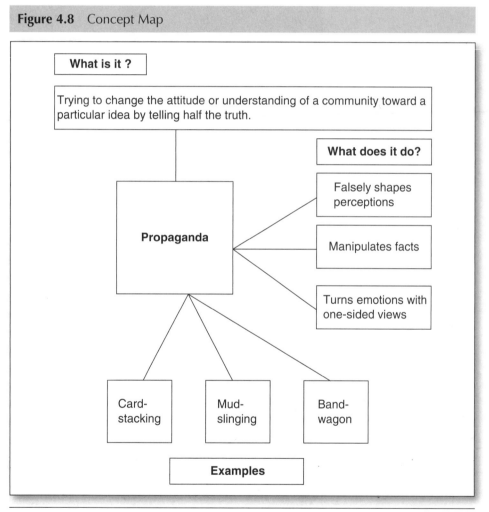

Source: Adapted from Echevarría, J., Vogt, M., & Short, D. (2012). *Making content comprehensible for English language learners: The SIOP model* (4th ed., p. 81). Needham Heights, MA: Allyn & Bacon.

Semantic Feature Analysis (Johnson & Pearson, 1984). Using a chart or grid to identify similarities and differences among a group of related concepts, students use *Semantic Feature Analysis* to make distinctions between identified concepts in relation to a specific set of criteria. Using the grid can help students think critically and analyze text closely. This activity can support students' understanding of complex concepts and academic vocabulary as they are related to a finite set of identified characteristics of a selected topic. The following are steps to creating a *Semantic Feature Analysis* grid:

1. *Select a topic or category.* After examining the text or subject matter, choose a concept that students may compare such as two types of cells, plant and animal, or a group of related ideas, such as different forms of government.

2. *Identify characteristics and features.* Select words and phrases that are related to the characteristics and features of the key concepts.

3. *Create the grid.* Place the key concepts to be analyzed down the first column of the grid and the semantic features to be examined across its top row.

4. *Decide how students report their findings.* Identify how students will mark the features that both positively and negatively relate to each concept such as using plus (+) or minus (–) signs, check marks (✓), or other reporting indications.

Figures 4.9 (Plato's Five Regimes) and Figure 4.10 (Plant and Animal Cells) are completed examples of this strategy.

The *Semantic Feature Analysis* may be used as a before-, during-, or after-reading strategy. Some academically and linguistically diverse learners would benefit from completing this activity with peers in pairs or working in a small group alongside a teacher. Teachers may also consider reducing the number of concepts or features diverse learners compare at one time in order to differentiate the task.

Figure 4.9 Semantic Feature Analysis (Plato's Five Regimes)

Plato's Five Regimes	Class System	Elected Officials	Leaders Accumulate Wealth	Power to Assemble Armies	Based on Principle of Freedom
Aristocracy	+	+	–	+	–
Timocracy	+	+	–	+	–
Oligarchy	+	+	+	+	–
Democracy	–	+	+	+	+
Tyranny	–	–	+	+	–

Figure 4.10 Semantic Feature Analysis (Parts of a Cell)

Parts of a Cell	Golgi Vesicle	Mitochondrion	Chloroplast	Centrioles	Cytoplasm
Plant cell	+	+	+	–	+
Animal cell	+	+	–	+	+

Meaning and Tone Chart (Illinois State Board of Education, 2012). This strategy helps students to analyze the impact of word choices on the meaning and tone of the text. Students draw specific words, phrases, or sentences from the text they have read and identify their significance as well as how the author's word choices influence the quality and character of the text. Next, students rewrite the selected words/phrases/sentences and compare how the meaning and tone of the text might change due to the alternative way in which ideas have been expressed. Figure 4.11 is an example of a *Meaning and Tone Chart.*

Completing a *Meaning and Tone Chart* will be challenging for many diverse learners for whom reading such a complex academic text is new. This organizer requires students to self-select pertinent phrases and sentences as well as consider their effect on the overall tone of the text. Students with diverse learning needs will benefit from opportunities to have the strategy

Figure 4.11 Meaning and Tone Chart

Meaning and Tone			
Title: The Perils of Indifference by Elie Wiesel (1999)			
Phrases or Sentences Selected From Text	**Impact of Word Choices**	**Phrase or Sentence Rewritten**	**How Changes Alter Meaning and Tone**
Indifference, after all, is more dangerous than anger and hatred. Anger can at times be creative . . . But indifference is never creative . . . Indifference elicits no response.	The author's words express much passion and feeling about the subject.	When people are indifferent, they are detached and do not express any real emotion.	The passion and feeling are removed when the phrases are restated. The tone becomes dull and unexciting.

Source: Wiesel, E. (1999). *The perils of indifference.* Retrieved from http://www.historyplace.com/speeches/wiesel.htm

modeled and for guided practice. Initially, the teacher instead of the students might select the phrases or sentences to be examined. Moreover, using a *Think Aloud* strategy (see Anchor Performance 1) in combination with this strategy can help give students insight into how to critically think about the meaning and tone of the text.

K. I. M.—Key idea, Information, and Memory clue (Beck, McKeown, & Kucan, 2002). Students are better able to remember the meaning of new academic vocabulary using this organizing activity. To begin, develop a three-column chart as in Figure 4.12. Have students write a vocabulary word or key idea under *K*, its definition (or essential information) under *I*, and a picture or drawing under *M* to commit the word to memory.

Figure 4.12 K.I.M.

K (Key Idea)	I (Information)	M (Memory clue)
republic	A form of government in which the power lies with its citizens, who are entitled to vote for people to represent their interests.	

Anchor Performance 5: Recognize Text Features and Organizational Structures of Informational Texts

Informational texts vary in their organization and the features they contain. For this reason, students need to be aware of the distinct ways in which texts are structured so that they will be better prepared to find information and more closely analyze the texts they read. Identifying and focusing in on text features such as headings, subheadings, illustrations, tables, and graphs, help students to more readily answer text-based questions. These features can also guide students to find supporting evidence for their formed opinions and conclusions about the text.

In addition to text features, being aware of the different organizational structures further enhances students' abilities to carefully examine text for a variety of purposes. Table 4.1 identifies different structures of informational text.

Table 4.1 Organization of Informational Text

Organization	Description
Enumeration	A list of major ideas is followed by supporting details.
Time Order	Major ideas and details are expressed in a particular sequence of events.
Compare/Contrast	The details of two major ideas or concepts identify the similarities and differences between them.
Cause/Effect	The details of a stated concept or event reflect both the aftermath of the event and its causes.
Question/Answer	Similar to enumeration, the key ideas are expressed in question form and the supporting details as answers.

Source: Adapted from Marinak, B. A., & Gambrell, L. B. (2009). Ways to teach about informational texts. *National Council for Social Studies, 22*(1), p. 20.

For this anchor performance as well as to meet grade-level expectations for Reading Standards for Informational Texts, Grade 6 students are expected to analyze how a piece of text adds to the expansion of ideas in the overall text, whereas in Grade 7, students also need to examine the organizational structure of the text used and how major sections of text help to build the text as a whole. Moreover in Grade 8, students must carefully examine the role of how specific sections of text help to clarify key concepts. In addition to these skills, students in Grades 9–10 must determine how claims made by the author are supported by both smaller and larger pieces of text, and in Grades 11–12, students also need to determine if the text structure clearly and convincingly expresses the author's ideas, arguments, or points of view.

With regard to the Reading Standards for Literacy in History/Social Studies for this anchor performance, students in Grade 6–8 must be able to identify how information is revealed according to the structural organization of the text (e.g., compare and contrast, cause and effect), whereas students in Grades 9–10 additionally must determine how the text structure clarifies key points. Furthermore, students in Grades 11–12 must also identify how key sections (e.g., sentences, paragraphs) of the text contribute to the whole.

With consideration for the Reading Standards for Literacy in Science and Technical Subjects, students in Grades 6–8 must be able to analyze text structure in order to determine how the structure contributes to the understanding of the topic. Students in Grades 9–10 additionally must analyze the relationship between and among key ideas and concepts, and students in Grades 11–12 must also be able to determine how information is organized into categories and hierarchies to demonstrate understanding of the subject matter.

Essential Strategy to Support Anchor Performance 5: Examine the Key Elements of Informational Texts

Academically and linguistically diverse learners may not be well versed in the elements of informational texts written in formal English. The characteristics unique to nonfiction writing are often explored individually rather than as a set of binding elements. It is important to explore informational texts in this way as a whole. The following are identified as elements of informational texts (Marinak & Gambrell, 2009):

- *Author's purpose.* The reasons why the author is writing the text, whether it is to provide information, persuade or convince the reader of a particular point of view, or entertain
- *Major ideas.* The major concepts, convictions, or thoughts expressed by the author
- *Supporting details.* Information that verifies or further illustrates the main ideas in the text
- *Visual support.* Graphic representations that offer helpful information, including charts, drawing, photographs, and tables
- *Vocabulary.* Words that are pertinent for understanding and writing about the text

The following are some activities to promote student understanding of the organizational elements found in informational texts. The purpose of some of these strategies is to engage students in game-like, low-anxiety tasks to remove the fear some students have of expository texts and promote skills such as text skimming and scanning to find information.

Text Structure Treasure Hunt (Robb, 2003). With newspapers, magazines, online news articles, or any informational text sources, have students play a game in which in pairs or teams, they identify the text structures of selected texts. Students may use a T-chart to note the name of the text and the type of text structure. Teams win by labeling the most text structures within a particular time frame.

Text Structure Sort (Florida Center for Reading Research, 2007). Similar to the strategy *List-Group-Label* (Taba, 1967)—a vocabulary strategy in which students group a list of words according to their similarities (see Anchor Performance 4)—students use a set of prepared paragraphs and sort them according to their text structure. To begin, print at least ten articles or paragraphs for each team of students that contain different informational text structures (e.g., cause/effect, compare/contrast; see Table 4.1 for additional text structures). Students not only must sort the different pieces of text but also must identify evidence in the text that were used as clues to its structure. Some diverse learners might benefit from having a list of words that signal different text structures (see Anchor Performance 3—*Structured Note Taking*—for a list of signal words).

Self-Questioning. This strategy engages students in asking and answering a set of questions to themselves while reading. This reflective process encourages students to think more critically while they read, a strategy that capable readers do automatically. To support this anchor performance, students focus on questions that examine the features and organization of informational texts. The following are sample questions for students to consider:

- What information can I find about the topic from the titles and subtitles?
- What can I understand about the topic from the photographs, drawings, tables, and charts?
- Are there any key words printed in boldface? Are there explanations for these key words anywhere in the text?
- What organizational framework (e.g., compare/contrast, cause/effect) might the author have chosen for this piece of writing? How is this evident?
- Has the author chosen to use multiple organizational frameworks? How do I know?
- Which text features helped me the most to understand the reading? Why is this so?

Self-Questioning can be modified to best serve the needs of some diverse learners by using this reflective questioning technique as part of a shared or guided reading lesson during small-group instruction. Students can also work in pairs to examine the questions, discuss the information, and note the answers in writing.

THIEVES (Manz, 2002). A prereading strategy that helps students "steal" information from their textbook before they read, this activity encourages students to preview a text chapter using the following guide for finding information. THIEVES stands for seven key text features to examine:

- *Title.* The title frequently identifies the topic and the context of the chapter.
- *Headings.* An important text feature that identifies the various subject sections in the chapter, headings can be turned into questions in order to establish a framework for their reading.
- *Introduction.* The introduction furnishes an overview of the chapter's contents. The goals and objectives are often stated in the introduction.
- *Every first sentence of a paragraph.* For a quick and complete chapter preview, students read the first line of every paragraph, which generally contains the topic sentence.
- *Visuals and vocabulary.* Reviewing all visual information, including photographs, drawings, tables, charts, timelines, and maps as well as captions and labels, can reveal pertinent information about the text.
- *End-of-chapter questions.* Having students read the end questions before they begin the chapter helps them to establish a purpose for their reading and focuses their attention on pertinent content.
- *Summary.* End summaries provide students with a great deal of information about the chapter. Reading the summary before reading the chapter provides students with a preview of the detailed content it contains.

THIEVES may be used with a variety of informational texts and not just textbook chapters, even though all the text features the strategy outlines may not be present. Figure 4.13 is a graphic organizer that supports students to preview text with the THIEVES strategy.

Anchor Performance 6: Understanding Point of View

Informational texts, written predominantly with the intent of either informing or persuading the reader, often express the particular points of view of their authors. For this reason, students must be able to appreciate the author's role in devising the structure and content of a text as well as distinguish between various viewpoints and sources of information.

For this anchor performance as well as to meet grade-level expectations for Reading Standards for Informational Texts, Grade 6 students are expected to identify the point of view of authors and how it is expressed in the text, whereas in Grade 7, students also need to define how authors differentiate their own positions from others. Moreover in Grade 8, students must carefully examine how authors recognize and react to differing viewpoints. In addition to these skills, students in Grades 9–10 must

Figure 4.13 THIEVES Text Preview Strategy.

A Text Preview Strategy: THIEVES
Directions: Survey the reading using the following text features and guiding questions. Make note of any information uncovered about the text.
Title: *What does the title tell me about the reading? What might I know about this subject?*
Headings: *What clues to the reading do the headings present? What topic will I be reading about? How might I turn the headings into questions that might be answered by information from the text?*
Introduction: *Does the first paragraph identify the content of the chapter? Does it give any clues to what the reading is about?*
Every First Sentence of a Paragraph: *What information about the reading can be found in each sentence? How might a combination of these sentences be used to create a preview summary?*
Visuals and Vocabulary: *What visuals are present in the text? What can be learned from them? Are there any boldface or italicized words? Are there clues to the meaning of these words?*
End-of-Chapter Questions: *What information can be learned from these questions? How might these questions be used as a focus for the reading?*
Summary: *What information does the summary provide?*

Source: Adapted from THIEVES template, Exeter Township Senior High, Reading, PA: http://www.exeter.k12.pa.us/Page/5338

analyze how authors use language to progress their viewpoints, and in Grades 11–12, students also need to examine how authors' language and style contribute to the impact or beauty of the text.

With regard to the Reading Standards for Literacy in History/Social Studies for this anchor performance, students in Grades 6–8 must be able to determine which parts of the text reveal the author's point of view, whereas students in Grades 9–10 additionally must make comparisons between the points of view of two or more authors. Furthermore, students in Grades 11–12 must also weigh the different points of view of the same historical event.

With consideration for the Reading Standards for Literacy in Science and Technical Subjects, students in Grades 6–8 must be able to deconstruct the author's purpose for explanations, descriptions, or discussions. Students in Grades 9–10 additionally must uncover the question the author wants to address, and students in Grades 11–12 must also be able to recognize key issues that may remain unanswered.

Essential Strategy to Support Anchor Performance 6: Closely Examine the Author's Point of View

When an author's purpose is to inform the reader by sharing information or explaining a concept, the author's point of view generally remains neutral. However, when the author wants to persuade the reader or convince the reader to think in a certain way, the expressed point of view is a mirror image of the author's attitude about the subject in question. When closely examining text, students must develop the skills to discern an author's point of view, which sometimes may be stated outright but at other times is implied. The following strategies will help students to think more critically in order to uncover an author's point of view.

Questioning the Author (QtA) (McKeown, Beck, & Worthy, 1993). *QtA* is a protocol that invites students to critically think about a shorter selection of text and evaluate the author's intent. To begin, select an inspirational quote such as, "He who is devoid of the power to forgive is devoid of the power to love" by Martin Luther King Jr. or a short intriguing passage such as the following from President Franklin Delano Roosevelt's first inaugural address in 1933:

> This is preeminently the time to speak the truth, the whole truth, frankly and boldly. Nor need we shrink from honestly facing conditions in our country today. This great Nation will endure as it has endured, will revive and will prosper. So, first of all, let me assert my firm belief that the only thing we have to fear is fear itself— nameless, unreasoning, unjustified terror, which paralyzes needed efforts to convert retreat into advance. (http://www.bartleby .com/124/pres49.html)

Next, create questions to spark students' interest and to support their independent, deep thinking as well as meaningful discussion of the text. Table 4.2 identifies some such questions.

Table 4.2 Question the Author (QtA) Protocol

Question the Author Prompts
What do you think the author is attempting to say?
What do you think is the author's point of view?
Was the author's message communicated clearly?
Why do you think the author chose to express himself or herself in this way?
How could the author's point of view be expressed differently?
Did the author explain why he or she thinks this way?

Display the quote or passage and begin to read it aloud to the students. Pause as needed to discuss vocabulary and word phrases as well as check students' understanding of the text. Ask students questions from the *QtA* protocol to facilitate discussion. At times, stop and share your own thoughts and ideas about the text to model thinking aloud and to add authenticity to the class discourse. Encourage students to ask their own questions of the author to further the class discussion.

Compare/Contrast (Illinois State Board of Education, 2012). This strategy helps students to examine different authors' points of view on the same subject. With this exercise, they begin to understand the importance of author bias and how it can alter the information an article contains. To prepare for this activity, gather written information about the same topic drawn from various sources and authors. Have students work in pairs or trios to read and compare the writing of the different authors, focusing in on how they unfold arguments or examining particular word choices in the writing and how these choices affect the overall expression of point of view. The following are some questions students may use to guide them to complete this task:

- Is the author's purpose to inform, explain, or advocate? How do you know?
- Why is this author's opinion or argument relevant?

- Is the author associated with a particular organization, think tank, or political party?
- Does the author's argument appear to be based on research, practical experience, or opinion?
- Why does the author quote the exact words of . . . ?
- Why does the author want the reader to think that . . . ?
- Why does the author begin his or her story by . . . ?

To introduce this task, consider comparing only two articles or short excerpts from each of the selected writings. Complete the reading as a whole-class, shared-reading activity. As an alternative, configure a combination of teacher-led and peer-assisted small groups to differentiate according to diverse learners' needs. In these groups, review the topic, build students' background knowledge, and preview vocabulary. Students may also benefit from using some type of graphic organizer such as a Venn diagram or the *Compare and Contrast Chart* depicted in Figure 4.14 to complete this activity.

Point-of-View Analysis. This activity helps students to gain insight into media bias, special interests, stereotyping, and the misuse of information that is sometimes present in multimedia sources. It works well with opinion pieces such as newspaper editorials, television news segments, weblogs, or political speeches. Students become aware of how writers attempt to persuade readers to embrace one point of view or another. Students are asked to read critically to detect an author's partiality and viewpoint by means of overgeneralizations and exaggerated language as well as use of inflammatory words and images. Students should consider the following in order to complete their analysis:

What are the author's . . .

- opinions?
- arguments?
- overgeneralizations?
- exaggerations?
- pieces of evidence?
- sources?
- emotionally biased words?
- points of view?

As with many activities suggested for diverse learners, teachers need to discern what preteaching, grouping strategies, structural supports (e.g., graphic organizers, response logs), and additional

Figure 4.14 Compare and Contrast Chart

Compare and Contrast Chart	
Text 1	**Text 2**
Title:	**Title:**
Author:	**Author:**
How are they similar?	
How are they different?	

Source: Adapted from http://www.readwritethink.org/files/resources/lesson_images/lesson275/compcon_chart.pdf

preparation may be necessary for their particular students to complete this task. For a different discussion of point-of-view analysis, see Chapter 6.

Integration of Knowledge and Ideas

Anchor Performance 7: Analyzing Multiple Text Formats to Support Meaning

In the age of technology, information is readily accessible through a variety of formats and mediums, and students often take advantage of these different vehicles of information to conduct research. It is certain that students find a considerable amount of research material on the Internet, and they have access to data not only from the text information it contains but also from the illustrations, diagrams, charts, and other text aides it may provide. Additionally, online material is often accompanied by audio and visual representations, which offer similar and sometimes enhanced information in alternative formats. Diverse learners need to be able to understand, evaluate, and make meaningful connections between and among the different mediums and sources of information in order to gather accurate and reliable data and answer text-dependent questions.

For this anchor performance as well as to meet grade-level expectations for Reading Standards for Informational Texts, Grade 6 students are expected to incorporate material offered via different formats (e.g., audio, visual, multimedia) in combinations with written text to develop an overall understanding of the presented topic, whereas in Grade 7, students also need to compare and contrast these formats and how they convey the subject. Moreover in Grade 8, students must carefully judge the benefits and drawbacks of using different formats to gather information. In addition to these skills, students in Grades 9–10 must consider the various versions of the topic as revealed in different mediums and identify the details each contain, and in Grades 11–12, students also need to examine and evaluate the information obtained from an assortment of sources and merge the data in order to answer questions or problem solve.

With regard to the Reading Standards for Literacy in History/Social Studies for this anchor performance, students in Grades 6–8 must be able to combine information obtained from charts, graphs, maps, and other visual media with information from text, whereas students in Grades 9–10 additionally must incorporate a detailed analysis of visual information with text. Furthermore, students in Grades 11–12 must also analyze multiple sources of information to problem solve and answer questions.

With consideration for the Reading Standards for Literacy in Science and Technical Subjects, students in Grades 6–8 must be able to merge text data received from quantitative and technical sources with visual information such as graphs, diagrams, and flowcharts. Students in Grades 9–10 additionally must be able to convert text data into visual form and change visually displayed or mathematical data into words. Students in Grades 11–12 must also be able to incorporate and judge the value of different sources of information.

Essential Strategy to Support Anchor Performance 7: Compare Information Sources

Although there are various media sources, most young people obtain their information from the Internet, where there is a vast amount of news and data available in different forms—news and television broadcasts, video recordings, audio podcasts, online newspapers, radio shows, and magazine and journal articles. Due to the seemingly boundless information available, it is important for students to consultant a wide range of these sources in order to cross-check data as to their validity, reliability, and accuracy. The following strategies guide students to examine different pieces of information to gather data that is precise and dependable.

The Big6 (Eisenberg & Berkowitz, 2011). An approach to teaching information and technology skills, Big6 presents a model for gathering information for solving problems. It incorporates strategies for locating, applying, and evaluating information, and offers six steps for determining a solution. The steps in the process are as follows:

1. *Task definition.* Define the problem and identify what information is needed to resolve it.

2. *Information-seeking strategies.* Identify and select the best sources to explore to gather information.

3. *Location and access.* Locate selected sources and discover what information they contain.

4. *Use of information.* Carefully examine and gather pertinent information.

5. *Synthesis.* Organize and present information obtained from multiple sources.

6. *Evaluation.* Determine the effectiveness of the results.

The skills identified by the Big6 can be applied to problem solving across a wide range of subject areas. Many academically and linguistically diverse learners would benefit from its step-by-step process combined with self-reflection questions such as these: *Do I understand what this step is asking? Do I know how to perform this step? Do I need more information or guidance to complete this task?*

Media Mash. With this strategy, students compare information drawn from various sources in order to answer a question or gather information to solve a problem. Questions might address issues in content-area studies such as the causes of a species becoming endangered or the repercussions of a war. To facilitate this activity, teachers need to gather data sources from different media (e.g., video clips, newscasts, articles, political cartoons) about the topic in question and have them available for students to watch, listen to, read, and examine. These media pieces may be experienced as a whole class, in small groups, or a combination of both. After students have the opportunity to access all the media, they reexamine each piece of data using the *Media Mash Comparison Sheet* (see Figure 4.15).

Figure 4.15 Media Mash Comparison Sheet

Media Mash Comparison Sheet			
Question:			
Media Notes			
Information from Medium 1 Title:_____	**Information from Medium 2** Title:_____	**Information from Medium 3** Title:_____	**What information was the same from all three media?**

For a different discussion of media analysis, see Chapter 6.

SIGHT (Illinois State Board of Education, 2012; Marzano, Pickering, & Pollack, 2001). This strategy is a simple framework for teachers to follow in order to plan a lesson for students to examine different media on the same topic. The steps are as follows:

- Select two media pieces on the same subject.
- Identify the particular reference points for students to judge each medium.
- Guide students to examine and compare each media form.

- Have students determine the similarities and differences of each piece.
- Tie the pieces together by having students synthesize the information.

Teachers may also ask students to make generalizations or draw conclusions about the topic as well as use a graphic organizer to compare the different media.

Anchor Performance 8: Evaluate Text Claims According to the Evidence

Students must be able to judge the relevancy of evidence that supports an author's assumptions or identify if there is proof of sound reasoning for an author's claims. To support these complex tasks, students need to develop strategies to focus their attention on relevant text information.

For this anchor performance as well as to meet grade-level expectations for Reading Standards for Informational Texts, Grade 6 students are expected to outline and assess the evidence or claims in a text, identifying claims that are supported by text information and those that are not, whereas in Grade 7, students also need to evaluate if the text identifies sound reasoning and relevant information as well as if that reasoning and information are adequate enough to support any claims made. Moreover in Grade 8, students must be able to recognize when extraneous information is introduced. In addition to these skills, students in Grades 9–10 must identify statements believed to be false and reasoning that is illogical, and in Grades 11–12, students also need to weigh the reasoning, premises, purposes, and arguments presented in seminal U.S. texts such as U.S. Supreme Court opinions and presidential addresses.

With regard to the Reading Standards for Literacy in History/Social Studies for this anchor performance, students in Grades 6–8 must be able to tell the difference between fact, opinion, and evaluation, whereas students in Grades 9–10 additionally must evaluate the degree to which the reasoning and evidence in the text reinforces the author's claims. Furthermore, students in Grades 11–12 must also use additional information to judge the validity of an author's premise or evidence.

With consideration for the Reading Standards for Literacy in Science and Technical Subjects, students in Grades 6–8 must be able to separate the facts from speculation or research-based judgment. Students in Grades 9–10 additionally must be able to evaluate the degree to which the evidence in the text supports the advancement of a solution for a scientific or technical problem, and students in Grades 11–12 must also make judgments concerning the data analysis and conclusions in the text by comparing and contrasting them to other sources of information.

Essential Strategy to Support Anchor Performance 8: Unpacking the Evidence

Finding strategies to support the reading of struggling learners is a challenging task. Students often benefit from different approaches to break down complex texts to be better able to gather information, identify an author's claims, and find supporting evidence. One approach is for students to use learning logs or journals in which they select particular sentences from the text and analyze them. The following are some other techniques to help students find and evaluate authors' claims and unpack textual evidence.

Annotation (Zywica & Gomez, 2008). This strategy can help students understand more complex texts and be better able to identify the way in which an author forms an argument. When students annotate, they become more engaged in reading and focus more carefully on the content and structure of the text. Zywica and Gomez (2008) identified the strategy as follows:

> Annotation as a cognitive literacy approach helps students recognize how words and phrases and their definitions can be embedded skillfully in text yet in ways that (for struggling readers at least) are difficult to recognize, extract, and use to make meaning. It helps students begin to analytically approach texts by looking for structures and patterns that are used to convey information. (p. 156)

To develop this approach, teach students in increments the different ways in which they can mark and label a text as well as write marginal notes to highlight important information, identify an author's claims, and gather evidence that is apparent in the details of the text. Porter-O'Donnell (2004) identified some of the ways to annotate text as follows:

- *Before reading.* Mark the titles and the subtitles; examine the print and highlight any bold or italicized words; consider the illustrations and highlight any important information found in the captions.
- *During reading.* Circle the names of individuals, events, or ideas; place a box around words or phrases that are essential for understanding the topic; underline important information; write margin notes to summarize, make predictions, form opinions, ask questions, and make connections.
- *After reading.* Review annotations and draw conclusions; reread the introduction and the summary to derive something new; consider if there are any noticeable patterns or repetitions and determine what they might mean; write a journal entry that identifies the author's claims and the found evidence to support them.

Evidence Tracker (Whitfield, 1998). With this strategy, students are asked to read with a specific focus on identifying the author's claims and the evidence that supports those claims in the text. Using a graphic organizer (Figure 4.16), students note each claim they find as well as the text details as evidence. Finally, students analyze and judge whether or not the author's reasoning is thorough and the evidence is sufficient to support the stated claims.

Figure 4.16   Evidence Tracker

Evidence Tracker	
Author's claim:	Evidence 1
	Evidence 2
	Evidence 3
Is the author's reasoning sound and the evidence sufficient? Explain.	

Anchor Performance 9: Compare and Contrast Information From Multiple Sources

Students must be able to compare information from both primary and secondary sources as well as other media and analyze different representations and interpretations of the same topic. To this end, students need to develop organizational skills to connect the ideas gathered from each media source, evaluate the importance of each piece of data, and eliminate information that is superfluous. In addition, to support the needs of all learners, specific vocabulary words and phrases to express comparisons of texts such as *similarly, likewise, on the contrary,* and *in contrast to* must be explicitly taught and modeled in context to increase students' ability to complete comparative tasks.

For this anchor performance as well as to meet grade-level expectations for Reading Standards for Informational Texts, Grade 6 students are expected to make comparisons between two author's presentation of events, whereas in Grade 7, students also are expected to examine how multiple authors interpret the same topic placing different emphasis on key ideas and details. Moreover in Grade 8, students must analyze two or more texts that contain contradictory information on the same topic. In addition to these skills, students in Grades 9–10 must examine how seminal U.S. documents such as the *Gettysburg Address* give an account of themes or topics, and in Grades 11–12, students also need to evaluate U.S. historical documents for their purpose and rhetorical features.

With regard to the Reading Standards for Literacy in History/Social Studies for this anchor performance, students in Grades 6–8 must be able to examine the similarities between a primary and secondary source of information, whereas students in Grades 9–10 additionally must compare and contrast how the subject is presented in several primary and secondary sources. Furthermore, students in Grades 11–12 must also combine data obtained from a number of different sources into a comprehensible understanding of events and identify any inconsistencies among the sources.

With consideration for the Reading Standards for Literacy in Science and Technical Subjects, students in Grades 6–8 must be able to make comparisons between multiple sources of information (e.g., experiments, simulations, text, video) on the same subject. Students in Grades 9–10 additionally must document how findings uphold or challenge previous accounts, and students in Grades 11–12 must also incorporate data from a range of sources and clarify conflicting information when possible.

Essential Strategy to Support Anchor Activity 9: Use Compare/Contrast Organizers

Some academically and linguistically diverse learners need assistance with organizing information. Remaining focused, staying on task, recognizing the "big picture" ideas, and paying close attention to details may also present a problem for some learners. When students engage in compare/contrast activities, using a tool such as a graphic organizer and working in teacher-led or peer-assisted small groups, they are much better able to extract relevant information from the text not only to make comparisons but also to make better sense of what it is they are reading.

Graphic organizers such as the Venn-diagram or variations of the T-chart guide students to successfully select and manipulate essential information from the text as well as make comparisons between two authors' renditions of events or ideas. We have included samples of these organizers in the strategies that follow. However, in Grades 7–12, students are expected to compare and contrast accounts from multiple authors in primary, secondary, and multimedia sources and incorporate the information from these sources in order to arrive at an understanding of a particular subject. Therefore, we have included in this section, organizers for comparing multiple pieces of work.

Venn Diagram. The overlapping images of a bi-circle Venn diagram create three writing areas to compare the similarities and differences between two texts. The tri-circle Venn diagram allows students to compare three texts. In these organizers, there are spaces for students to write information that is exclusive to each text and areas in which they can include information that the texts have in common. Figure 4.17 illustrates an example of each of these Venn diagram configurations.

Figure 4.17 Bi-Circle and Tri-Circle Venn Diagrams

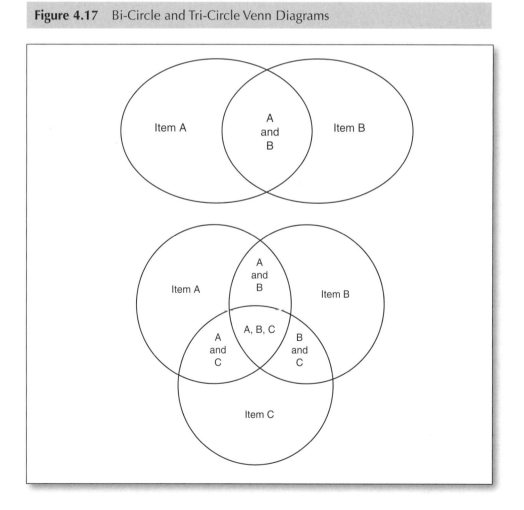

Compare Three. A variation on the tri-circle Venn diagram, *Compare Three* incorporates triangular shapes to give students separate writing surfaces to identify similarities and differences in each text (see Figure 4.18).

Figure 4.18 Compare Three

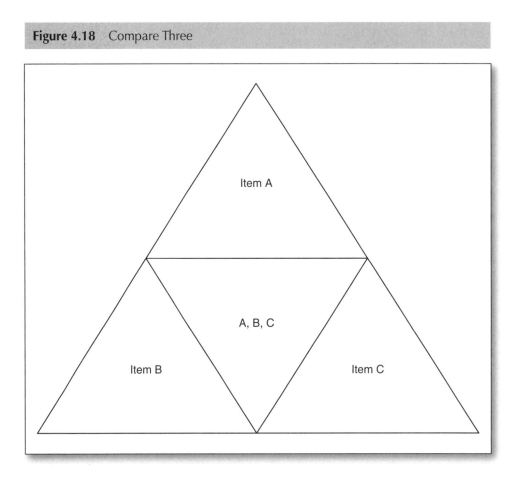

Compare Four. Similar to *Compare Three*, this strategy offers spaces to compare four pieces of text. This organizer can be used as a group activity. Have students work in teams, each reading one of four selections on the same topic. After reading, team members summarize their reading on one of the item spaces. Students then share what they wrote, compare the information, synthesize the common data, and document their commonalities in the center of the organizer (see Figure 4.19).

Graphic organizers are ideal tools to be differentiated for multilevel classes since they can be presented blank or with various amounts of preentered information depending on the amount of support students need to complete the task.

Figure 4.19 Compare Four

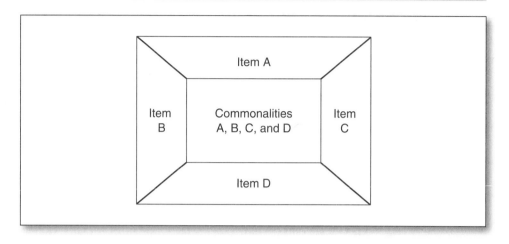

Range of Reading and Level of Text Complexity

Anchor Performance 10: Reading Informational Texts Independently

Reading instruction in the content-area class is a challenging task for many teachers who are most accustomed to concentrating on providing students information and understanding in specific subject areas but not building the overall or discipline-specific reading and writing capabilities of their students (Grant & Fisher, 2010). Middle and high school content-area teachers need to provide explicit literacy instruction particularly to students reading below grade-level expectations using texts from their own disciplines in order to meet this anchor performance.

Some students will benefit from reading a wide range of informational texts to increase their facility with reading tasks. To build their literacy skills and ability to read independently, teachers should actively engage and support these students to make meaning from text and teach them a broad range of reading strategies to support their learning. On the other hand, a small group of students may have persistent and severe reading difficulties. They may have complex reading problems brought about by identified disabilities. These learners will need even more intense instruction and support and may require individually adapted programs to meet with success.

For this anchor performance as well as to meet grade-level expectations for Reading Standards for Informational Texts, students at each grade level are expected to read and understand nonfiction texts independently and proficiently. Similar expectations are in place for the Reading Standards for

Literacy in History/Social Studies and in Science and Technical Subjects in that students must be able to comprehend texts at the complexity level of their grade band specific to each discipline.

Essential Strategy to Support Anchor Performance 10: Identify and Apply Literacy-Learning Practices in Content-Area Classes

Numerous cognitive processes for comprehension are employed while reading, and competent readers commonly use only a handful of strategies consistently to make sense of what they read (Block & Pressley, 2002). Teachers of all disciplines teach reading strategies to some degree; however, certain literacy practices are more effective than others. The following is a list of such research-based practices employed to increase students' overall reading achievement (Torgesen, Houston, & Rissman, 2007):

1. *Comprehension strategies.* Instruction and supporting practice that improves the use of effective reading strategies before, during, and after reading. Comprehension strategies are behaviors students can consciously apply to improve their understanding and learning from text.

2. *Discussion.* Opportunities for deeper, more sustained discussion of content from text. Extended discussions of text can be facilitated by the teacher, or can occur as structured discussions among students in cooperative learning groups.

3. *High standards.* Setting and maintaining high standards for the level of text, conversation, questions, and vocabulary reflected in discussions and in reading and writing assignments.

4. *Reading-writing connection.* Strengthening the reading-writing connection to improve student opportunities to reflect on the meaning of text and receive feedback on their reflections.

5. *Motivation and engagement.* Creating more engaging and motivating classrooms, and interacting with students in a way that promotes internal motivation for reading. Students will learn to process text more deeply if their reading is relevant to their lives and they are pursuing meaningful learning goals in an atmosphere that supports their initiative and personal choice.

6. *Content learning.* Teaching content knowledge to ensure learning of the most essential concepts by all students, even those who struggle to read the textbook. Teachers should use instructional methods, such as graphic organizers or concept comparison routines, that deepen understanding and show students better ways of learning new content on their own. (p. 6)

In addition to the broad-based strategies listed previously, students often benefit from being assigned a task while reading to better focus on the overall reading. A task may include asking students to read to find out one of the following: why or how something occurred, how the author described certain events, or where evidence to answer a question might be found. Other tasks may include practicing particular reading strategies that were already explicitly taught.

ANTICIPATED OUTCOMES

Making informational texts accessible for diverse learners can appear to be a daunting and challenging task. The strategies presented above are particularly designed to assist students to accomplish the following:

1. Cite and organize textual evidence

2. Activate inferential thinking

3. Organize summary information

4. Understand the structure of informational texts

5. Closely examine authors' point of views

6. Compare informational sources

7. Evaluate authors' claims and find relevant evidence for those claims

INSTRUCTIONAL CHALLENGES

The challenges associated with adolescents developing the skills to read discipline-specific texts are multifaceted. First and foremost, teachers need to be aware of the types of reading strategies students must learn and apply in order to comprehend informational texts. Being able to use general reading strategies such as making predictions, rereading, asking questions, and summarizing are often not sufficient to understanding complex texts. Lee and Spratley (2010) identified a list of discipline-specific reading strategies for students to become competent readers in their content-specific classes. These strategies focus on the ability to do the following:

- Build prior knowledge
- Build specialized vocabulary
- Learn to deconstruct complex sentences
- Use knowledge of text structures and genres to predict main and subordinate ideas

- Map graphic (and mathematical) representations against explanations in the text
- Pose discipline relevant questions
- Compare claims and propositions across texts
- Use norms for reasoning within the discipline (i.e., what counts as evidence) to evaluate claims (p. 16)

They further suggested that content knowledge and reading strategies be taught in conjunction with one another. In essence, students can learn to read while reading to learn. For this reason, teachers need to provide ongoing, guided support while students are engaged in reading, foster students' responsibility to make sense of texts on their own, and sequence tasks and "the reading of a range of discipline focused texts in ways that build knowledge and dispositions over time" (p. 16).

Literacy instruction can no longer be the sole responsibility of English teachers in secondary schools. Each content-area discipline presents its own literacy demands in terms of the course content, including the structure of discipline-specific texts and the challenging, academic vocabulary they contain. Therefore, all teachers need to support students to become successful readers in their own content-specific disciplines. For this reason, we offer the following guidelines for providing reading instruction for students with various language and academic challenges:

- Support students' development of comprehension strategies by providing repetitive modeling of strategy use and class time for students to practice them.
- Provide both low-tech and high-tech visual and auditory aids, displaying photographs, graphic organizers, and other print media that support reading content.
- Make available multimedia technology, including video, personal computers, and iPod/iPad applications to build background knowledge and motivate students to read.
- Promote the use of standard English and content vocabulary through cooperative and collaborative group activities focused on reading and interpreting informational texts.

PROMISING CLASSROOM PRACTICES

Unlocking the Common Core in a New Hampshire High School

Linda Chick, an English teacher at Manchester High School, New Hampshire, teaches a parallel English Department curriculum to English language learners (ELLs) in Grades 9–12 and identified pupils, some with both individual education programs (IEPs) and ELL designations. In her twelfth-grade English IV class, she teaches mostly high beginner and low-intermediate ELLs and one SIFE (student with interrupted formal education) from Somalia. Considering her students are about to enter higher education or the workforce, her main goal is to enhance their expressive language skills both in writing and speaking, as well as their production of academically sound arguments based on authentic texts used as resources for support.

In a recent unit, Linda gave great consideration to the CCSS and unlocking several of their components, including craft and structure, identifying text types and purposes, and recognizing the conventions of standard English when reading literary nonfiction. Therefore, as part of a yearlong unit tracing the evolution of the American Dream through fiction, nonfiction, speeches, poetry, music, drama, as well as authentic documents, Linda's English IV class read both a biographical sketch on and an excerpt from the autobiography of Benjamin Franklin. These lessons from this unit addressed three components of the Standards around a very interesting and memorable character whose work ethic and values embody the theme of the course. The expected concepts and skills for part of the unit were (a) to identify relevant information about Ben Franklin, (b) to understand purpose and point of view, (c) to understand subject/verb agreement, (d) to be able to compare/contrast two genres, and (e) to be able to develop a personal narrative using what we have learned of craft and structure.

Within these parameters, Linda included activities such as a prereading jigsaw, a close reading of both pieces of text, unpacking structures of each genre (tense, register, organization, etc.), examining the use of descriptive versus action words, and an analysis of sentence structure, a critical skill for ELLs. To enhance instruction, Linda explicitly pretaught a list of academic vocabulary found in each text. As a daily *exit slip*, students generated an active study guide formulating both "right there" and higher-order thinking questions as well as questions about grammatical form and linguistic functions. Linda also provided sentence starters using Bloom's Taxonomy for this activity. Assessments included a final test drawn from the student-generated questions and the vocabulary, a compare/contrast Venn diagram and essay, and the creation of a personal narrative of a key event in each student's life. Taken as a whole, these lessons combined both literacy and linguistic challenges, embraced the CCSS, and engaged the students in a variety of tasks and activities to build knowledge and skills useful in any content area.

Using Stop-and-Process Strategies in U.S. History Class in Massachusetts

Kelley Brown teaches a tenth-grade U.S. history class in Easthampton High School in Massachusetts. Of the 26 students in her class, 15 of them have IEPs. Many of these students deal with cognitive processing and organizational challenges. They require strategies such as scaffolded instruction, extended time, shortened assignments, copies of notes, opportunities to augment answers, quiet and separate testing areas, graphic organizers, and one-on-one check-ins for understanding.

During the first week of school, Kelley shared the following scenario with her students:

How many of you had this experience? Your teacher assigns you a few pages of reading from your textbook. You sit down, ready to do your homework. You read all three pages and when you finish you say to yourself, I have no idea what I just read.

Every hand in the classroom went up, including hers. She then suggested, "How about we solve that problem?" The students nodded as if some big secret had just been exposed and they finally realized they were not alone.

From Day 1, Kelley established a procedure and model for students to read carefully and take notes in order to help them learn the skills to identify the main idea and key details in the texts they read. Most of her tenth-grade course focuses on inquiry-based historical learning. For this reason, students needed to be able to answer historical questions and use primary and secondary sources with conflicting and concurring views to draw reasoned conclusions. Students must have the skills to analyze authors' biases, determine context, and closely read for meaning, rhetorical styles, and historical significance. However, students cannot perform any of these tasks if they cannot read and understand the main idea and details of a text.

To better prepare her students to accomplish multiple challenging tasks, Kelley began the process by modeling skills for her students. Handing each student a copy of a memo titled, *In the Event of a Failed Moonlanding*, she asked her students to follow her lead. She demonstrated how to mark the reading off in sections and began to read aloud. Instead of reading through the whole text, she stopped after the first paragraph and conducted a *Think Aloud* saying, "What did I just read?" She then proceeded to answer her own question and wrote down a short note on a graphic organizer that was displayed. She instructed students to do the same with their individual copies. The next paragraph was read as a class, and the one that followed was completed in pairs. By the end of the reading, students were working independently. When the document was completed, students reread their notes and filled in the main idea box at the bottom of the page.

Kelley believes that most students have the habit of reading an entire text without taking notes or stopping to think about what they are reading. Therefore, she encourages her students to stop and process information often with the help of a graphic organizer in order to set a procedural framework for reading and a method for her students to take notes. Her experience has shown that once the use of graphic organizers becomes routine and has been practiced many times, students come to class better prepared to analyze and closely read historical sources because they are better able to understand what they are reading. Kelley also uses graphic organizers as a method of formative assessment for her students.

At the end of the semester, Kelley's students identified the use of graphic organizers as making a significant change in their schoolwork. Likewise, several teachers reported that they have also instituted the same process for reading and research in their classes. Additionally, the special education department confirmed the use of graphic organizers as a tool for teachers in meeting reading accommodations for students.

In a recent professional development workshop, Kelley distributed one of the graphic organizers to teachers during a discussion of the CCSS. Every teacher took one, and most listed it as "something they would use tomorrow." Ms. Brown firmly believes that a simple change in instruction has made a significant difference for many students.

Teaching Literacy Skills in Social Studies Classes at an Iowa High School

In cotaught classes at Ames High School in Iowa, social studies teacher Sunday Ogunsola and English-as-a-second language (ESL) specialist Shaeley Santiago are challenged to engage their ELLs with key concepts and information, particularly in the case of U.S. history since many of them lack background knowledge about the United States. Shaeley and Sunday incorporate various literacy strategies in their social studies classes in order to build students' acquisition of both language and subject content.

To increase students' reading comprehension, one focus of instruction is on building content vocabulary. One way these teachers ensure that students understand key terms is having them create their own vocabulary notebook. In this notebook, students write key content words with accompanying definitions, visual representations, and sentences illustrating and exemplifying the significance of each term.

Another strategy Shaeley and Sunday use is to select texts that are matched with students' independent reading levels. Students work together in small groups with an appropriate set of texts and are guided to summarize key information from their reading, which they then share with the whole class. Working in small groups provides additional support for students who may struggle on their own.

To assist their students in identifying key content concepts, Sunday and Shaeley codevelop and provide graphic organizers that list important unit topics to guide students to essential information while they read. This teaching pair almost always provides a reading guide or some type of scaffolded tool containing questions or specific categories of information that help students focus when they are reading or completing individual research projects. They also hand out select texts that build students understanding of needed background information to support their study of essential themes and topics.

Beyond any doubt, Shaeley and Sunday work together to keep their students motivated and on task. After their group reading is completed, students are given the freedom to self-select texts they are particularly interested in to read within the broad themes of the unit. Their use of a variety of strategies to scaffold students' development of language and content is an essential part of their overall instruction for ELLs.

COMMON CORE READING STANDARDS— UN(COMMON) REFLECTION QUESTIONS

1. Which of the ten anchor standards or the grade-appropriate equivalents will present the greatest departure from your previous literacy instructional practices regarding teaching informational texts?

2. Which of the ten anchor standards or the grade-appropriate equivalents will present the greatest challenge to your students? Why?

3. How are you planning to strategically address the difficulties your students will face with select standards?

KEY RESOURCES

Professional Resources

Calderón, M. E. (2007). *Teaching reading to English language learners, grades 6–12: A framework for improving achievement in the content area.* Thousand Oaks, CA: Corwin.

Ellery, V., & Rosenboom, J. L. (2011). *Sustaining strategic readers: Techniques for supporting content literacy in grades 6–12.* Newark, DE: International Reading Association.

Lee, C. D., & Spratley, A. (2010). *Reading in the disciplines: The challenges of adolescent literacy.* New York, NY: Carnegie Corporation of New York. Retrieved from http://carnegie.org/fileadmin/Media/Publications/PDF/tta_Lee.pdf

Silver, J. F. (2001). *Real-life reading activities for grades 6–12: Over 200 ready-to-use lessons and activities to help students master practical reading skills.* San Francisco, CA: Jossey-Bass.

Online Resources

Access to nonfiction selections
http://www.readworks.org
http://www.k12reader.com
http://www.wiki-teacher.com
http://www.newseum.org
http://www.loc.gov/teachers

Adolescent Literacy
http://www.adlit.org

Documents in Law, History, and Diplomacy
http://avalon.law.yale.edu/default.asp

English Language Learner Instruction in Middle and High School
http://www.colorincolorado.org/webcasts/middle/

Graphic Organizers
http://aim.cast.org/learn/historyarchive/backgroundpapers/graphic_organizers
Cause and effect: http://www.educationoasis.com/curriculum/GO/cause_effect.htm

Compare and contrast: http://www.readwritethink.org/files/resources/lesson_images/lesson275/compcon_chart.pdf

Sequence: http://www.educationoasis.com/curriculum/GO/sequence.htm

Time order: http://www.eduplace.com/graphicorganizer/pdf/timeorder.pdf

Middle School Reading Strategies
www.asdk12.org/middlelink/about/Strategies_Can_Triumph.pdf

Reading for the 21st Century: Adolescent Literacy Teaching and Learning Strategies
www.all4ed.org/files/Reading_21stCentury.pdf

Text Mapping
http://www.textmapping.org

 # Writing Strategies

Writing is thinking with a pencil.

—Anonymous

OVERVIEW

As students progress through the secondary grades, they have to produce more and more complex writing to be college and career ready, and they must do so in a variety of genres about a range of topics. Among many other writing skills, the Common Core State Standards (CCSS) emphasize that students need to learn how to gather information, evaluate sources, and cite material accurately as well as report findings from their research in a clear and persuasive manner. When commenting on the CCSS and writing instruction in their opening chapter of *Pathways to the Common Core*, Calkins and her colleagues Ehrenworth, and Lehman (2012) suggested that

> once students become fluent, fast, structured, and proficient writ-
> ers across a range of genres, it is easy to take those skills on the
> road, using writing as a tool for thinking across all the disciplines.
> When students write across the curriculum, it not only escalates
> their engagement in other subjects but also makes teachers more
> accountable and more responsive. (p. 14)

The goal of this chapter is to offer numerous ideas on how to make the CCSS for writing meaningful and accessible for the not-so-common learn-ers of standard academic English, so they, too, can become as *fluent, fast, structured,* and *proficient writers* as they can be in English language arts

(ELA) and all the secondary content areas. Nonetheless, we cannot forget that teaching writing takes time: "time for practice, time to share writing, time to complete pieces of writing, and time to respond to and evaluate all of that writing" (Kirby & Crovitz, 2012, p. 9).

WHY SCAFFOLDING AND EXPLICIT SKILLS INSTRUCTION IMPROVE THE WRITING OF DIVERSE LEARNERS

We also concur with Hillocks (2011), who suggested that "in teaching any sort of process, when the process is new to learners, it is important to provide as much coaching and modeling as necessary" (p. 30). Successfully engaging in the process of writing in multiple genres is especially challenging for some learners since both complex, discipline-specific content must be mastered and advanced writing skills developed. Additionally, these skills and newly gained knowledge must be demonstrated through a range of secondary school writing assignments. Students need to see excellent, yet attainable models and also need to practice writing in the required genres with ample guidance and carefully planned, incrementally removed support.

After reviewing current research, Goldenberg and Coleman (2010) pointed out that structured writing instruction and specific teacher or peer feedback has improved linguistically diverse students' writing. Supporting diverse learners as they hone their writing skills through a variety of ways continues to be imperative in the secondary classroom. Scaffolding is one critical way to offer the necessary support to all students regarding all ELA-skill areas but especially to struggling writers of standard English at the middle and high school levels. Gibbons (2009) identified the three major characteristics of scaffolding as follows:

> It is *temporary* help that assists a learner to move toward new concepts, levels of understanding, and new language.
>
> It enables a learner to know *how to do something* (not just what to do), so that they will be better able to complete similar tasks alone.
>
> It is *future oriented:* in Vygotsky's words, what a learner can do with support today, he or she will be able to do alone tomorrow. (p. 15)

Thus, teaching writing—as one of the most challenging skills for diverse or struggling learners—must focus on carefully designed temporary supports that could and should be adjusted as students learn each new writing skill. For at-risk secondary learners, all content-area teachers must find a way to embrace the process of writing and offer students opportunities for structured direct instruction in various genres as well as guided practice and time for revisions so students can refine their writing skills and polish the final product.

CORE WRITING STRATEGIES

The strategies contained in this chapter follow the expectations of the ten College and Career Readiness Anchor Standards (CCRAS) for Writing both in (a) ELA and (b) science, social studies, and the technical subjects (see Box 5.1). The writing standards are divided into four subcategories:

- Text types and purposes, which are designed to ensure that students know how to produce opinion and argument pieces and that both informational and narrative writing structures are practiced
- Production and distribution of writing, which focuses on the writing process and the product as well as the use of technology across all genres
- Research to build and present knowledge, which ensures that students learn to take an analytical approach to both literature and nonfiction
- Range of writing, which parallels a similar anchor standard for reading, reminding teachers to expand the types of writing experiences students should have in the secondary grades

What makes this chapter unique is that it has its own organizational pattern—more than one essential strategy is presented for several anchor standards because of the broad reach of writing across all the secondary content areas.

Box 5.1 College and Career Readiness Anchor Standards for Writing

Text Types and Purposes

1. Write arguments to support claims in an analysis of substantive topics or texts, using valid reasoning and relevant and sufficient evidence.

2. Write informative/explanatory texts to examine and convey complex ideas and information clearly and accurately through the effective selection, organization, and analysis of content.

3. Write narratives to develop real or imagined experiences or events using effective technique, well-chosen details, and well-structured event sequences.

(Continued)

(Continued)

Production and Distribution of Writing

4. Produce clear and coherent writing in which the development, organization, and style are appropriate to task, purpose, and audience.

5. Develop and strengthen writing as needed by planning, revising, editing, rewriting, or trying a new approach.

6. Use technology, including the Internet, to produce and publish writing and to interact and collaborate with others.

Research to Build and Present Knowledge

7. Conduct short as well as more sustained research projects based on focused questions, demonstrating understanding of the subject under investigation.

8. Gather relevant information from multiple print and digital sources, assess the credibility and accuracy of each source, and integrate the information while avoiding plagiarism.

9. Draw evidence from literary or informational texts to support analysis, reflection, and research.

Range of Writing

10. Write routinely over extended time frames (time for research, reflection, and revision) and shorter time frames (a single sitting or a day or two) for a range of tasks, purposes, and audiences.

Text Types and Purposes

The first three writing standards focus on argument, informative, and narrative writing skills across all content areas. Here, each of these three standards is given careful consideration since the remainder of the writing standards is built on them.

Anchor Performance 1: Write Arguments About Grade-Appropriate Topics

According to the first standard, elementary school (K–5) students learn to write about their opinions. In the secondary grades, a notable shift occurs as students develop skills in argument writing. While moving through the middle school grades, they learn to identify their own claims in Grade 6 and incorporate claims and opposing claims in their writing in

Grade 7, and finally in Grade 8, they not only acknowledge but also clearly distinguish the claims they make from alternate or opposing claims. In high school, the progression continues.

Students in Grades 9–10 are expected to "develop claim(s) and counterclaims fairly, supplying evidence for each while pointing out the strengths and limitations of both in a manner that anticipates the audience's knowledge level and concerns" (*Common Core State Standards*, 2010a, p. 45). In Grades 11–12, the expectations are further refined, requiring students to offer the most relevant evidence in their writing and also to evaluate the available information critically. In addition, students should be able to consider the audience's concerns, values, and possible biases, thus anticipating how the target audience for the written argument will receive the product. To accomplish all this—in ELA, science, social studies, and technical subjects (where the arguments must focus on *discipline-specific content*)—is no small feat! Of all the Common Core writing standards, this might prove to be the most challenging for teachers when they work with diverse learners who need *to translate* their thoughts into standard academic English. We recommend a careful look at Appendix A of the CCSS (*Common Core State Standards*, 2010b), where the genre of argument writing is further discussed. See our summary of the key ideas in Table 5.1.

Table 5.1   What Constitutes an Argument Across the Content Areas?

"An argument is a reasoned, logical way of demonstrating that the writer's position, belief, or conclusion is valid" (Common Core State Standards, 2010b, p. 23).		
In English Language Arts	**In Science**	**In Social Studies/ History**
• Students make claims about the worth or meaning of a literary work or works. • They defend their interpretations or judgments with evidence from the text(s) they are studying.	• Students make claims in the form of statements or conclusions that answer questions or address problems related to scientific investigations. • They use data in a scientifically acceptable form. • They present evidence and draw on their understanding of scientific concepts to argue in support of their claims.	• Students analyze evidence from multiple primary and secondary sources to advance a claim. • They support their claim with the evidence. • They use historically or empirically based reasoning.

Source: Adapted from Appendix A (*Common Core State Standards*, 2010b, p. 23.)

Since arguments are used for many purposes—such as "to change the reader's point of view, to bring about some action on the reader's part, or to ask the reader to accept the writer's explanation or evaluation of a concept, issue, or problem" (*Common Core State Standards*, 2010b, p. 23)—explicit lessons are needed to help students understand the expectations of the genre and to develop their own well-constructed arguments in all content areas using discipline-specific norms. English as a second-language learners and speakers of nonstandard English will require additional support to the native languages or home dialects and standard English, which Joanne Kilgour Dowdy, professor of adolescent and adult literacy, calls ADE (AcaDemEse) (personal communication, February 12, 2013). We agree with Ladson-Billings (2009) who emphasized that "the language they [speakers of nonstandard English] bring with them serves as a tool that helps them with additional language learning, just as speakers of standard English use English to help them acquire new languages" (p. 92). The challenge all teachers face is to acknowledge, value, and effectively build on the language students bring with them to school and to help them develop academic language skills in standard English while being validated for the language they already possess.

We concur with Calkins et al. (2012), who emphasized that students need well-planned, sustained learning experiences with writing arguments so they can explore this genre in a variety of ways, "with some of those opportunities allowing writers to work over both long and short periods of time on a piece of writing, receiving coaching and instruction along the way" (p. 138).

Essential Strategy #1 to Support Anchor Performance 1: Argument Writing Structures

Below we present a number of brief strategies that are structured and scaffolded, may be directly connected to the topic or text the course is exploring, and are frequently tied to enhancing other language skills such as reading, listening, or speaking. For designing high-quality, teacher-tested tasks, also see assignment templates developed by the Literacy Design Collaborative (http://www.literacydesigncollabora-tive.org).

The genre of argument writing readily calls for public sharing and presentations, so have students share what they have written. Thus, they can see "(1) that writing is part of learning, (2) that such writing assignments are integral to the lesson and not merely busywork, and (3) that what they write is valued" (Walling, 2009, p. 19).

Scaffolded Argument Charts and Graphic Organizers. When students seem to be stuck on merely stating an opinion (which may be expected with adolescents) and do not make a well-supported argument, they need practice with the elements of arguments, which are (a) claim (*What is your point?*), (b) evidence (*Why do you say so? What is your proof?*), and (c) explanation (*What is the logical connection between the evidence and your point?*)

To learn the genre of argument writing, students can be introduced to the structured graphic organizers presented in Figures 5.1 and 5.2, which will help them shift from expressing their own opinion to producing well-supported argument writing. Please note that the scaffolded steps in Figure 5.2 encourage students to consider the viewpoints and arguments of others.

Gallagher (2011) suggested a four-square argument chart to help explore more sides of an issue. He expects his students to use a version of Figure 5.3 so they can take notes and plan their writing as they draft key ideas from multiple perspectives.

To generate a balanced set of arguments and counterarguments, the V-diagram in Figure 5.4 may also serve as a helpful visual tool. The target question (such as *"Should cell phones be allowed in the classroom?"*) is placed in the center; one side of the V contains the arguments for and the other side against allowing access to cell phones during class time.

Figure 5.1 Scaffolded Argument Analysis Chart

1. Identify the major claim in the text: (What is the main point?)
2. Find a quote that supports the claim: (Where is the proof or evidence?)
3. Explain the quote: (What does it mean? What is implied?)

Figure 5.2 Expanded Argument Analysis Chart

1. Identify a major claim made in the text:
2. Find a quote that supports the claim:
3. Explain the quote:
4. Take your own position about the claim:
5. Offer one or two reasons why you are for the claim, or offer a counterclaim:
6. Support your reasoning with evidence from one or more other sources, including a target text:

Figure 5.3 Four-Square Argument Chart

Your side of an argument	Your parents' or friends' side of the argument
Your parents' or friends' main counterarguments (response to your arguments)	Your counterarguments to respond to your parents or friends

Source: Adapted from Gallagher, K. (2011). *Write like this: Teaching real world writing through modeling & mentor texts* (pp. 177–178 and Figure 7.1). Portland, ME: Stenhouse.

Figure 5.4 V-Diagram for Arguments and Counterarguments

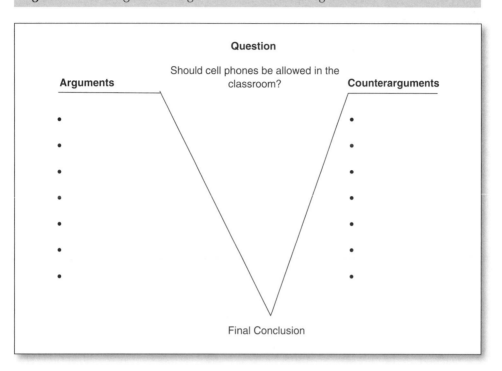

Question

Should cell phones be allowed in the classroom?

Arguments   Counterarguments

• • • • • • •   • • • • • • •

Final Conclusion

Take a Stand. At the completion of a lesson or after having read and discussed a text that presents multiple perspectives, provide students with a list of *Agree, Disagree, Strongly Agree, Strongly Disagree* prompts. On an index card, have them develop a brief written argument using the following sentence frame:

I (strongly) (dis)agree with this statement because _____.

Name the four corners of the room as Agree, Disagree, Strongly Agree, and Strongly Disagree. Invite students to select one of the four positions to which they will respond by (a) *taking a stand* at a designated corner of the classroom, (b) sharing their own arguments and listening to their classmates' ideas, and (c) responding in writing by using sentence stems and word boxes. As they interact with their classmates, students should be encouraged to refine or add to their original responses. Alternatively, this activity lends itself to be turned into a game in which students on each side of the issue try to gain members. Box 5.2 has some possible prompts about climate change.

Box 5.2 Sample Agree, Disagree, Strongly Agree, and Strongly Disagree Prompts About Climate Change

Climate change may be caused by the hole in the ozone layer.

Climate change is the greatest natural threat to humanity.

Climate change and global warming are often used interchangeably but have a different meaning.

Climate change is a natural process: The Earth has been getting warmer for hundreds of years.

Anticipation Guides With Extensions. Anticipation guides help build student interest about a subject, establish a purpose for reading, or tap into learners' prior knowledge. As students agree or disagree with a few carefully written statements that are closely aligned to the upcoming lesson/text, they get a quick preview of what is about to be taught. For oral language development, Fisher, Frey, and Rothenberg (2008) suggested that students read the statements individually and also discuss them with a partner. To connect anticipatory guides to writing, have students write a brief explanation for their choices. Ask them to revisit the guide at the end of the unit or lesson to note any changes in their thinking. At this time, they may write a statement explaining the change in their thinking and cite evidence from the text (see samples in Box 5.3).

Box 5.3 Anticipation Guide Extension Samples

Prior to this unit, I thought climate change and global warming were the same. Now I know . . .

Originally I thought global warming was . . . Evidence from my readings shows . . .

Essential Strategy #2 to Support Anchor Performance 1: Questionnaires and Surveys

To engage students in authentic argument writing experiences, use student-generated questionnaires and surveys. If necessary, first have students respond to teacher-generated questionnaires based on a text or a topic studied in class (see Box 5.4 for possible grade-appropriate topics). As a next step, create questionnaires and surveys collaboratively as a class and engage students in pair-work activities to share questions and answers to their questionnaires. Based on the responses students collect, they prepare arguments and counterarguments related to the topic explored.

Box 5.4 Sample Topics for Questionnaire and Survey Design

Grades 6–8

Ecosystems

Organization of governments around the world

Globalization

Art media, techniques, and processes

Personal health and fitness

Grades 9–12

Water pollution

Technology and ethics

Informed decisions about college and career choices

Historical figures and modern times

Musical genres

Source: Based on the *2012 Amplification of the English Language Development Standards, Kindergarten–Grade 12* (World-Class Instructional Design and Assessment Consortium, 2012)

Anchor Performance 2: Write Informative/Explanatory Texts Related to Grade-Appropriate Content

Throughout the secondary grades, both in ELA and in history/social studies, science, and all technical subjects, students will have to be taught (a) to introduce and develop an informational topic effectively, (b) to use precise language and domain-specific vocabulary as well as transitions as they maintain a formal writing style, and (c) to offer a well-supported conclusion. Students in Grades 6–8 are expected to write informative/ explanatory texts to examine a topic and convey ideas, concepts, and information through the selection, organization, and analysis of relevant content, with a gradual increase in attention to detail and careful choice of facts.

By Grades 9–10, students work with complex ideas and need to show more clarity and accuracy in their selection, organization, and analysis of the content. In addition, they consider the audience's knowledge of the topic and use an objective tone while observing the norms and conventions of the discipline in which they are writing. In their conclusions, they also discuss the implications or the significance of the topic. To further refine their expository writing style, students in Grades 11–12 are expected to use techniques such as metaphors, similes, and analogies.

When it comes to writing in the disciplines—history/social studies, science, and all technical subjects—students will write informative/ explanatory texts, including the narration of historical events, scientific procedures/experiments, or technical processes. The subskills involved in reaching these goals parallel the expectations in ELA.

Essential Strategy to Support Anchor Performance 2: Visual Frameworks for Expository Writing

Getting students ready for informative/explanatory writing and helping them plan their work is a critical step to success. Visual frameworks, such as select graphic organizers can aid in the writing process by offering the necessary support for all students.

Timelines. Following a structured research activity or shared directed reading/thinking session, have students summarize the key events by first mapping their sequence on a scaffolded timeline. For example, if students are studying the history of New York State, they can complete the timeline in Figure 5.5 to help organize their ideas by jotting down key notes connected to each century.

Timelines can also be used to support sequencing fictional events that take place in a short story or novel (see Standard 3 in Box 5.1). We also encourage teachers to use interactive, web-based timelines presented on educational sites or on virtual museum web pages. Box 5.5 lists some recommended links that lend themselves to either independent study or group exploration.

Box 5.5 Sample Interactive Timelines From Select Virtual Museums and Educational Sites

John F. Kennedy: http://whd.jfklibrary.org/Timeline

Anne Frank: http://www.annefrank.org/timeline#!/timeline

One Hundred Years of Flight: http://teacher.scholastic.com/activities/flight/timeline .htm

Ancient Egyptian History: http://www.ancientegypt.co.uk/time/explore/main.html

Figure 5.5 Scaffolded New York State Timeline

16th Century

1524—Giovanni da Verrazano sailed from _____

17th Century

1609—Henry Hudson was the first European to _____.

1624—The Dutch settled _____and ruled over the colony of New Netherland for 40 years.

1625—The Dutch purchased Manhattan Island from _____.

1664—The Colony of New Netherland was conquered by the English and was renamed "New York" in honor of _____.

18th Century

1765—New York City hosted a colony conference to _____.

1776—**July 9**—New York declared _____.

1777—The first governor was _____.

1788—With the Revolutionary War ended, New York became _____.

1797—Albany became _____.

1789—**April 30**—New York City became the first capital of _____, where President George Washington was _____.

1792—The New York Stock Exchange was founded by _____.

19th Century

1825—Erie Canal was _____.

1853—Railroads _____.

1886—The Statue of Liberty _____.

20th Century

1929—The New York Stock Market _____.

1932—Lake Placid hosts the _____.

1939—World Fair opens in _____.

1946—The United Nations _____.

1964—World Fair opened (again) in _____.

21st Century

2001—World Trade Center _____.

Summary Chart. A summary chart assists students in categorizing all key ideas related to a topic that aids them in developing language chunks into complete sentences and paragraphs. Figure 5.6 offers a sample, partially completed summary chart comparing Hinduism and Buddhism. Similar summary charts may be generated collectively as a class, in small groups, in pairs, or individually. To support learners who need it, we suggest differentiating the chart by offering scaffolded answers as models for students to emulate.

Figure 5.6 Summary Chart Example

Hinduism	Shared Characteristics	Buddhism
• No one founder • Developed over 3,500 years	• To live a moral life	• Buddha was the founder • Late 500s BC

Taylor Volpe, social studies teacher candidate at Molloy College, New York, uses the partially completed summary matrix presented in Figure 5.7 when she teaches about the thirteen colonies. Structured summary charts help students understand the task globally and also see the expectations in the concrete examples given.

Figure 5.7 Summary Matrix for the Thirteen Colonies

Colonies	Settlements	Characteristic Features	Reasons Founded
New England	Massachusetts, New Hampshire, Rhode Island, Connecticut	Fishing and ship building	
Middle Colonies			
Southern Colonies			

Transition Phrase Poster. A poster-size version of the chart presented in Table 5.2 offers a quick reference to the common logical relationships expressed in expository text structures and the most frequently occurring transition words associated with each. A printable version of this poster may be used in students' notebooks to remind them of the different choices they have to indicate transitions in their writing. Another way to introduce this tool is for the teacher to start the poster and have students add to it throughout the year.

Table 5.2 Transition Phrase Poster

Logical Relationships	Transitional Phrases
Addition	and, in addition to, furthermore, moreover, likewise, as well as, equally important
Comparison/Similarity	also, similarly, in the same way, likewise, in similar fashion
Contrast/Exception	but, however, on the contrary, nevertheless, in spite of, in contrast, yet, on one hand, on the other hand, conversely, at the same time, while this may be true
Time	to begin with, previously, in the meantime, immediately, recently, earlier, simultaneously, currently, subsequently, after, afterward, eventually, later, meanwhile
Place	here, there, wherever, opposite to, adjacent to, above, below, nearby
Example/Illustration	thus, for example, for instance, to illustrate, in particular, such as, namely, specifically, to illustrate
Emphasis	above all, in fact, even, indeed, of course, truly, certainly, surely, really, also, furthermore, in addition
Sequence/Order	first, second, third, . . . next, then, finally
Clarification	to clarify, in other words, that is to say, to explain, i.e. (that is)
Cause	because, since, on account of, for that reason
Effect	consequently, accordingly, thus, hence, so, therefore, as a result
Summary	in summary, in sum, to summarize, to sum up, in short, on the whole, finally
Conclusion	in conclusion, to conclude

Fact Cards. Distribute two to three index cards to students to individually record one carefully selected fact about the target topic per card (Figure 5.8). Have them read their cards in pairs. After they agree on the five (or more) most important facts about the topic, have them arrange the cards so they can collaboratively write a summary using the cards as scaffolds. For example, when studying the Maurya Empire of Ancient India, students might generate fact cards about the empire by identifying the dates, the location, the government type, the predominant forms of economy, the role of Buddhism, the importance of schools and libraries, and so on. Using the individually drafted fact cards, they then collaboratively develop a well-crafted summary.

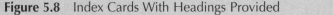

Figure 5.8   Index Cards With Headings Provided

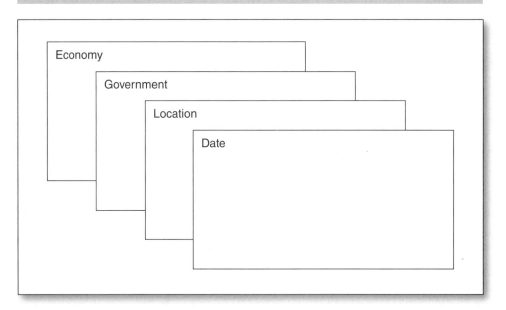

Anchor Performance 3: Write Narratives About Real or Imaginary Events and Use Descriptive Writing

Although most students are likely to have considerably more experience writing personal narratives and developing their descriptive writing skills, struggling learners and English language learners (ELLs) will continue to rely on scaffolding techniques to perform these writing tasks successfully. Scaffolding is especially needed since the expectations for narrative writing become gradually more complex and demanding. In Grade 6, the task is quite complex already; some highlights of the expectations include but are not limited to the following: establishing a context, organizing an event sequence that unfolds naturally and logically, and using both a variety of narrative techniques and a variety of transition words, phrases, and sentence types.

By Grade 7, students establish a point of view as well as show the relationships among experiences and events through transitions; by Grade 8, writers also reflect on events in the conclusion. Students in Grades 9–10 introduce multiple points of view and use well-chosen details and multiple plot lines. By Grades 11–12, writers will not only create a coherent whole but also build toward a particular tone and outcome, such as a sense of mystery or suspense. Although this standard does not directly apply to literacy in history/social studies, science, and technical subjects, it is expected that students will be able to

> incorporate narrative elements effectively into arguments and informative/explanatory texts. In history/social studies, students must be able to incorporate narrative accounts into their analyses of individuals or events of historical import. In science and technical subjects, students must be able to write precise enough descriptions of the step-by-step procedures they use in their investigations or technical work that others can replicate them and (possibly) reach the same results. (*Common Core State Standards*, 2010a, p. 65)

Essential Strategy to Support Anchor Performance 3: Visual Frameworks for Narrative Writing

Similar to Anchor Performance 2 earlier, visual frameworks also support secondary learners as they develop narrative and descriptive writing skills. Select graphic organizers that match the narrative and descriptive genres are presented below.

Story Lines (Timelines). To encourage students to see the sequence of events in historical fiction or chapter books, have them map the story on a timeline showing the key dates (or times) and abbreviated events associated with each date or time. For example, to offer a narrative account, students may first work with a graphic organizer—such as the one in Figure 5.9—to map the key events by jotting them down on each diagonal line.

Figure 5.9 Blank Story Planning Timeline

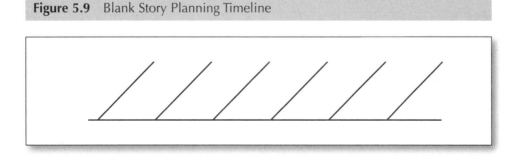

Sequencing Flow Charts. Flow charts are effective graphic organizers to represent the order or sequence of events. Creating a game on an interactive board allows students to move around events, indicating their relative position in the sequence (see Figure 5.10).

Figure 5.10   Flow Chart for Sequencing Events

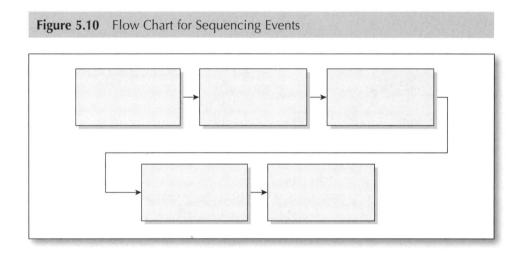

Sensory Chart. Thinking about details captured by the five senses is not just a K–5 strategy. As students plan a vivid description of the setting, they can first sketch out what can be seen, heard, smelled, tasted, or felt by the characters. See Table 5.3 as a sample completed sensory chart based on a scene in *The Hunger Games* (Collins, 2010) right before the contest begins.

Table 5.3   Sensory Chart

See	Other contestants scanning for suitable weapons, neon numbers flashing, rugged terrain
Hear	Clock ticking, heartbeats accelerating, wind blowing through the leaves, insects warbling
Smell	Freshly cut tree branches, dirt piles, gun powder, perspiration odor
Taste	Dry bitterness in their mouths
Feel	Sweat rolling down their temples, tension building up in their muscles

Plot Plan. In Figure 5.11, we offer a frequently used graphic organizer that contains the key elements of literary fiction. When it is presented visually and used frequently, students recognize and remember the essential components of narrative texts more easily and make plans for their own writing.

When supporting narrative writing for secondary learners, the planning tools and scaffolding templates presented here cannot be viewed as final products. They are intended to help students plan or organize their writing and put the much needed forethought into the task before sitting down to write. Other scaffolds may be necessary for students who have completed certain aspects of the writing task but need guidance with combining the elements and incorporating the features of good writing into their product.

Figure 5.11 Plot Plan Template

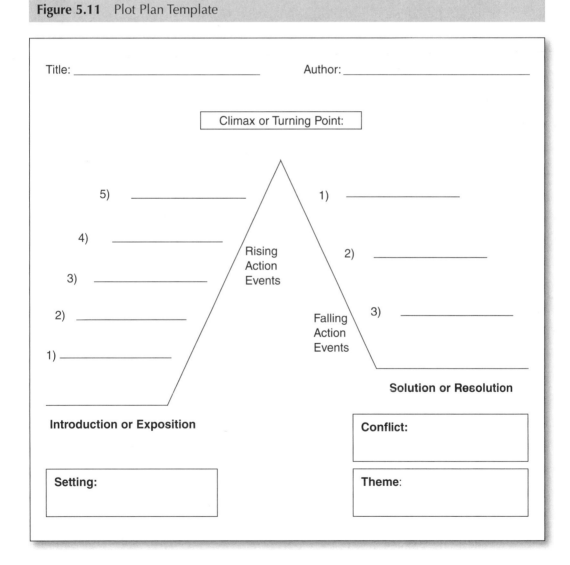

Production and Distribution of Writing

The next three writing standards focus both on successfully participating in the writing process and on producing and sharing the outcome or the finished written product. To be able to do so, students need to develop specific subskills and must have ample opportunities to respond to varied writing tasks in which they write for a variety of audiences and multiple purposes. We like to say, "Read the genre, to write the genre," by which we suggest that students have the opportunity to read model texts in all genres. The models—used as mentor texts—can come from published sources (not even intended for instructional purposes), previously written and edited student work, or teacher-generated examples.

Anchor Performance 4: Produce a Written Response With Grade-Appropriate Organization and Development

Secondary students are expected to produce clear and coherent writing that shows the development, organization, and style of ideas that are appropriate for the assigned task, the grade-level content, the target audience, and the purpose of the written work. We have found that many speakers of nonstandard English, ELLs, or struggling secondary students may not be able to achieve this standard without (a) carefully designed direct instruction, (b) opportunities to transfer what they know in their native language or home dialect, and (c) scaffolded assistance with writing in academic English.

Essential Strategy to Support Anchor Performance 4: Scaffolding Writing Instruction

Scaffolding writing can take various forms and can offer various degrees of support. The purpose of scaffolding instruction may focus on the actual outcome or product of the writing, thus offering students fully or partially developed examples at the sentence, paragraph, and text levels. Some students who have their ideas clearly developed in their native languages or home dialects will need opportunities to *translate or code-switch* their thoughts into standard academic English (Joanne K. Dowdy, personal communication, February 12, 2013). Another approach to scaffolding writing instruction will support students throughout the entire writing process, from drafting through editing to publishing the final written piece.

Sentence Starters With or Without Word-Level Support. For producing written responses at the sentence level, have students complete sentence starters either independently or with additional support such as the use of mentor texts, word lists, glossaries, word walls, or word boxes. Grant and Fisher (2010) suggested that in addition to offering the typical headings for a science report—*problem, hypothesis, data analysis,* and *conclusion*—teachers should offer sentence starters for the data analysis section such as the following:

My data show that over time _____.

The evidence for this is _____.

Based on this evidence, I determine that _____. (p. 65)

Structured Analysis of Written Resources. When students participate in structured, scaffolded tasks that guide them step-by-step to analyze specific aspects of published documents, they not only work on a carefully designed activity that helps develop a better understanding of the target content, but they also develop their discipline-specific writing skills. For example, for analyzing point of view expressed in primary sources in a social studies class, students may complete the scaffolded outline in Figure 5.12. A letter, a speech, a diary entry, a political cartoon, or virtually any authentic source will serve well as a target document to be analyzed this way.

Once the template is completed either in small groups or individually, students may need a paragraph frame or sentence starters to transfer their analysis into a well-constructed final paragraph.

Figure 5.12 Structured Analysis of Point of View in Primary Documents

Title	
Author	
Point of view: (SOAP)	
Speaker	
Occasion	
Audience	
Purpose	

Paragraph Frames and Essay Outlines. Another way to scaffold student expository writing is to offer them paragraph frames or essay outlines that will help further their understanding of the most frequently encountered expository text patterns, including (a) description, (b) sequence, (d) compare-contrast, (e) cause-effect, and (f) problem-solution or narrative text. Figure 5.13 is a sample paragraph frame designed to assist students in writing a comparative paragraph.

Figure 5.13 Comparative Paragraph Frame

Even though _____ and _____
are different in many ways, they also share several similarities. Both _____
_____ and _____ are _____.
Some differences between _____ and _____
include _____. In conclusion, _____
_____.

To support students in the development of the commonly required five-paragraph essay, try the graphic organizer template in Figure 5.14. Initially, have students only jot down key words and phrases in each designated section of the template; then gradually model for the students and encourage them to provide short sentences, more complex sentences, and finally paragraphs.

Anchor Performance 5: Edit and Revise Written Work

Students who are not proficient writers will rarely know how to edit and revise their own work. Most students in Grades 6–8—as recognized by the CCSS—will need some guidance and support from peers and adults to develop and strengthen their writing skills. By Grades 9–12, writers are expected to implement the writing process independently and also be able to focus on "what is most significant for a specific purpose or audience" (*Common Core State Standards*, 2010a, p. 46).

To prepare all students for such a challenging task, provide them with mentoring: opportunities to read high-quality mentor texts and opportunities to watch you model how you plan, revise, edit, rewrite, and try new approaches to writing. Gradually release the responsibility to students through guided and collaborative practice (Fisher & Frey, 2008) so they may also work with their classmates and offer peer support and mentoring to each other.

Essential Strategy #1 to Support Anchor Performance 5: Explicit Instruction in the Revising and Editing Steps of the Writing Process Through Modeling and Guided Support

Gallagher (2011) noted, "If students are to become better writers, they need to recognize that sometimes their first idea is not always their best

Figure 5.14 Five-Paragraph Essay Planning Template

Introductory Paragraph With a Thesis Statement		
Topic Sentence (first supporting paragraph)	Topic Sentence (second supporting paragraph)	Topic sentence (third supporting paragraph)
Key details	Key details	Key details
Closing or Summary Paragraph		

idea. . . . Their richest thinking may be found in their second, or fifth, or ninth idea" (p. 229). Students must develop persistence and skills to revise the content and edit their writing for style and mechanics.

Write Aloud. Similar to read alouds and think alouds, the purpose of *writing aloud* for and with students is to model the entire writing process by showing not only the thoughts that go into planning the written piece but also how a writer handles false starts and how to revise and rewrite at the word, sentence, paragraph, and text level. Such modeling will help develop metacognitive awareness in students about the editing and revisiting process.

Interactive Editing. Similar to interactive writing, defined as collaboratively composing and constructing a written message *while sharing a pen* (McCarrier, Fountas, & Pinnell, 1999), interactive editing allows for a collaborative rereading of a student's original written piece, while teacher and student jointly check for content and form, looking for errors in conventions and editing or revising at the word, sentence, or text level. This activity affords opportunities for meaningful dialogues in which the teacher validates students' ideas expressed and their native language or home dialect use, while also guiding them to use standard English forms.

Feed Forward. After modeling writing in the target genre, allow students to work in small groups to generate similar drafts collaboratively. During the process, circulate the room and teach on purpose; offer immediate personalized assistance—or *feed forward*—to each student in anticipation of what he or she might be trying to work out. Feed forward can take any of the following forms:

- Remind students of writing strategies you previously introduced.
- Guide them with word selection.
- Model a more complex sentence structure.
- Offer transition words choices.
- Help recast what the student says in nonstandard, informal English to standard, academic English.

Mentor Text. We concur with Anderson (2007), who noted that "editing instruction starts with students observing how powerful texts work" (p. 13) one sentence at a time! Anderson's and many others' use of mentor texts involve guiding students in understanding what they can learn from *effective* and *correct* writing, thus making teaching editing inquiry based and open-ended. We adapted the guiding questions Anderson suggests when examining mentor texts (see Box 5. 6).

Box 5.6 Guiding Questions to Analyze Mentor Texts

What do you notice about the way the author uses the word/phrase _____?

What else do you notice about it?

How does it sound when we read it?

How would you say the same ideas?

What would change if we removed _____ from the sentence?

Which do you prefer? Why?

Source: Adapted from Anderson, J. (2007). *Everyday editing: Inviting students to develop skill and craft in writer's workshop* (p. 13). Portland ME: Stenhouse.

Essential Strategy #2 to Support Anchor Performance 5: Prepare Students to Engage in Self- and Peer-Editing Tasks

To be proficient writers of academic English, bridges must be built between how students currently use English, what knowledge they have of their home language or nonstandard dialect, and how to shift that to academic writing. When students learn to edit their own writing, they develop increased awareness of how well their ideas are developed and how closely they have observed writing conventions. Focusing on specific features helps students become more self-directed, independent learners as well as more confident writers. Peer editing helps create both a community of engaged writers and a supportive learning environment in which mistakes are accepted and feedback and comments are welcome.

Peer Editing Through Read Around Groups. Susan Lafond, National Board Certified ESL Teacher has used a peer assessment/feedback technique called Read Around Groups (RAGs) (Gossard, 1996), in which students give each other advice on one of these four dimensions: formatting of the paper, the introductory paragraph with a thesis statement, the body of the paper, and the conclusion. Students work in small groups completing one row of the RAGs Comment Sheet (see Figure 5.15). As they read peer papers (with author names removed), they write comments,

Figure 5.15 Read Around Groups (RAGs) Comment Sheet

Name of Assignment _____   Date _____

What to Look for	Comments	Comments	Comments
Form • Four paragraphs: intro, two body paragraphs, conclusion			
Introduction • First sentence grabs attention. • Thesis statement reflects headline on style. • Personal beliefs about the thesis statement are clearly stated.			
Paragraph Structure • Paragraphs are grouped by main ideas. • Topic sentence is used per paragraph. • All sentences provide detail for topic sentence.			
Conclusion • Thesis statement and topic sentences are included. • They are restated in different terms.			

suggestions, and/or recommendations for improvement in the corresponding boxes. When the group is finished, the papers are switched to the next group, where peers will offer feedback on the next dimension of the paper.

Self-Assessment/ Reflection Tools. Make self-assessment and reflection on students' own writing a regular practice. Have students use sticky notes to mark a section (sentence or paragraph) of their own writing that contains a *well-developed idea.* Next, have students look for a section (sentence or paragraph) that is less than completely developed and may be lacking in clarity or detail. Move on to having students complete the self-reflection checklist in Figure 5.16, or use a similar one codeveloped with your class.

Figure 5.16 3-2-1 Self-Assessment Reflection Tool

3 ideas I successfully expressed
2 ideas/sections I improved upon with a friend's help
1 idea I still need to work on

Lapp and Fisher (2012) suggested a self-assessment checklist to help students evaluate the power of their persuasion (see Figure 5.17). It is especially effective since it is a scaffolded tool that can be adapted for the context or writing proficiency level of any secondary class. It is not merely a checklist but also serves as an open-ended reflection and summary in one.

Rubrics and Checklists. Use editing and revising tools such as checklists and rubrics that are grade appropriate and are written at the students' cognitive and linguistic levels. The best way to approach implementing the use of such tools is to collaboratively generate them with your students. For sample rubrics and for templates to develop your own rubrics, see one of these sites: www.rubrics4teachers.com/ or www.teachnology .com/web_tools/rubrics/. Another recommendation is to examine the existing rubrics aligned to your state assessments, familiarize yourself with the criteria in them, and use them during the year since they are the benchmarks toward which students are working.

Figure 5.17 Evaluating the Power of My Persuasion

Evaluating the Power of My Persuasion

Introducing My Persuasive Claim

_____ My clearly stated claim is . . .

_____ My audience is . . .

_____ The authority of my claim has been established by . . .

Supporting My Claim

_____ Evidence is included to support my claim. The evidence is . . .

_____ The knowledge, concerns, and questions of my intended audience have been addressed by . . .

_____ The formalness of tone matches my familiarity with the audience. My tone is . . .

Illustrating Language Power

_____ Rhetorical questions have been asked. These are . . .

_____ Power verbs and adjectives have been included. These include . . .

_____ An unforgettable power phrase has been included. It is . . .

Summing It Up

_____ My claim or position is clearly presented, developed, and supported as shown in lines . . .

_____ A powerful conclusion reinforces the authority of my original claim. It is . . .

Source: Adapted from Lapp, D., & Fisher, D. (2012). Persuasion = Stating and arguing claims well. _Journal of Adolescent & Adult Literacy, 55,_ 641–644.

Code-Switching. As recommended by Wheeler (2005, 2008), Fogel and C. Ehri (2000), and many others, one effective strategy to be woven into the editing process is code-switching from informal (or vernacular) to formal (or standard) English. Once nonstandard speakers of English are given the opportunity—through explicit contrastive analysis—to discover how the grammar of their home language compares and contrasts with standard English, they are able to notice the differences between the two and limit how much informal grammar use transfers into their formal writing. Wheeler (2008) identified the following five areas for starting with contrasting grammar analysis (with examples of vernacular English added in parenthesis):

- Subject-verb agreement (*Mama walk the dog every day.*)
- Showing past time (*Mama walk the dog yesterday or I seen the movie.*)
- Possessive (*My sister friend came over.*)
- Showing plurality (*It take 24 hour to rotate.*)
- "A" versus "an" (*a elephant, an rabbit*) (p. 55)

This strategy helps students who speak and write in the vernacular dialect of their home communities to improve their academic writing, as noted by Wheeler (2005), "*after* students have done the content work on their essays—homing in on a main idea, brainstorming, organizing, drafting, elaborating, and revising. After the *content* is in place, then comes code-switching" (p. 111).

Anchor Performance 6: Use Computers or Digital Devices to Register Ideas

Information technology standards are incorporated throughout the CCSS, so all students are expected to use computers and web-based resources as well as other nonprint-based media to access information and to communicate their own ideas. Across all secondary grades, Writing Standard 6 emphasizes the use of technology to produce new writing and to collaborate with others via the Internet. By Grade 6, students will have to develop sufficient keyboarding skills; in Grade 7 linking to and citing resources is expected, whereas in Grade 8 the new skill is to establish relationships between information and students' own ideas, thus becoming critical consumers of online sources. In the high school context, students in Grade 9–10 will use technology's capacity to share their work in a flexible and dynamic way, whereas by Grades 11–12, they will also incorporate feedback as they update individual and shared written work using technology tools.

Essential Strategy to Support Anchor Performance 6: Introducing Technology Tools in the Classroom

Most adolescents use technology to a much greater extent outside of school than inside the classroom: texting on their smartphones, video chatting on their iPads, posting personal updates on their Facebook pages, sharing photos and videos on Instagram or Tumblr, or engaging in multiplayer, synchronous, virtual games are daily occurrences in their lives. Rosen (2011) described the *iGeneration*, as frequently observed by their parents and teachers, "being online, using computers offline, listening to music, playing video games, talking on the telephone, instant messaging, texting, sending and receiving e-mail, and watching television" (p. 12). November (2011) went as far as encouraging teachers to use *reverse mentoring* and rely on their most tech-savvy students for learning about new technology tools and skills. The bottom line is that making technology similarly engaging for instructional purposes, especially for writing or creating multimedia products, is a challenge teachers must embrace. As Kirby and Crovitz (2012) noted,

> Advances in technology and communications are poised to open new vistas for teachers and schools. When we constructively channel students' interests in gadgets, media, and social networks, we help create sophisticated and agile communicators, comfortable with and skilled in a variety of both new and conventional "literacies." (p. 3)

Below is a brief selection of some favorite websites that can engage students with technology tools and help develop their writing, collaboration, and literacy skills.

Student Publishing Websites. Web-based publishing is not only highly motivating and in line with students' out of school literacies, it also promotes collaboration with peers, teachers, parents and community members, as well as a global audience (if teachers decide to allow it) across multiple forms of media. Here are some sites to consider for student collaboration or sharing student work online:

- *Glogster* (http://www.glogster.com). A safe and secure web-based publishing platform where students can share their interactive web posters complete with text, graphics, music, and videos.
- *Wikis* (http://www.wikispaces.com): This website allows students (with their teachers) to publish and regularly update pages that many contributors may develop collaboratively. At the same time, the site also allows for published content to be discussed.
- *Fakebook* (http://www.classtools.net/fb/home/page): Students create imaginary profile pages in Facebook-style for study purposes.
- *Storybird* (http://storybird.com): Contributors to this free online digital storytelling platform create, share, and read others' visual stories.
- *Topics* (http://www.topics-mag.com/index.html): This is a magazine published by and for English learners and their teachers.

Blogs. In addition to the sites listed above, teachers can create their own password-protected blogs for their classes at sites such as www.edublogs .org, www.kidblog.org, and www.classblogmeister.com. A unique blog called Youth Voices (http://youthvoices.net/about) has recently been voted best student-written blog by Scholastic; it offers a platform for students, their teachers, and their authentic readers from around the world to participate in a "colossal ongoing discussion about everything." Langer de Ramirez (2010) pointed out that "students feel a connection to a broad audience or readers—and subsequently writers who may post comments to their blogs" and that "there is a strong sense of autonomy in blogging" (p. 17) since students develop ownership of their work published online. Blogging is personal or may be closely tied to instructional topics. Since writing with a purpose for a real audience is both intrinsically and extrinsically motivating for linguistically and academically diverse learners, reluctant or struggling writers may significantly benefit from blogging.

Research to Build and Present Knowledge

The next three writing standards emphasize how students need to become adept at gathering and synthesizing information from multiple sources, evaluating the sources they use for their research, and also citing the material using a standard style format.

Anchor Performance 7: Participate in a Grade-Appropriate Research Project

Students in Grades 6–8 are expected to engage in short research projects in ELA and the content areas using multiple resources. By Grade 8, students are also encouraged to generate their own research questions and to explore multiple pathways to answer more complex questions. In Grades 9–12, students must demonstrate that they can adjust their investigation, thus narrowing or broadening their inquiry as deemed necessary. Additionally, at the high school level, students are also asked to synthesize the information gleaned from multiple sources to demonstrate a higher level understanding of the target topic.

Essential Strategy to Support Anchor Performance 7: Collaborative Writing Projects

Group Explorations. Author studies, topic studies, and genre studies lend themselves to a guided group research activity, in which the entire class or smaller groups of students read a selection of related books, articles, or other materials—such as a selection of books by the same author or on the same topic, or written in the same genre. As a follow-up, students collaboratively generate a report to summarize and evaluate their research findings.

Group explorations also allow for students' funds of knowledge and expertise to be recognized and nurtured—acknowledging that there might be a disconnect between the taught curriculum and the students' own knowledge and that students bring varied backgrounds and knowledge bases to the class that should be valued and used. Collaborative writing can use traditional paper and pen(cil) methods or new web-based technologies. Kessler, Bikowski, and Boggs (2012) noted the advantage of using web-based collaborative tools for collaborative writing as follows:

> The use of tools such as Google Docs also allows teachers to establish practices of monitoring student progress throughout the writing process without the need to formally collect drafts. By monitoring student contributions teachers will gain greater insight into how their individual students and groups use these tools as they continue to evolve. (p. 105)

The activities we suggest below—jigsaw writing and gallery walk—are select strategies that pave the way for students to write independently from multiple sources. Since these tasks are collaborative, students have an opportunity to practice analyzing and writing about multiple sources in a less threatening or overwhelming way.

Jigsaw Writing. Before each student can tackle complex writing tasks independently, structure the writing assignments that require the use of multiple sources for input in the form of a jigsaw activity. Each individual student in a group of three to five will be responsible for providing answers based on the reading assigned to them only (be it a paragraph, a page, an article, a webpage, a book, or other resource). The individually constructed short responses will have to be combined into one final product, which must have an introduction and a conclusion and must also include the use of transitional words and phrases (see earlier Table 5.2 Transition Phrase Poster).

Gallery Walk. In this strategy, kinesthetic learning is coupled with pair work. Select and place around the classroom five to six selections related to the topic you are studying with the class. Make sure to include a variety of sources and types of *exhibits* such as brief poems, songs, proverbs, famous sayings, images with or without text, photographs, cartoons, and so on. Invite students (in pairs first, then later in the year give them the choice to work alone) to walk around and study at least three selections they find in your gallery. Ask them to fill out a scaffolded gallery response sheet that will invite students to reflect on the exhibits and make connections to their prior knowledge and among the items in the gallery (see sample Gallery Walk Response Questions in Box 5.7).

Box 5.7 Sample Gallery Walk Response Questions

Which two or three exhibits were the most meaningful to you? List them and explain why.

Which two exhibits may be connected?

Establish and explain a logical connection between them.

Cite evidence from the exhibits to support the connection you established.

Anchor Performance 8: Take Notes, Organize, and Evaluate Information

Students in the elementary grades are expected to recall information from experiences or gather information from sources provided by the teacher. They also learn to take notes, organize information, and in the upper grades, cite their sources. In the secondary context, Common Core Writing Standard 8 indicates significantly more complex expectations. Secondary students gather relevant information from multiple print and digital sources, assess the credibility of each source, and quote or paraphrase findings, providing bibliographic information for sources.

Starting with Grade 6, students need to make sure they understand plagiarism and know how to avoid it. Students in Grades 7–8 start using search terms effectively, assess sources not just for credibility but for accuracy, and apply a standard format for citing their sources. In addition to the skills gained during the middle school years, students in Grades 9–10 are going to conduct more complex searches, assess the usefulness of each source, and selectively integrate the information they locate into their own writing. Finally, students in Grades 11–12 will also assess the strengths and limitations of each source in terms of the task, purpose, and audience. In their writing, they must be mindful of not overrelying on one source.

Essential Strategy #1 to Support Anchor Performance 8: Structured Note Taking

Note taking based on one or more reading materials involves sifting through the text "to determine what is most relevant and transforming and reducing the substance of these ideas into written phrases or key words"

(Graham & Hebert, 2010, p. 16). During structured, scaffolded note-taking activities, teachers guide their students to organize the target material in a way that connects the new ideas found in the text with the students' prior knowledge gained both in and outside the classroom. Note-taking scaffolds help establish relationships between key concepts and supporting details, while also encouraging students to use analytic and evaluating skills. Charts that offer space for questions and answers are especially helpful.

I-Charts (Inquiry Charts). These charts were developed by Hoffman (1992) to encourage critical reading and note taking across the content areas. The adapted template presented in Figure 5.18 invites students to use multiple sources to answer the same three guiding questions. This template is also conducive to collaborative or jigsaw reading/writing in which each group focuses on one source only and completes one column of the chart.

Figure 5.18 Adapted I-Chart Template

Topic	Source 1	Source 2	Source 3	Source 4
Title and Author				
Question 1				
Question 2				
Question 3				
Summary				

Graphic Organizers for Information Gathering and Organization. Graphic organizers help students become familiar with different text structures through a range of reading and writing activities as presented in this book previously. They will also aid learners in applying their understanding of how ideas are organized in different genres by gathering information and organizing ideas using a visual tool. A favorite note-taking graphic organizer is in Figure 5.19, showing prompts for key ideas, details, and summary/evaluation of the source.

Additionally, see www.thinkingmaps.com for eight graphic organizers that promote analytical thinking while providing visual support. Examples from ELA, science, and social studies lessons are presented in Table 5.4.

Essential Strategy #2 to Support Anchor Performance 8: Web Source Evaluation

Since the expectations for secondary writers clearly state that they need to assess their print and online sources for credibility, accuracy,

Figure 5.19 Structured Note-Taking Template

Key Points	Details
Summary and Evaluation	

Table 5.4 Thinking Map Examples

Thinking Map	Purpose	Examples From Grade 6–12 ELA, Science, and Social Studies Lessons
Circle Map FOR DEFINING IN CONTEXT	Contextualization (adding a frame of reference)	Create a frame of reference for Scout Finch, the narrator and protagonist in Harper Lee's *To Kill a Mockingbird*
Tree Map FOR CLASSIFYING AND GROUPING	Classification	Summarize the achievements of the Sumerian Empire
Bubble Map FOR DESCRIBING USING ADJECTIVES	Description	Describe Cassie Logan in Mildred D. Taylor's *Roll of Thunder, Hear My Cry*
Double Bubble Map FOR COMPARING AND CONTRASTING	Comparison and contrast	Compare and contrast animal cells and plant cells

Thinking Map	Purpose	Examples From Grade 6–12 ELA, Science, and Social Studies Lessons
Flow Map FOR SEQUENCING AND ORDERING	Sequence or order of events	Track the events leading up to World War I
Multi-Flow Map FOR CAUSES AND EFFECTS	Cause and effect	Discuss what led to the Boston Tea Party and what events followed it
Brace Map FOR ANALYZING WHOLE OBJECTS AND PARTS	Part-whole relationships	Identify the major systems of the human body and the organs found in each system
Bridge Map as FOR SEEING ANALOGIES	Analogies	Explore the analogies in Walt Whitman's "O Captain! My Captain!"

and usefulness, they need explicit instruction on how to do all that, as well as needing a user-friendly tool to accomplish a source evaluation task. We suggest sharing and using (or adapting) the Web Evaluation Rubric in Figure 5.20 that assigns point values to a limited, but carefully selected set of criteria so students can evaluate websites with guidance and support. If a site receives a score below 16, students are to look for a more credible source.

Anchor Performance 9: Offer Text-Dependent Answers Using Grade-Appropriate Literary and Informational Texts

Students in all secondary grades are expected to apply grade-appropriate reading strategies to literature, literary nonfiction, and discipline-specific informational texts while they draw evidence from the target readings to

Figure 5.20 Web Evaluation Review

Criteria	Evaluation Techniques	Low Quality	Medium Quality	High Quality
Who is the author of the page?	• Is his or her name listed? • Can you figure out what makes the author an expert? (Look for an about me link.) If the author's name is not listed, does the credibility of the organization cover the author's reputation?	Not Qualified Or not available (0 pts)	Somewhat Qualified (3 pts) →	Highly Qualified (5 pts)
Is the sponsoring organization reliable?	• Is the organization's name prominent? • Is there an about us link on the home page? • What is the organization's reputation? Who links to the site?	Not Reliable (0 pts)	Somewhat Reliable (3 pts) →	Highly Reliable (5 pts)
Is the information helpful and important?	• How much information is there? • Is most of the information important and relevant to your topic? • Is the information accurate? • Is the spelling/grammar correct?	1 page or less Not relevant Many errors (1 pt)	2 pages Somewhat relevant Few errors (3 pts) →	3 pages or more Very relevant No errors (5 pts)
When was the information written and last updated?	• Is there an update date listed at the top or bottom of the page? • Is there a copyright date at the bottom?	6 yrs or more (1 pt)	3–5 years old (3 pts) →	2 yrs old or less (5 pts)

Source: http://brockport.k12.ny.us/webpages/hslib/evaluation.cfm/

support analysis, reflection, and research. In a recent report titled *Writing to Read: Evidence for How Writing Can Improve Reading,* Graham and Hebert (2010) concluded that "writing about a text proved to be better than just reading it, reading and rereading it, reading and studying it, reading and discussing it, and receiving reading instruction" (p. 14). Responding to readings in writing using analytical thinking skills may prove to be rather challenging for many students, for various reasons. If students do not have adequate background knowledge, text-dependent questioning must be supplemented with opportunities to understand the context.

Additionally, Bellanca, Fogarty, and Pete (2012) suggested a step-by-step approach to teach students to think and write analytically. The steps are summed up as the PART acronym presented in Box 5.8.

Box 5.8 PART Acronym for Analytical Thinking and Writing

Preview the whole text

Assess similarities and differences

Reorganize information by these similarities and differences

Turn the analysis into a summary or synthesis

Source: Adapted from Bellanca, J. A., Fogarty, R. J., & Pete, B. M. (2012). *How to teach thinking skills within the Common Core: 7 key student proficiencies of the new national standards* (p. 17). Bloomington, IN: Solution Tree.

Students who are learning standard English as a new language or new dialect or who may be struggling with linguistic expression must have additional support with text-dependent answers, also dubbed as one of the CCSS six shifts (see http://www.engageny.org/resource/common-core-shifts).

Essential Strategy #1 to Support Anchor Performance 9: Connect Questions and Responses.

Students need to understand that there is an intricate system of connections between questions and answers. The more metacognitive strategies they develop about questioning techniques, the easier they can handle responding to more complex readings or assignments as they progress through the grades.

QAR (Question–Answer Relationship). In the early 1980s, Raphael (1982, 1986), introduced this strategy to help students categorize the types of questions (depicted in Figure 5.21) they are asked and give them a tool to

Figure 5.21 QAR (Question–Answer Relationship) Template

IN THE TEXT	IN MY HEAD
RIGHT THERE	AUTHOR AND YOU
THINK AND SEARCH	ON MY OWN

discover where to look for the answers. If the answers are *In the Book*, students will either find them in a specific place in the text (*Right There*), or they will have to look in several places in the text (*Think and Search*). The two subcategories of the *In My Head* category include *Author and You* questions, which refer to when students need to use a combination of textual information and their background knowledge and experiences and *On My Own* questions, in which students rely mainly on background experiences and knowledge to come up with the answer (a question type not promoted by the CCSS). (See Raphael, Highfield, and Au, 2006, and Chapter 3 of this publication as well.)

Read Something, Write Something. Working in small groups, have students read short passages of text—from one paragraph to one full page. After reading silently and/or aloud, ask them to write one sentence that responds to a text-dependent question, such as having students identify the main idea or an essential detail (with or without sentence starters or other scaffolds). This activity may continue until a summary paragraph is complete and students share their summaries in a small group. For subsequent tasks, vary the prompt and allow for a range of text-dependent questions to be practiced.

Essential Strategy #2 to Support Anchor Performance 9: Photography-Based Response Writing

When you first introduce text-based answers or when text-dependent questioning needs some visual support for some learners, consider photo-based writing as suggested on The Learning Network blog maintained by the *New York Times.* As described in a supplement to the "6 Q's About the News" feature on the blog (http://learning.blogs.nytimes.com/category/6-qs-about-the-news), students not only answer the classic questions journalists report on in the news—who, what, where, when, why, and how—but also examine photographs related to a variety of news events. Students are asked to look for answers to questions in a related *Times* story, analyze the picture as visual input, and also make personal connections to the picture and the related story. Try the following for prompts for photo-based writing responses:

- Make a personal connection to the photo (e.g., "This reminds me of when _____").
- Write a question the photo brings to mind (e.g., "Why can you see only _____?").
- Write a detailed observation about the photo (e.g., "The color _____ is everywhere: _____").
- Make a guess as to what information the caption of this photo imparted (e.g., "This looks like _____").

Source: Adapted from http://learning.blogs.nytimes.com/2010/01/11/picture-this-building-photo-based-writing-skills/.

An additional tool, the *Photo Analysis Worksheet,* helps students to conduct a detailed analysis of any photograph (see Figure 5.22).

Range of Writing

Anchor Performance 10: Express Ideas and Thoughts in Writing Through a Variety of Tasks Ranging From Very Short to Extended Writing Assignments

As benchmarked by the Common Core and as suggested by common sense, for students' writing to improve, they need opportunities for sustained, extensive involvement in multiple, meaningful writing tasks. Students in all secondary grades will "write routinely over extended time frames (time for research, reflection, and revision) and shorter time frames (a single sitting or a day or two) for a range of tasks, purposes, and audiences" (*Common Core State Standards*, 2010a, p. 44).

For writing to become a powerful tool for learning, it must become an integral part of every class. To expand the daily independent writing tasks, we suggest inviting diverse learners to produce writing that is collaboratively generated over a period of time and edited as well as published for a real audience, including parents and the entire school community.

Figure 5.22 Photo Analysis Worksheet

Step 1. Observation	
A.	Study the photograph for two minutes. Form an overall impression of the photograph and then examine individual items. Next, divide the photo into quadrants and study each section to see what new details become visible.
B.	Use the chart below to list people, objects, and activities in the photograph.

People	Objects	Activities

Step 2. Inference

Based on what you have observed above, list three things you might infer from this photograph.

Step 3. Questions

A.	What questions does this photograph raise in your mind?
B.	Where could you find answers to them?

Source: http://www.archives.gov/education/lessons/worksheets/photo_analysis_worksheet.pdf/.

Essential Strategy #1 to Support Anchor Performance 10: Structured and Unstructured Daily Writing Opportunities

We cannot take this challenge lightly. Writing develops only when students have nonthreatening opportunities for sustained, ongoing, nongraded practice, so writing every day for a variety of purposes and in a variety of genres should become an integral part of every classroom. Some writing experiences should be naturally flowing, whereas other writing tasks should be structured to help students master craft elements (text structure or character development), writing skills and mechanics (spelling or punctuation), and process strategies (planning, drafting, and revising tactics).

Quick Write and Quick Draw. Frey, Fisher, and Everlove (2009) proposed using quick writes not only for inviting students to jot down some key ideas they have but also to practice writing quick responses to literature or content learning. Quick writes serve as a starting point as well for student-to-student dialogues, pair work, or small-group interactions during which students engage in a discussion with one another more successfully since they have previously collected their thoughts and are more prepared to share their ideas. Alternatively, they sketch a diagram or draw a graphic representation of their thoughts.

Use the following quick write prompts and invite students to offer their ideas:

- Today we investigated/examined/discovered_____.
- I find investigating/examining/discovering _____ challenging/interesting/intriguing _____ because _____ _____.

Alternatively, make up prompts that are specifically aligned to the lesson you are teaching:

- What do you think the protagonist will do next in the story?
- What does [key concept from lesson/text] mean? What evidence leads you to think so?
- Why should we care about [key concept from lesson/text]?

Journaling. Experiment with a variety of journal writing tasks to engage students in a range of brief forms of response to a topic or text. *Dialogue journaling* allows two students or the teacher and a student to exchange ideas in writing in the same journal, passing the journal back and forth periodically and in essence creating a personal written "dialogue" between them. *Response journals* invite students to share the most important word/

idea/sentence/or piece of information they encountered in a text and offer their opinions/feelings/personal reactions/connections they made. *Word journals* encourage students to collect, organize, illustrate, and regularly review newly acquired vocabulary. *Learning logs* help students develop ways to reflect on and organize what they have learned. The sample student response journal presented in Figure 5.23 was completed in conjunction with studying *To Kill a Mockingbird* (Lee, 1960).

Figure 5.23 Sample Page from a Ninth-Grade Student's Literature Response Journal

Quotations	Responses—Making Connections to Prior Knowledge
"The other boys attended the industrial school and received the best secondary education . . ." (p. 10)	I noticed that this feature has appeared in many other cultures, such as Greece, where only boys and men were educated.
"I suppose he loved honor more than his head . . . " (p. 13)	I have heard of nations and people who value honor and courage above all else, even their own personal safety. One example is the militaristic nation of Sparta.

Essential Strategy #2 to Support Anchor Performance 10: Writing Process

Follow the steps of the writing process with special attention to the initial stages: Most ELLs and struggling learners will need a considerable amount of time and support given to the prewriting and drafting stages. One possible framework for teaching and assessing writing is the 6+1 Trait® Writing model, which is made up of 6+1 key qualities that define strong writing (see Box 5.9 for basic definitions adapted from http://educationnorthwest.org/traits). Features of the 6+1 Trait® Writing aligned to the appropriate stages of the writing process will be helpful in keeping the process focused on essential skills (see Table 5.5).

Box 5.9 Features of the 6+1 Trait® Writing model

- **Ideas**: What is the main message?
- **Organization:** How is the writing internally structured?
- **Voice:** What is the author's personal tone like?
- **Word Choice:** How does the writer choose the vocabulary to convey the intended meaning?
- **Sentence Fluency:** How does the language flow on the page?
- **Conventions:** Are the writing mechanics observed?
- **Presentation:** How does the writing look on the page?

Table 5.5 Stages of the Writing Process Aligned to the *6+1 Trait* Writing

Step	Main Focus	6+1 Traits®
Prewriting	Build background, gather information, establish purpose, audience, and form	Ideas, Voice
Drafting	Generate first version of the written piece Organize ideas, make choices about word selections and sentence structures	Ideas, Organization, Word Choice, Voice
Sharing and Responding	Receive feedback on draft	Ideas, Organization, Word Choice
Revising	Revise for content and clarity of expression	Voice, Ideas, Organization, Word Choice, Sentence Fluency
Editing	Make corrections to language usage, grammar, conventions	Conventions
Publishing	Finalize the piece Prepare it for sharing in print	Voice, Presentation

Essential Strategy #3 to Support Anchor Performance 10: Daily Writing

Students need to write regularly in every subject matter, including the technical subjects such as art or music. To make the writing assignments even more personally relevant, current, and meaningful, Gallagher (2011) suggested that teachers keep a chart similar to the one in Figure 5.24 handy and in collaboration with students, fill it with ideas based on recent events, shared readings, or individual contributions by students as ready topics for students to write about.

Figure 5.24 Idea Chart

School Issues	Community Issues	State Issues	U.S. Issues	Global Issues

ANTICIPATED OUTCOMES

When linguistically and academically diverse secondary students are given a writing task, they may struggle with the rigorous expectations. They need to be given ample opportunities to develop and enhance their craft of writing; they are most likely to improve their writing skills if carefully structured, scaffolded writing instruction is embedded in other rich literacy experiences such as reading and discussing both literary and nonfiction texts that are engaging and meaningful. Though not limited to only these outcomes, the strategies presented previously are designed to accomplish the following:

1. Reinforce for students that writing is a form of learning

2. Help students explore and internalize the stages of the writing process

3. Motivate and engage students in a variety of writing tasks

4. Improve students' overall language skills in the other language domains of reading, speaking, and listening as well

Generally speaking, when students' learning needs are accommodated, they reap benefits that are rarely quantified. Writing lessons made accessible to diverse learners through scaffolding and other supports create actively engaged learners who can accomplish academic tasks they were unable to complete previously. From these positive learning experiences, diverse learners gain self-confidence, self-esteem, and a sense that they are able to succeed academically.

INSTRUCTIONAL CHALLENGES

It is widely recognized that writing is the most challenging to teach of the four language skills (listening, speaking, reading, and writing). Akhavan (2009) insightfully noted:

Writing is a gatekeeping skill. Those students who write well do well in the upper-elementary grades, in high school, and beyond. Those who are never given the opportunity to learn to write never get the chance to think, connect, and excel in classes that demand of them the ability to show what they know. (p. xii)

For diverse learners, on-demand writing in standard English (which for some is their second or third language or dialect) in a range of academic genres is just one of the major challenges. Additionally, some students are less than motivated to tackle them. Teachers we know who have successfully overcome these challenges shared one common characteristic with us also recognized by Mazur and Doran (2010). They refused to fall into a "deficit" model of thinking and turned what others might have perceived as limitations of students' linguistic, cultural, physical, cognitive, and other diversities into opportunities: opportunities to express themselves in the language or dialect they know best but also learn to write in academic English; opportunities to write about meaningful, engaging topics; opportunities to learn cooperatively in a safe, supportive environment; and opportunities to be guided and mentored personally and through the great writings of others.

PROMISING CLASSROOM PRACTICES

Turning Reluctant Writers to Zine Authors in Wantagh, New York

Elizabeth Oldendorp, a Wantagh, New York English-as-a-second-language (ESL) teacher, used to struggle to engage her middle school and high school students in writing until she introduced a writing project that transformed them from reluctant writers into enthusiastic learners and authors. Her solution was having students work on their own Zines, which are multigenre magazines focused on a single topic (Oldendorp, 2011). Customarily, a Zine includes a title page, a table of contents, a Dear Reader letter, poetry, a fiction story, a nonfiction piece, and an About the Author biography.

Building on their personal interests, out-of-school knowledge base, and cultural heritage, students became engaged empowered and successful writers. Elizabeth has implemented the Zine project as an "anchor activity"—which allows for differentiated instruction after all the required classwork was finished in her multiage, multilevel ESL class and which kept students engaged as they researched their self-selected subject matters. In the past, Elizabeth's students developed Zines about the Taj Mahal, gardening, the saber-toothed tiger, Egypt, playing cricket, and Sri Lankan culture in clothing. In Elizabeth's own words:

> The Zine Project helped my students develop language proficiency by requiring them to write in several different genres on a single topic. It walked them through the stages of process writing: planning, drafting, revising, editing, and publishing. It gave them

access to computer technology that was not available to them in their homes. Finally, and perhaps most important, the Zine Project provided the personal connections necessary to make learning English more meaningful. Thanks to the Zine Project, my English language learners are now enthusiastic writers and communicators! (Oldendorp, 2011, para. 12)

Question–Answer Relationships in California

Jim Burke (2010)—a San Francisco, California, high school English teacher and noted author (see www.englishcompanion.com)—guides his students to make observations while reading a literary selection. He requires a series of short, text-based answers that may address, for example, the exposition, the rising action, key characters, inferences, and the mood expressed in the selection. For each assigned chapter in a novel or other type of reading, he also has his students develop two test questions:

a. Right There (Literal) Question: This is a factual question that you can answer by pointing "right there" on the page to find the answer.

b. Between the Lines (Inferential) Question: This question is more complex. The answer cannot be pointed to on the page but must be inferred from other details in the story. (Burke, 2010, p. 165)

Students not only generate test-like questions, they are also expected to answer their own test questions and explain their significance. Thus, they ensure that they have put some thought into their questions and answers and can argue their importance.

Cornell Notes Adapted for an Inclusive Classroom in Lacona, New York

Coteaching allows for teacher collaboration for the sake of diverse learners. To meet the needs of their students (including some with learning disabilities, hearing impairment, and autism spectrum disorder) and the rigor of the Common Core, Ms. Kim Manfredi and Ms. Jonna St. Croix use a variety of strategies—one of which is known as Cornell Notes—with their ninth-grade, cotaught, inclusive, global history and geography class in the Sandy Creek Central School District. They have adapted this strategy for taking notes during a close reading of an assigned text (see Figure 5.25). Students are required to read the text, record notes that include the main ideas and key details, review those notes to formulate essential questions, and finally write a summary. The teachers use this strategy within each unit taught but often vary the method. For example, they use Cornell

Figure 5.25 Adapted Cornell Notes Template

Questions	Notes
Summary	

Notes for whole-group cooperative instruction, small-group collaboration, and independent learning as well.

At the start of the year, the coteachers model note taking for their students, providing them with a common scaffold for using this strategy by composing class-generated notes on the SMART Board in an organized manner. As the school year progresses, students become familiar with the format of Cornell Notes and no longer require modeling.

When using Cornell Notes for whole-group instruction, the teachers have the students all read the same text selection. In the cotaught setting, they determine and chunk the reading selection, and the students take turns reading aloud. After each section, the teachers ask scaffolded questions to guide their students in determining the main ideas and key details that they record as notes.

Once notes are complete, students reread the notes they have taken, and the teachers ask guiding questions to help students generate essential questions. Essential questions serve multiple functions such as processing course content, connecting and synthesizing key ideas and concepts, and serving as a study tool for students to review course material at a later date. Next, students summarize their notes or, in other words, answer their essential questions.

Students are required to complete state-assessment-quality writing when answering essential questions. Students are encouraged to construct summaries that consist of one to three declarative sentences with the ultimate goal being that students will compose a strong thesis statement. Students will frequently share their summaries with the class by writing them on the SMART Board. Through class discussion, students collaborate to edit peers' summaries using SMART Board technology, editing for both content and grammar. All students then review and edit their own summaries. The teachers assist individual students as they edit their written work. Small-group collaboration requires that students apply the same process. Teachers group students heterogeneously prior to class and facilitate group progress as needed.

When the Cornell Note-Taking System is assigned to foster independent learning, teachers differentiate text selections based on students' abilities. For example, teachers may assign a sixth-grade textbook excerpt to some, a standard ninth-grade text selection to many, and an academic journal article to a few. As is evident, such a strategy may be used to analyze a wide variety of texts. In a coplanned and cotaught class, this adaptation of the Cornell Notes strategy successfully addresses various aspects of the CCSS, including those for reading and writing as well as speaking and listening.

COMMON CORE WRITING STANDARDS— (UN)COMMON REFLECTION QUESTIONS

1. Which of the ten anchor standards will present the greatest challenge to your students, and how will you overcome the difficulties you may face?

2. How will you differentiate writing instruction in multilevel classes while keeping in mind the common goals the anchor standards present?

3. How will you validate students' home language skills (be it another language or nonstandard dialect) and bridge those skills to enhance their academic writing skills in English?

4. What authentic opportunities for writing do students have in the secondary content areas?

5. How will you ensure that writing becomes a regular part of your lesson so students can write routinely in a variety of genres?

KEY RESOURCES

Professional Books

Anderson, J. (2011). *10 things every writer needs to know.* Portland, ME: Stenhouse.

Gallagher, K. (2011). *Write like this: Teaching real-world writing through modeling & mentor texts.* Portland, ME: Stenhouse.

Walling, D. R. (2009). *Writing for understanding: Strategies to increase content learning.* Thousand Oaks, CA: Corwin.

Online Resources

CCCC Statement on Second Language Writing and Writers
http://www.ncte.org/cccc/resources/positions/secondlangwriting

Education Northwest (Home of 6+1 Trait® Writing)
http://educationnorthwest.org

Genre Studies Planning Guide
http://www.noycefdn.org/documents/ecrw/curriculum/GenreStudy
PlanningGuide.pdf

Graphic Organizers
www.thinkingmaps.com

Jeff Anderson's Site
http://www.writeguy.net

Kelly Gallagher's Site
http://kellygallagher.org

Mentor Sentences
http://www.greatsentences.blogspot.com

National Gallery of Writing
http://galleryofwriting.org

National Writing Project
http://www.nwp.org

NCTE Beliefs About the Teaching of Writing
http://www.ncte.org/positions/statements/writingbeliefs

Scholastic Art and Writing Awards
http://www.artandwriting.org/alliance

6 Speaking and Listening Strategies

Many ideas grow better when transplanted into another mind than the one where they sprang up.

—Oliver Wendell Holmes

OVERVIEW

The Common Core State Standards (CCSS) (2010a) offer the possibilities to provide equitable opportunities for all learners to enrich their receptive and expressive oral language skills, to expand their listening and speaking vocabulary, and to build new skills and strategies in literacy as well as knowledge in the content areas through interaction. Focusing on listening and speaking skills—especially finding the time to meaningfully engage students in tasks that improve these skills—can no longer remain merely an option. Instead, we must recognize that careful attention to oral literacy is needed. Listening to extended teacher-directed lectures or answering in single words or short phrases will not suffice.

Based on a careful examination of the grade-appropriate speaking and listening standards, we must conclude that meeting the new oral language goals at the secondary level will be closely tied to helping students develop critical-thinking skills, offering opportunities for reasoning, and creating an instructional framework for frequent, meaningful student collaboration and extended language use.

WHY SPEAKING AND LISTENING SKILLS IMPROVE THE OVERALL ACADEMIC PERFORMANCE OF DIVERSE ADOLESCENT LEARNERS

Among many others, Allyn (2013) has established a strong relationship between oral communication skills and academic performance. She made a powerful connection between and among opportunities for speaking and listening skills development on the one hand and college and career readiness on the other. She claimed that

> the more we allow our students to practice making their arguments orally, articulating their thoughts on a particular topic, and voicing their opinions, the more adept and comfortable they will become with doing this on a daily basis. Likewise, the more we allow our students to use their deep listening skills, especially with their fellow classmates, the easier it will become for them to use that skill as they move through college and the workplace. (p. 14)

The literature also supports the connection between listening/speaking and literacy as well as academic proficiency. Applebee, Langer, Nystrand, and Gamoran (2003) carefully reviewed the literature on discussion-based learning and nonmainstream students—defined by them as low achievers, children of the poor, and second-language learners. They concluded that rather than learning in a traditional classroom environment, these diverse learners

> do much better when instruction builds on previous knowledge and current ideas and experiences, permits students to voice their understandings and refine them through substantive discussion with others, and explicitly provides the new knowledge and strategies that students need to participate successfully in the continuing discussion. (p. 689)

Specifically, Saunders and O'Brien (2006) confirmed that "there is no controversy about the fundamental importance of English oral language development as part of the larger enterprise of educating ELLs" (p. 14). August and Shanahan (2006) (National Literacy Panel) found that strong oral language skills enhance the development of literacy in second language learners. Additionally, Genesee and his colleagues (Genesee, Lindholm-Leary, Saunders, & Christian, 2006) reported that oral language proficiency in the native language and second language both contribute to literacy development.

CORE SPEAKING AND LISTENING STRATEGIES

There are only six Speaking and Listening Anchor Standards (*Common Core State Standards*, 2010a), which are organized into two subgroups (see Box 6.1). The first three standards emphasize listening comprehension and student collaboration, whereas the last three standards require students to refine their presentation and oral language skills to successfully deliver a formal speech or report. The use of multimedia—both for listening and speaking or presentation—is incorporated into these standards, indicating that 21st-century technology skills must be an integrated part of any class.

Box 6.1 College and Career Readiness Anchor Standards for Speaking and Listening

Comprehension and Collaboration

1. Prepare for and participate effectively in a range of conversations and collaborations with diverse partners, building on others' ideas and expressing their own clearly and persuasively.

2. Integrate and evaluate information presented in diverse media and formats, including visually, quantitatively, and orally.

3. Evaluate a speaker's point of view, reasoning, and use of evidence and rhetoric.

Presentation of Knowledge and Ideas

4. Present information, findings, and supporting evidence such that listeners can follow the line of reasoning and the organization, development, and style are appropriate to task, purpose, and audience.

5. Make strategic use of digital media and visual displays of data to express information and enhance understanding of presentations.

6. Adapt speech to a variety of contexts and communicative tasks, demonstrating command of formal English when indicated or appropriate.

From each of the six College and Career Readiness Anchor Standards for Speaking and Listening, we derived and aligned a series of related *Anchor Performances*—skill sets that all students need to develop—and suggest strategies to help diverse learners build these skills in order to meet the standards. Some strategies may be more appropriate than others depending on the grade levels or language proficiency levels of the students. To that end, we also include suggestions on how to adapt strategies to meet the needs of diverse individual learners.

Comprehension and Collaboration

The first three speaking and listening anchor standards emphasize the importance of students interacting with each other based on the content they are learning while using academic English. To become successful collaborators, they need frequent, meaningful opportunities to work in groups of all sizes to accomplish the following oral language development tasks: to exchange ideas, to consider input from teachers and peers, to express themselves clearly and coherently, to defend or adjust their own point of view, and many others as demanded by the curriculum.

Anchor Performance 1: Participate in a Range of Small and Large Group Discussions

At the middle school level, students are expected to "engage effectively in a range of collaborative discussions (one-on-one, in groups, and teacher led) with diverse partners on *[grade appropriate] topics, texts, and issues*, building on others' ideas and expressing their own clearly" (*Common Core State Standards*, 2010a, p. 49). Students in Grades 6 prepare for group discussions based on assigned materials; students in Grade 7 and up also include independently researched information in their contributions. Students in Grades 7–8 will take more initiative in discussions and demonstrate more advanced skills when it comes to responding to others and reflecting on their own contributions. All middle schoolers have to follow established rules for discussion, ask questions, and respond to multiple perspectives presented in a discussion.

In the high school grades, there is a marked emphasis on students' initiating and participating in a range of collaborative discussion in which they (a) build on their own research, (b) set rules for discussion and decision making with classmates, and (c) "clarify, verify, or challenge ideas and conclusions" (p. 50). By Grades 11–12, the expectations also indicate that students will accept divergent and creative perspectives and are fully prepared not only to respond thoroughly to diverse viewpoints but also to synthesize contrasting ideas and determine how to deepen their discussion and understanding of the topic.

Essential Strategy to Support Anchor Performance 1: Support Student Participation Through Collaborative Practices

Using flexible grouping with linguistically and academically diverse learners ensures that they learn to work with varied groups of peers rather than seeing themselves and others as belonging to set groups based on ability. Thus, all students should be given the opportunity to accomplish tasks in large, medium, and small—both heterogeneously and homogenously designed—groups, depending on the goals and objectives of the lesson. They must engage in dialogue both with their friends and others with whom they do not have any social contact outside school. As Parker (2006) noted, the classroom is the place for the much needed "social occasions that provide opportunities for discussants to think, speak, listen, and learn together, with and across their differences, about a specified topic" (p. 11).

If you simply assign students to complete pair work or small-group work without any guidance or support, some conversations will take off, whereas others may falter or become less than fruitful. We are not suggesting that assigning specific roles is always necessary for productive conversations to take place, although defined responsibilities in group work can help scaffold the process in some cases. Rather, we are presenting a few effective structures below for oral language development that authentically engage all those involved.

Turn-and-Talk. Prior to inviting students to offer a response to a reading or a question in front of a larger group, have them turn to a partner and briefly share some ideas. Other versions of this strategy involve more personal planning, preparation, and rehearsal time as in *Think-Pair-Share* (Lyman, 1981) or jotting down some ideas as in *Think-Jot-Pair-Share*. Dutro and Kinsella (2010) suggested enhancing partner interaction with *Think-Write-Pair-Share*, which begins by having "students independently compose a response to a question or task using a response frame or scaffold that guides them in successful use of target vocabulary, sentence structure, grammar and register" (p. 196). Soto (2012) claimed that one of the most basic yet powerful techniques for enhancing academic oral language development is *Think-Pair-Share*. Students are invited to individually read a selection or reflect on a question posed by the teacher, then pair up, and share their ideas. Even at lower levels of language proficiency, students can participate when sentence starters or oral language development stems are offered.

To present additional opportunities for students to evaluate another speaker's ideas, pairs double up and form groups of four with *Think-Pair-Share-Square*. In this setup, students first complete the Think-Pair-Share portion of the task and then summarize their own discussion with another pair as well as compare both of their conclusions. One more type of pair work activity is called *Pair-Plus-One* in which a third person observes the two conversing students in order to offer feedback on how effective their interaction is (Zwiers & Crawford, 2011).

Request: Reading With Questions. Grant and Fisher (2010) described a range of reading, writing, and oral literacy tasks to help all students develop these skills for content-area study, also known as disciplinary literacy. One of their suggested activities is called *Request: Reading With Questions*, in which students work in pairs with a target text and act both as questioners and respondents. Box 6.2 outlines the steps each student will have to take as he or she participates in such a structured, text-dependent discussion. To be best aligned to the Common Core expectations, middle schoolers may follow the recommended steps below, whereas in high school, students should be expected to engage in a similar exchange based not only on teacher-assigned readings but also on independent research.

Box 6.2 Request: Reading With Questions

Questioner

1. Read a chunk of text silently and think of two or three questions to ask your partner.

2. With the text in front of you, ask your partner to answer each of your questions.

3. If your partner needs a hint, you may provide one.

4. If your partner needs more help, you may show him or her where the answer may be found in the text.

Respondent

1. Read a chunk of text silently and think of two or three questions that your partner might ask you.

2. Cover the text and try to answer each of your partner's questions.

3. If you need a hint you may ask your partner for one.

4. If you need more help, you may ask your partner to show you where the answer may be found in the text.

Source: Adapted from Grant, M. C., & Fisher, D. (2010). *Reading and writing in science: Tools to develop disciplinary literacy.* Thousand Oaks, CA: Corwin.

To differentiate this strategy, consider the difficulty of the text to be read as well as the reading abilities of the students. Try adapting the content or selecting texts that are at students' independent reading levels so the information will be more accessible. Alternatives to silent reading with texts that are above students' independent reading abilities include students listening to an audio rendition of the text while they follow along with the printed version or the teacher's conducting a shared reading for students who need support before they proceed with the protocol for questioning their partners.

Inquiry Circles. Similar to literature circles, students can also engage in meaningful, deep conversations focused on content-area topics within the framework of inquiry circles. Harvey and Daniels (2009) suggested a sequence of three guiding questions to help students discuss content-based readings. They named the three types of questions as (a) definition, (b) consequence, and (c) action questions. See generic and content-specific examples in Table 6.1. Students can be invited to generate the discipline or topic-specific questions based on the generic guiding questions so they develop an even more enhanced ownership of the discussion.

To scaffold this activity, consider giving students model questions that can be used to generate topic-specific questions or sentence frames that require students to fill in the blank spaces of partially completed questions.

Table 6.1 Guided Questioning for Inquiry Circles

Question Type	Generic Guiding Questions	Examples From a Lesson on Biotechnology or Genetically Modified Foods
Definition Questions	What is it? What is taking place?	*What is bioengineering? What is happening to the genetic makeup of foods that are genetically modified?*
Consequence Questions	Why does it matter? Why is it important?	*Why should we learn about genetically modified foods? Why does it matter if the food we consume is bioengineered?*
Action Questions	What can be done? What actions should be taken?	*What choices do we have as individuals? What actions can we take individually and as a community?*

Coaching, Listening, and Speaking. In her seminal work, "The Silenced Dialogue," Delpit (1988) concluded that teachers who are successful with children of color and those who come from low-income families understand the need for two seemingly different approaches: "the need to help students to establish their own voices, but to coach those voices to produce notes that will be heard clearly in the larger society" (p. 296). Roberts and Billings (2011) proposed that teachers support their students' listening and speaking skill development through one-on-one or small-group coaching sessions, during which students role-play various scenarios in which they can demonstrate active listening skills and engaged participation. For example, they can role-play interactions with classmates, teachers, community members, college admission counselors, and so on. In preparation for whole-class, student-led seminars, Roberts and Billings suggested specific skill building during the coaching sessions as summarized in the Table 6.2.

Table 6.2 Target Skills for Coaching

Sample Active Listening Skills	Sample Speaking Skills
• Look at the person speaking. • Paraphrase what you hear. • Respond to what someone else says before changing the subject. • Wait your turn to talk. • Give way. (Be quiet if you begin talking at the same time someone else does.) • Help make sure no one dominates the discussion in your group.	• Speak loudly enough so that everyone can hear. • Speak voluntarily three times. • Make clear and accurate statements. • Use appropriate grammar. • Use relevant vocabulary. • Use a collaborative tone and gestures. • Ask questions. • Ask for clarification or elaboration. • Disagree respectfully or in a neutral tone.

Source: Adapted from Roberts, A., & Billings, L. (2011). *Using seminars to teach the common core's speaking and listening standards* (p. 2). Larchmont, NY: Eye On Education.

Send a Question/Send a Problem (Kagan & Kagan, 2009). This activity encourages students to have an authentic discussion about open-ended, personally relevant questions or problems. We recommend the following steps:

1. Have students generate an authentic question or problem related to a target topic of instruction. Ethical questions, students' views about scientific discoveries, current events, character development issues, or problems students face themselves as teenagers or as members of their own school or broader community will all work well in the secondary classroom.

2. Using a manila folder, students staple the problem to the outside of the folder. Assign an ambassador in each group, whose role is to hand deliver the problem/question to the next group. The ambassador is also responsible for (a) keeping the group on task, (b) clarifying the question if needed, and (c) taking notes based on the answers received on a sheet inserted in the folder.

3. Within a specified time, each group responds to their visiting ambassador's question/problem with as many viable answers as possible.

4. When time is called, the ambassador thanks the group and delivers the folder to the next group. The second group also generates as many possible answers to the question within the time limit, and the ambassador takes notes on a new sheet without comparing the answers to the previous set of responses.

5. At this point, the folder is returned to the original group. The ambassador reports the findings and leads a discussion in which the group evaluates and ranks all responses. A secretary—appointed by the ambassador—writes a summary statement based on the group discussion. A possible frame for such a summary can be offered:

In response to our question _____, we have received many possible answers. We appreciated your suggestions. Of all the responses, we found that the following were the most helpful: _____

_____, _____,

_____.

6. The secretary appoints a speaker, whose job is to report to the class based on the group's summary statement and conclude whether the question has been fully answered or not.

7. As a final step, the teacher as facilitator may synthesize the responses and offer his or her own input. It is also suggested that the folders are collected and reviewed by the teacher before the groups reconvene to summarize the findings in case there is a need for checking whether all the information gathered is factual or appropriate.

In one version of this activity, students are asked to generate test-like questions based on a recently completed unit of study. Each group prepares one carefully written question that requires constructed responses (shorter, one- to two-paragraph long answers), written in the same academic style in which test questions are typically presented. Students thus review the unit in a highly interactive, student-directed fashion, and by doing so prepare to be more college and career ready.

In sum, one of the most profound changes the CCSS may ultimately bring is shifting teachers' practices from teacher-directed instruction to inquiry-based, interactive learning that requires more advanced research and critical-thinking skills, independent and group accountability, and frequent, thoughtful participation from all students (Bellanca, Fogarty, & Pete, 2012). Additionally, Wolsey and Lapp (2009) suggested that classroom discussions could extend beyond the school walls using web cameras, Internet technology such as chat software, or asynchronous tools, such as blogs and discussion boards. Students can interact with others from around the United States or even from other countries.

Anchor Performance 2: Listen to, Discuss, and Evaluate Information Presented in Diverse Formats

As with the previous standard, the expectations for middle school compared with high school students are somewhat different, indicating the cognitive skills involved in the communicative tasks at hand. Students in Grade 6 interpret and explain information, whereas students in Grade 7 analyze the main ideas and supporting details and offer an explanation on "how the ideas clarify a topic, text, or issue under study" (*Common Core State Standards*, 2010a, p. 49). In Grade 8, students conduct further analysis into the purpose of the information and evaluate the motives that drive the presentation. In high school, the focus is on students' ability to integrate information derived from multiple sources: Students in Grades 9–10 evaluate the credibility and accuracy of the sources, whereas students in Grades 11–12 also make informed decisions and solve problems based on the resources they analyzed.

What is common in all the grades is that this standard emphasizes students' skills to interact with and comprehend information presented through multiple sources, including multimedia channels. Thus, this standard should be considered a critical example of, and opportunity for, visual literacy and technology integration and for building research skills as well.

Essential Strategy to Support Anchor Performance 2: Structured, Accountable Academic Talk

Schmoker (2009) suggested, "Give students an interesting text and the chance to argue about the characters and issues within it, and they will do the rest" (p. 525), an idea that might work for many students but definitely not all. With diverse learners in particular, there is certainly a need to devise some ways to keep students' discussions on track and make them accountable for their contributions. Moreover, the research and professional literature support the idea of establishing organized conversational frameworks such as structured academic discourse (Kinsella, 2012), instructional conversations (IC) (Goldenberg, 1992), curricular conversations (Applebee, Burroughs, & Stevens, 2000), accountable talk (Michaels, O'Connor, Hall, & Resnick, 2010), and intentional interaction (Sanchez & Harper, 2012), all of which are more likely to promote student engagement. When defining accountable talk, Michaels et al. (2010) aptly stated that "not all talk sustains learning. For classroom talk to promote learning it must be accountable: to the learning community, to accurate and appropriate knowledge, and to rigorous thinking" (p. 1). We therefore offer the following strategies to support the idea of structured, accountable, and academic student discourse.

Authentic Teacher-Led Dialogues. For students to be actively engaged in classroom discourse, teachers must move away from asking only the type of questions that merely test what the students already know or are supposed to know. Jacobs (2006) cautioned that "such questions encourage students to take on the role of completing the classroom script rather than voicing authentic opinions" (p. 84). Instead, the goal of authentic teacher-led discussions—ones that also align to the Common Core expectations—is to support students' open expression of different ideas and beliefs. To sustain this goal, regularly include in your discussions with students question/prompt stems that request students' varied opinions and promote higher-order thinking. Try the following:

- Why do you think so?
- What difference does it make in your life/future if _____?
- What impact does _____ have on you/your community/ your future?
- Can you give an example of _____ to justify what you just stated?
- I would like to add to what you/_____ said _____.
- How would you persuade someone who _____?
- Is that (what you are saying) true for all cases?

An active listening and questioning technique to try when engaging students in authentic teacher-led discussions is using *question uptake,* which means that the teacher's (or fellow classmate's) question takes up and builds on a previous comment, thus creating an authentic continuity in the class discussion. The ultimate goal of modeling authentic teacher-led discussions is that students learn to engage each other in similar conversations aligned to target curricular goals. As a Common Core-driven expectation, we can train our students to respond to a previous comment before sharing their opinion or offering their input.

Scaffolded Language Frames. Among many others, Ross, Fisher, and Frey (2009) suggested the use of language frames to scaffold accountable talk in the science classroom. For example, for providing evidence, they offer the frames for students to use either on card stock, as posters, or even as table tents (see Box 6.3):

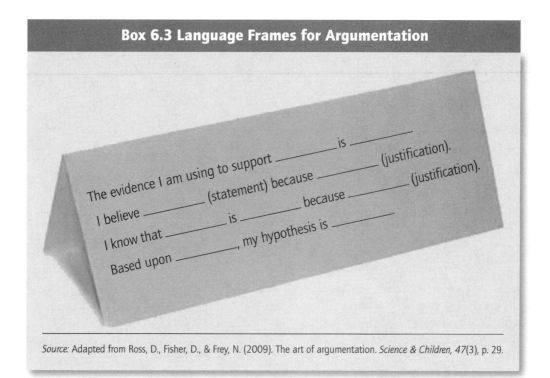

Box 6.3 Language Frames for Argumentation

The evidence I am using to support _____ is _____.

I believe _____ (statement) because _____ (justification).

I know that _____ is _____ because _____ (justification).

Based upon _____, my hypothesis is _____.

Source: Adapted from Ross, D., Fisher, D., & Frey, N. (2009). The art of argumentation. *Science & Children, 47*(3), p. 29.

In their work on oral language development, Dutro and Kinsella (2010) built on the scaffolding tradition commonly used with English learners and speakers of nonstandard English. They suggested a much more carefully structured response frame that supports all learners of academic English. We concur with them that sentence starters are critical for supporting accountable talk, but we cannot stop there. Offering varied sentence frames to accomplish the same task is aligned to principles of differentiated instruction, and the leveled frames can be used both simultaneously in the classroom to address different students' needs or developmentally to show progression of text complexity. Adding appropriate grammatical and lexical support will help students produce more complex responses to questions such as, "Why do people decide to go to college?" (see Box 6.4).

Box 6.4 Sample Differentiated Scaffolded Response Frames

Level 1:

People go to college for better _____.
(Nouns: jobs, lives)

Level 2:

Many people decide to go to college because they want _____.
(Noun phrases: a better life, a better-paying job)
Many students go to college for _____.
(Noun phrases: more opportunities)

Level 3:

Students decide to go to college because _____.
(Independent clauses: they want to pursue a career)
Some people got to college in order to _____.
(Verb phrases)

Source: Inspired by Dutro, S., & Kinsella, K. (2010). English language development: Issues and implementation at grades six through twelve (p. 199). In *Improving education for English learners: Research-based approaches* (pp. 151–207). Sacramento: California Department of Education.

Reader/Writer/Speaker Response Triads. In addition to pair work, students can be placed in groups of three to work cooperatively while taking turns having three different roles:

- One student (the reader) reads aloud the assigned selection (a portion of the text the entire group is going to tackle). The text could be adapted or annotated since students will need to decode the text independently and process the meaning in small groups, not with direct teacher support. The other two students each jot down at least one clarifying discussion question (which could be scaffolded as needed).
- The next student (the writer) writes responses to the questions about the text based on a small-group discussion. It is critical that the writer does not take sole responsibility for providing the answers;

instead, his or her role is to be the note taker or scribe who gathers information from the others in the triad and jots down the important details.

- Finally, the third student (the speaker) will use the notes recorded by the second student and report the answers to the whole class. This step helps students gain practice in public speaking for which they are well prepared through the previous two steps.

To ensure that each member of the triad takes turns, an effective way to set up this activity is to assign each student one of the three possible roles before the activity begins. The roles will be rotated so each student will read, write, and speak publically. So by the completion of the activity, all language skills are practiced within the context of the lesson (Vogt & Echevarria, 2007).

Self-Assessment Tool for Accountable Talk. When accountable talk is first introduced, teachers lead the discussion and model the academic language usually derived from the content-area topic of the lesson necessary for participation. With appropriate scaffolding, teachers gradually release the responsibility, and students take ownership of their participation, both as initiators and responders in the dialogue. In this way, teachers can encourage students to take responsibility for their own active participation in the classroom. The adapted self-assessment tool in Figure 6.1 invites students to examine subskills of their participation in accountable classroom talk, reflect on each subskill, identify barriers to participation, and set goals for future discussions.

Self-Assessment Tool for Accountable Talk can be used after any one of these activities: partner sharing, small-group discussions, or whole-class conversations.

Anchor Performance 3: Listen and Assess the Speaker

In the middle grades, students are expected to develop advanced listening and reasoning skills that will allow them to identify what arguments a speaker presents and to outline what claims are made. Students in Grade 6 determine whether a claim is sufficiently supported or not; students in Grade 7 evaluate the quality of the reasoning and the relevance and sufficiency of the evidence the speaker provides; finally in Grade 8, students are also expected to identify irrelevant evidence. In high school, the focus of this standard shifts to evaluating a speaker's point of view, reasoning, and use of evidence and rhetoric. Students in Grades 9–10 will identify false reasoning and exaggerated or distorted evidence, whereas

Figure 6.1 Effective Discussion Self-Assessment Rubric

Name:_____ Date:_____ Discussion Topic:_____

	Not at All	Somewhat	Extensively	Reflection Notes
I took a position, explained it clearly, and used evidence to support my ideas.				
I answered people's questions about my position.				
I respectfully explained or defended my position.				
I asked my classmates to clarify or justify their positions when appropriate.				
I listened actively and respectfully to my classmates' positions.				
I compared and contrasted their ideas with my own.				
I kept an open mind and was willing to modify my own position.				
Throughout the discussion, I summarized in my mind the things that others had said.				
I was actively involved in the conversation.				

Source: Adapted from Silver, H. F., Dewing, R. T., & Perini, M. J. (2012). *The core six essential strategies for achieving excellence with the common core* (p. 43). Alexandria, VA: ASCD.

students in Grades 11–12 also evaluate for the position the speaker takes, how his or her ideas are connected, and what types of rhetorical devices are used.

Essential Strategy to Support Anchor Performance 3: Scaffolded Listening and Note Taking

The anchor performance to support the third standard helps students focus their attention on what the speaker says and how the message is communicated. To introduce this type of careful listening for details, students can first respond to speeches or presentations within the framework of a checklist, then move on to taking more elaborate, structured notes with appropriate linguistic and grouping scaffolding.

Listen and Check. Have students listen to a short, two- to three-minute speech or media message for a brief analysis. Recorded presentations from television programs or video podcasts are ideal since the selection can be replayed multiple times. During the first listening/viewing, students should focus on overall understanding of what the intended message is, providing opportunities for open discussion about the topic and the meaning of the message in the presentation, as well as time for clarification of what was presented as needed. During the second listening/viewing, students pay attention to the *underlying meaning* and use the checklist in Figure 6.2 (see p. 208) to identify whether the speaker addressed the identified features of a speech. A third listening lends itself to taking notes on how each of the target speaker behaviors was demonstrated in the clip. We encourage our readers to modify or add to the prompts in the first column of this chart to match the grade-level goals for their students.

Structured Comparative News Analysis Template. Carefully select a news account presented on CNN and on one or more other news organizations for a comparative analysis. As students watch and listen to the same news event presented from various perspectives, they jot down notes in response to the prompts given in the structured note-taking template presented in Figure 6.3 (see p. 209).

To vary this listening/note-taking activity, students can watch advertisements for various products and analyze the evidence and the rhetorical devices used in each ad to persuade the potential buyer to purchase the item. For example, have students watch advertisements for various hand-held devices or electronic gadgets that teenagers would be interested to use or own. Ads for sports equipment, local theater performances, or movie trailers could also be used. If feasible, several guest speakers can be invited to the school or classroom to participate on a panel discussion about a complex topic, including career choices, language rights, and

Figure 6.2 Speaker Evaluation Checklist

	Yes or No	Notes
Speaker clearly states a main claim.		
Speaker supports the claim in a logical way.		
Speaker offers facts, rather than opinions.		
Speaker presents evidence that is relevant and focused.		
Speaker exaggerates.		
Speaker is credible.		
Speaker uses persuasive techniques.		
Speaker is aware of the audience's needs.		
Speaker has a personal style.		

Figure 6.3 Structured Comparative News Analysis Template

	CNN	Alternate News Organization 1	Alternate News Organization 2
Main claim reported			
Evidence offered			
Biased language or exaggeration			
Conclusion			
Length of news event			

response to adversity such as various disabilities. To further illustrate this activity, consider a topic that is frequently discussed in secondary schools such as bullying. Connected to bullying prevention, set up a panel discussion on experiences with bullying presented by a police officer, a parent of a teen, a nurse, a social worker, and any other easily accessible panelist who can offer a different perspective.

When students are ready, they can prepare brief presentations based on their research that the rest of the class can analyze using a structured note-taking framework. Additionally, radio news reports or historical speeches can be used to challenge students to listen to various perspectives.

Political Speech Analysis Chart. Figure 6.4 offers an adapted framework (Giouroukakis & Connolly, 2012) for comparing Martin Luther King Jr.'s speech "I Have a Dream" (King, 1963/1992) and a speech of your choice (or excerpts from it). Selection of an appropriate target speech can be based on the curriculum you teach or on current events such as the latest State of the Union address by the president of the United States. One possible comparison we suggest is former President Bill Clinton's speech titled

Figure 6.4 Political Speech Analysis Chart

	"I Have a Dream" (line # and pg. #)	Teacher-Selected Speech (line # and pg. #)
Introduction How does the speaker introduce the speech?		
Organization What are the main sections of the speech?		
Narration What are some essential facts presented?		
Conclusion How does the speaker end the speech?		
Imagery What are some vivid words or phrases that convey mental imagery?		
Repetition What are some words or phrases that are repeated for emphasis?		
Alliteration What are some sounds that are repeated?		
Metaphor What are some comparisons that are used to convey meaning visually?		
Rhetorical Questions What are some questions that are asked for effect and for which there are no answers?		
Delivery What are some gestures and facial expressions?		
Tone What is the tone of the speech?		

Source: Adapted from Giouroukakis, V., & Connolly, M. (2012). *Getting to the core of English language arts, grades 6–12: How to meet the common core state standards with lessons from the classroom* (pp. 187–188). Thousand Oaks, CA: Corwin.

"Remarks to the Convocation of the Church of God in Christ" (www
.presidency.ucsb.edu/ws/?pid=46115) delivered on November 13, 1993, in
which he frequently refers to Martin Luther King as well as talks about
gun control, which remains to be an urgent current topic.

Students analyze the two speeches in terms of structure, rhetorical
devices, and delivery. Their task is to find examples of target features from
each speech and include the line numbers and the page numbers where
the sources are located.

As a summary activity, Giouroukakis and Connolly (2012) suggested
exploring the following questions:

- What can we conclude about the two speeches?
- How do they compare and contrast?
- What effect does each one have on the audience?
- What makes an effective speech?

Listening and note taking with the purpose of evaluating the speakers'
point of view or the evidence the speaker offered can be introduced and
practiced on television news reports or podcasts and then further refined
during in-class oral presentations by students. As students watch a news
report (such as a "human interest" story), half the class completes the first
column by focusing on and capturing actual quotes from the subject of the
news report. The other half of the class takes notes on the person's actions
as portrayed in the video clip (see Figure 6.5 for the structured, collaborative note-taking template). Once students watch the video two or more
times, they work in small groups with others who took notes in the same
column of the template to make their own notes more complete. Just as
with close reading, this *close viewing activity* allows for a more in-depth
analysis (T. D. Wolsey, personal communication, March 1, 2013). As a final
step, students are paired up to complete an information gap activity, during which they take turns sharing their own notes orally and adding notes
from their partners.

Figure 6.5   Collabrative Note-Taking Template With Complementary Prompts

What are the main points stated?	What documented evidence is offered?

Presentation of Knowledge and Ideas

The next three speaking/listening standards focus on presentation skills, with students being expected to draw on formal, academic English to hone their information organization and reasoning skills and to make use of technology tools. To be able to accomplish all this, students need to develop specific subskills (such as organizing a presentation, using technology tools and devices to support presentations, etc.) and must have ample opportunities to practice public speaking and communicating more formally for a variety of audiences and multiple purposes across the disciplines.

Anchor Performance 4: Give an Oral Presentation

Students in the secondary grades must be able to prepare and deliver a presentation that is logically organized and contains pertinent information while demonstrating that their public speaking skills are developing. Students in Grade 6 must be able to focus on sequencing ideas logically and use pertinent details. Students in Grade 7 will emphasize critical points, and students in Grade 8 employ sound valid reasoning and well-chosen details. All middle schoolers are expected to use appropriate eye contact, adequate volume, and clear pronunciation.

In high school, students in Grades 9–10 will refine their presentation skills by learning to be clear and concise while also responding to whether the style is appropriate to purpose, audience, and task. In Grades 11–12, students must be able to communicate a clear perspective and use communication styles appropriate for a range of formal and informal tasks.

Essential Strategy #1 to Support Anchor Performance 4: Scaffolding Oral Language Expression

The most critical support teachers can offer diverse learners to be successful with this standard is to scaffold their oral language production. Since scaffolding any task begins with strong teacher modeling, it is no different for oral language development. For this reason, model how to use extended academic language and rich vocabulary even when students do not understand every word or phrase. In other words, do not oversimplify your own language; instead, take advantage of the opportunity every interaction with your students provides to introduce and reinforce more complex sentence structures and more sophisticated word choices for your students to produce on their own (Kinsella, 2012). Brentwood High School English-as-a-second-language (ESL) teacher Lucille Purpura-Otto makes sure she uses complex language even when she takes a student into the hallway for a brief one-on-one conversation to address some discipline issues: "Unless you comply with my request, I will consider you as being insubordinate" (personal communication, March 12, 2013). Other examples of shifting teacher talk to show more academic register are in Table 6.3.

Table 6.3 Shifting Teacher Talk

Less Academic Word and Sentence Choice	More Academic Word and Sentence Choice
You guys	Mr. Mulligan's scientists (scholars/writers/mathematicians)
I'm gonna tell you what you have to do	These are my expectations for you . . .
Look at the _____	Examine the _____
What do you think?	What is your conclusion based on the information you have?
Let's come back together as a whole group.	Let's reconvene.
Read the next part and back up what you said with something from the text.	Read the subsequent paragraph and substantiate your claim with text-based evidence.

Regardless of their linguistic and academic background, students' receptive language skills (or listening comprehension) will be more advanced than their productive skills (such as speaking in cómplete sentences using academic discourse). Modeling will not be enough, though; Dutro and Kinsella (2010) noted that scaffolding oral language production is a must. It may include the following practices:

- Use questions and prompts that invite students to extend what they have said.
  - o *Ask open-ended questions, ones that begin with "why" and "how" to encourage students to add more details.*
- Expand students' thoughts by adding new vocabulary or using more complex syntax while recognizing their contribution to the discussion.
- Clarify and interpret information when students may not be able to clearly describe an idea or event.
  - o *For example, if a student describes his first experience with a tornado saying, "It went around and round like this and was very loud," while*

gesturing with his hands, you can comment by adding, "Tornados form a funnel and often sound as if a train were coming. It must have been very frightening when you first encountered one."

- Request clarification and teach them how to ask for clarification when they do not understand someone else.
  - *"What do you mean? Could you explain that again, please? How did you get your answer?"—are some possible model sentences to use and explicitly teach.*

- Provide frequent constructive feedback on students' language output to encourage, interpret, and evaluate their responses or their participation in small-group or class discussions.
  - *Instead of simply praising a student with a generic "Good job!" or even "Nicely stated," try to be more specific with your feedback and say "When you said _____, I was able to paint a picture in my mind because you used such a vivid adjective." or "First I was not sure what you meant by _____, but when you gave an example from your own life, I realized you were talking about _____."*

- Teach the process of developing and delivering a speech. In his recent publication titled *Well Spoken*, Palmer (2012) likened teaching speaking skills to teaching the writing process. The three distinct aspects of teaching public speaking or presentation skills entail the following:

  1. *Building a speech:* While developing a speech, students need explicit instruction in attending to the target audience, fully developing the target content, paying careful attention to the logical organization of the speech, deciding on appropriate visual aids, and planning on their physical appearance while delivering the speech.

  2. *Performing a speech:* Students will need coaching to deliver a speech with the right type of poise, to have control over the quality of their voice and the speed with which they perform the speech, to maintain eye contact with their audience, and to use appropriate gestures.

  3. *Evaluating a speech:* Once students have performed a speech, they need feedback that guides them to improve their public speaking skills.

Essential Strategy #2 to Support Anchor Performance 4: Scaffolding Presentations

Larmer and Mergendoller (2012) suggested project-based learning to help students develop speaking and presentation skills. Rather than simply assigning a project to students, it is important to scaffold the steps that lead up to presenting the final project to an authentic audience. After discussing what a good presentation looks and sounds like, students can watch sample presentations online and critique them. They can collaboratively develop a rubric or checklist for effective presentations. Larmer and Mergendoller also suggested a planning guide (see Figure 6.6) and practice sessions to enhance students' public speaking skills.

Figure 6.6 Presentation Planning Guide

My presentation is about _____.

My audience is _____.

I want my audience to (know, feel, or do) _____

_____.

In the beginning of my presentation, I will _____.

In the middle of my presentation, I will _____.

I will end my presentation by _____.

To make my presentation interesting, I will _____.

Source: Adapted from http://www.bie.org/tools/freebies/presentation_plan/.

Anchor Performance 5: Create a Visual, Audio, or Multimedia Illustration That Supports an Oral Presentation

Secondary school students are expected to develop visual literacy demonstrated by grade-level end-of-year goals. Adding multimedia and visual components to oral presentations are required for varied purposes across the grades. Students in Grade 6 use multimedia and visuals to clarify information; students in Grade 7 also do so to emphasize important points, whereas students in Grade 8 must be mindful of using multimedia and visuals to strengthen their claims and evidence as well as enhance the audience's interest. In high school, students make more strategic use of digital media tools primarily to enhance their audience's understanding of the findings and to add interest.

Essential Strategy to Support Anchor Performance 5: Slideshow Presentations

The need for integrating technology into instruction is apparent throughout the CCSS. As students develop language and literacy skills, their access to and development of proficiency with digital tools must be ensured. Developing a PowerPoint (Microsoft), Keynote (Apple), or Prezi (Internet-based) presentation may prove to be both a challenge and a source of satisfaction for students as they learn to accompany their oral reports with robust slides that come alive with images, sounds, perhaps even animation, and just the right amount of text. Students can also use digital storytelling tools (see resources at the end of this chapter) that consist of a single canvas the user may pan and zoom in and out of while including video clips, images, and short text among other digital components. The overall goal here is for teachers to develop their personal knowledge of these presentation tools so that they may direct students to use them. Keep in mind that diverse learners sometimes have less access to and may be less savvy with technology. They may need preliminary lessons or a *technology buddy* to complete such assignments.

Multimedia Show and Tell. A childhood favorite—*Show and Tell*—can be used for more academic purposes to help students practice using visual or multimedia tools strategically as they present self-selected information. Giouroukakis and Connolly (2012) created a *Show and Tell Preparation Guide* (Box 6.5.) to invite students to showcase literary examples they found to compliment taught curriculum. We further adapted that idea and suggest that students also add a multimedia component to their *Show and Tell* to enhance their audience's understanding of the selection. In English language arts, students can choose quotes, poems, or songs; in social studies, science, and the technical subjects, the *Show and Tell* can be based on students' independent research, current events, news items, and other pertinent information that connects directly to the course content.

Box 6.5 Show and Tell Preparation Guide

Directions: Complete this entire organizer before presenting. This will serve as your outline when you are standing in front of the class.

Introduction

How did you find this work?

_____

_____

_____

Why did you choose this work? What do you like about it? What do you find interesting?

_____

_____

_____

Passages

List two significant passages for discussion:

Passage 1:

_____

_____

Why did you like it?

_____

_____

Passage 2:

_____

_____

Why did you like it?

_____

_____

Discussion Questions:

1. _____

2. _____

_____

Source: Adapted from Giouroukakis, V., & Connolly, M. (2012). *Getting to the core of English language arts, grades 6–12: How to meet the common core state standards with lessons from the classroom* (pp. 140–141). Thousand Oaks, CA: Corwin.

Anchor Performance 6: Use a Variety of Registers and Adapt Speech to the Level of Formality Required in Various Contexts

The end-of-year goals for secondary students reveal that they need to adapt their speech to a variety of contexts and tasks, demonstrating command of formal English when indicated or appropriate. For specific expectations for using formal English, the CCSS document refers readers to the grade-appropriate Language Standards 1 and 3. For students to understand the way language is used in various contexts and to adjust their speech to various levels of formality, we suggest the following introductory activity we learned from Debra Cole, instructional specialist working for the St. Louis Regional Professional Development Center. Debra likes to ask high schoolers (or their teachers) to describe a Slinky as if they were speaking as

1. a friend to a friend,

2. an adult to a young child who does not know what a Slinky is and has never seen or used one,

3. a scientist explaining the physics behind the movement,

4. a historian who describes the origins of the Slinky,

5. an economist describing the cost of production and the expected or potential profits,

6. a poet who admires what a Slinky can do.

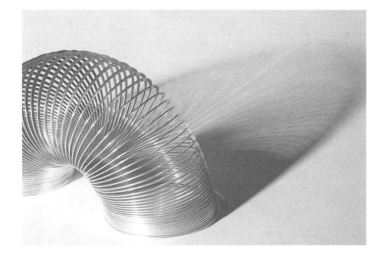

The activity reveals that the type and amount of technical vocabulary, word choice, sentence complexity, and level of formality when speaking in these various roles will vary dramatically. Other household or everyday objects or substances that can be discussed from multiple perspectives may include the following (see the perspectives included in parenthesis):

- *Water* (Living environment teacher, swim instructor, gardener, environmentalist, meteorologist)
- *Fire* (Boy or Girl Scout leader, firefighter, chef, mother to child, news reporter)
- *Book* (Librarian, book store owner, Amazon CEO, teacher, the inventor of Kindle, writer, publisher, child)

Essential Strategy to Support Anchor Performance 6: Kinesthetic Discussion-Based Activities

Many teachers have shared with us that when their students partake in a discussion or other interactive learning tasks while they are also encouraged or expected to move around the room—rather than merely sitting at their desks—the level of participation, engagement, and even productive noise, increase. This seems to be particularly the case with many diverse learners who perform instructional tasks more readily when removed from traditional classroom seating arrangements and are engaged in up-on-your feet activities. For younger learners, Gardner (1999) identified kinesthetic activities as vital for learning and emphasized that "merely passive experiences tend to attenuate and have little lasting impact" (p. 82). We would add that secondary school learners also need active engagement; thus, the suggested strategies that follow are simple yet powerful examples of kinesthetic activities.

Four Corners (Kagan & Kagan, 2009). This activity begins with the teacher assigning each corner of the room a category related to the curriculum. Depending on the grade level and the specific learning objective, the four corners might be labeled as the four causes of the collapse of the Roman Empire, as four characters in a story (any grade), as four types of chemical elements, or as *Agree, Strongly Agree, Disagree,* or *Strongly Disagree.* In preparation for the discussion and the kinesthetic component of the activity, students are given a specific task to be completed independently. For example,

- Students receive short descriptions of one of four characters or some key lines the characters have or could have spoken in the literary selection. After careful consideration, each learner will move to the corner labeled with the name of the character to create a match with the description or the quote.
- Assigning values such as *Agree, Disagree, Strongly Agree, or Strongly Disagree* to each of the four corners lends itself well to forming an opinion about any topic presented in the secondary curriculum. Facing History and Ourselves (2013) suggested complex

ideas to be explored with students through engaging activities, such as the *Four Corners*. Here are some possible statements to consider:

o *The needs of larger society are more important than the needs of the individual.*
o *The purpose of schooling is to prepare youth to be good citizens.*
o *One should always resist unfair laws, regardless of the consequences.*
o *I am only responsible for myself.* (para. 3)

• First students individually consider each statement. Next, the teacher calls out each statement and students express their ideas by moving to the corner of the room aligned to their opinion. It is critical that students are prepared to ask each other questions and share their decisions through scaffolded sentences, sentence starters, or model responses. Once they are in their chosen corners, a small-group discussion takes place, where participants take turns asking each other to explain their choices, justify their positions, and share evidence from their readings or own experiences along with their arguments for those choices.

Line Up and Fold (Kagan & Kagan, 2009). For another way for students to engage in active conversation and discussion on their feet, first have students line up in a particular order; ask them to line up in order of birthdays or alphabetically by first names or last names, or they may be given cards with information to sequence themselves. Once students have formed a straight line, the first student at one end of the line is directed to walk down to face the last student at the other end of the line, followed by the other students until the line is "folded in half" and everyone has a partner. This strategy is similar to the *Inside Outside Circle* (Kagan & Kagan, 2009), in which students form two circles facing each other to pair up; index cards or notes may be used to scaffold the interaction between the partners. The line closer to the teacher may start with a question, and the students on the opposite line will answer, and then the roles are reversed. After a few minutes of discussion, students in one of the lines are signaled to move down two people while the other line stays in place. When new pairs are formed, the process is repeated.

Stand Up, Hand Up, Pair Up. In this final kinesthetic discussion-based activity also suggested by Kagan and Kagan (1998), students are given a literacy or content-based task to prepare prior to the three steps outlined here:

1. Stand up holding your index card or note sheet in one hand.

2. Raise your other hand and look around the room for a partner.

3. Pair up with someone from another table (someone you do not talk to regularly).

Once students self-select their partners in this fashion, they engage in the discussion about the prepared topic. For example, they may have been given a sentence or paragraph from a target text and had to generate a key question to ask their partners. A class, exploring Chapter 1 of *The Namesake* by Lahiri (2004) for example, will each have a short excerpt from the novel, which they will study very closely to make sure they understand the meaning of their assigned selection as best as they can without the larger context of the entire chapter. Then they generate an authentic question or two related to their selection, which they write on the back of the card (see Figure 6.7).

Figure 6.7 Quote and Questions for a Stand Up, Hand Up, Pair Up Activity Based on *The Namesake* (Lahiri, 2004)

In Bengali the word for pet name is daknam, meaning, literally, the name by which one is called, by friends, family, and other intimates, at home and in other private, unguarded moments. Pet names are a persistent remnant of childhood, a reminder that life is not always so serious, so formal, so complicated. (p. 25)	*Why does the author use the Bengali word* daknam *in this selection when most readers do not speak Bengali?* *Is there a similar tradition in other cultures?*

When paired up, the first student reads his or her selection aloud and asks the question prepared ahead of time. Students take turns asking and answering questions or discussing the meaning conveyed in the reading selections. If the selections lend themselves to it, students should be asked to make connections between the short reading passages assigned to them. Once their exchange is complete, they raise their hands and look for new partners with whom they will repeat the verbal exchange, further exploring the topic or the text.

ANTICIPATED OUTCOMES

"Academic language is part of a cognitive toolbox for undertaking real content area tasks in the same or analogous ways to experts"(Wilhelm, 2007, p. 44). More specifically, oral language use, the type of formal, content-based, and academic task-driven interaction that leads to active, engaged school participation, is critical for student success. All learners—not just students with diverse academic and linguistic needs—benefit from explicit instruction in and about oral academic English use and ample structured, scaffolded opportunities for practicing formal English orally in all their classes. When such learning opportunities prevail, students incorporate newly acquired academic vocabulary in their speech, use more complete sentences rather than merely sentence fragments, and acquire more complex grammatical structures. In turn, strong academic oral language skills will support the development of advanced reading comprehension and writing proficiency.

INSTRUCTIONAL CHALLENGES

Designing and implementing discussion-based activities that support the six Speaking and Listening Standards may appear to be easy and simple at first. Most students like to talk, so put them in small groups and give them a task (a prompt or a question) to discuss and the lesson is on its way, right? Not always so! Students with diverse learning needs also demonstrate varied classroom participation patterns and comfort levels with speaking in public, even if that public speech means turning and talking to one another. Thus, the following overall recommendations will help overcome the challenges of involving reluctant speakers:

- Create a supportive learning environment, one in which risk-taking is fostered and part of the class culture.
- Allow for mistakes and struggles as class community members learn to express themselves.
- Model ways for students to communicate with one another and how students should respond when they do not understand a classmate who is speaking.
- Scaffold, scaffold, scaffold, and then release responsibility to students.
- Integrate listening and speaking with reading and writing, artistic expression, and technology use.

PROMISING CLASSROOM PRACTICES

Sociocultural Explorations and Presentations in New Hampshire

Students in the middle grades must read in pursuit of answering questions and considering themes as well as literary elements. This type of reading helps students to gain insight into human existence. Embedded in the practice of reading and writing are complex social relationships as well as avenues to talk.

Tina Proulx found that the rigors related to these skills are essential in the instruction of all learners, especially English language learners. In a social, cultural unit titled, "Cultures and Countries: Does a Person Have to Leave One Behind to Become a Member of Another?" Tina, in collaboration with preservice teachers and her English language learners, investigated this question through the anchor text, *Facing the Lion*, by Lemasolai and Viola (2005).

Tina teaches English as well as science classes in an urban school district in Manchester, New Hampshire, a city designated as a refugee resettlement site. Using dialogue journals to develop the skills necessary to be college-and-career-ready writers, students practiced narrative techniques to develop experiences, events, and characters related to the text. These middle school students, along with their paired preservice teachers, read a shared text, explored independent research on the author's country and cultural traditions, and viewed various video clips related to both the personal story of the author and the broader cultural rites and rituals of the Maasi nomads in rural Kenya.

Dialogue journal partners engaged in weekly written exchanges exploring a variety of questions surrounding the text. Some of the questions explored were, "How does sharing our stories help reveal values and beliefs shared by a group of people?" and "Can a person have two countries and/or two cultures?" As a culminating activity, students met face-to-face and collaborated to present claims and findings related to their joint exploration of the focus questions in a two- to three-minute oral/visual presentation. Through the use of a theme-based unit as well as multiple opportunities to develop listening, speaking, reading, and writing skills, these students showed great progress in both the acquisition of academic language and the development of a variety of Common Core skills for English language arts.

Rhetoric, Civil Rights, and Ourselves: A Unit of Speeches in New York

In her unit, "Rhetoric, Civil Rights, and Ourselves," Christine Rowland, high school English teacher and United Federation of Teachers (UFT) center coach, and her English learners explored this topic through the speeches of Sojourner Truth ("Ain't I a Woman?"; http://www.fordham .edu/halsall/mod/sojtruth-woman.asp), Dr. Martin Luther King Jr. ("I Have a Dream"; 1963/1992), and President Barack Obama (as senator in addressing the 2008 Annual Convention of the NAACP; http://blogs

.suntimes.com/sweet/2008/07/obamas_naacp_speech_cincinnati.html). One of the essential questions of the unit was, "How do great speakers use rhetorical devices to motivate their audiences?" The rhetorical devices selected for focus arose out of these speeches, which were first experienced either via the teacher's performance (for Sojourner Truth) or through viewing the actual speech on screen in the case of Dr. King and President Obama. Experiencing the delivery of the speeches was important in understanding aspects that may not come through in a text alone—such as the effective use of pause and emphasis. Rhetorical devices encountered included repetition, rhetorical question, extended metaphor, allusion, and anecdote.

In addition to writing an argumentative paper in response to a question arising from the Obama speech, "Does social and economic justice begin in the classroom?" students were required to create their own persuasive speeches on a topic about which they cared passionately. They needed to compose a two-minute speech using two of the devices they had learned about in the unit. The objective of the speech was to persuade their peers (along with the principal and the coordinator of the English department) to agree with their opinion and/or take certain actions.

Students chose to speak on a wide range of topics, including climate change, abortion, behavior in the cafeteria, and women in the military. A review of the end-of-semester student course evaluations revealed that a number of students identified this assignment as one of their favorite aspects of the course. This unit of study and culminating activity most certainly provided students with a strong overview of the aspects and use of rhetorical devices as well as furnished students the opportunity to apply what they had learned in delivering their own oral presentations.

COMMON CORE LISTENING/SPEAKING STANDARDS— (UN)COMMON REFLECTION QUESTIONS

1. Which of the six anchor standards or the grade-appropriate equivalents will present the greatest challenge to your students? Why?

2. How will you help your students overcome the difficulties they may face when speaking in front of others?

3. How will you support oral language development when complex reading and writing skills receive so much more attention due to their frequency on standardized tests?

KEY RESOURCES

Professional Books

Harvey, S., & Daniels, H. (2009). *Comprehension and collaboration: Inquiry circles in action.* Portsmouth, NH: Heinemann.

Kagan, S., & Kagan, M. (1998). *Multiple intelligences: The complete MI book.* San Clemente, CA: Kagan.

Kagan, S., & Kagan, M. (2009). *Kagan cooperative learning.* San Clemente, CA: Kagan.

Online Resources

Creating a Presentation with Other Web-Based Tools
 https://present.me
 www.slideshare.com
 www.voicethread.com
 www.kizoa.com
 www.helloslide.com
 http://animoto.com

Digital Story-Telling Tools and Sites
 www.storycenter.org
 www.microsoft.com/education/en-us/teachers/guides/Pages/digital_
  storytelling.aspx
 http://zimmertwins.com
 http://storybird.com
 http://www.piclits.com/compose_dragdrop.aspx
 http://generator.acmi.net.au/storyboard
 http://domo.goanimate.com/studio

Helpful Suggestions for Enhancing Any Presentation
 Http://www.presentationzen.com

Learning to Create a Prezi
 www.prezi.com

Library of Congress
 www.loc.gov/teachers

TED Talks for the Classroom
 http://edudemic.com/2012/03/25-ted-talks-perfect-for-classrooms/

Top 100 Speeches of the 20th Century
 www.americanrhetoric.com

7 Key to Successful Implementation

Collaborative Strategies

Creative teaching is disciplined *improvisation because it always occurs within broad structures and frameworks.*

—Keith Sawyer, 2004, p. 13

OVERVIEW

The broad structures and frameworks Keith Sawyer referred to in the above quote from 2004 today could very well mean both Common Core State Standards (CCSS) and collaborative contexts in which teachers co-construct meaning and new knowledge as well as codevelop new skills based on the Common Core expectations. Likewise, the goal of this chapter is to explore the collaborative practices that teachers may engage in to implement the Common Core English Language Arts Standards in the secondary school context. We will outline the types of collaboration among teachers that yield effective standards-based instruction to meet the diverse academic and language development needs of students. Both instructional and noninstructional collaborative activities focused on the Common Core Standards implementation are presented. Extensive research on both professional learning communities (PLCs) and teacher collaboration supports our notion that effective and successful implementation of any new initiatives, such as the CCSS, cannot happen without systemic collaboration.

WHY COLLABORATIVE PRACTICES HELP MEET THE COMMON CORE

Over a decade ago, Morse (2000) suggested that through collaboration, "educators will recognize they are not alone in searching for new modes of human exchange" and also noted that "rejecting collaboration is not an option" (p. xi). It has been recognized by many that the complexity of the challenges that diverse secondary students encounter on a daily basis calls for a collaborative approach so teachers are better able to pool their talents and resources and offer the best possible education to these learners. The implementation of the CCSS presents a unique opportunity for educators to collaborate on multiple levels to foster a shared mission and vision for diverse learners, to have in-depth conversations about standards-based teaching and data-driven instruction, to share instructional practices, to align curricula, to foster a student-centered approach to teaching, and to perpetuate avenues for effective professional learning.

When presenting low-cost yet highly effective instructional changes teachers can implement to enhance instruction for all learners, Schmoker (2009) included teacher collaboration as one such strategy. Based on the successful outcomes of the PLC movement, he emphasized that "authentic teams build effective curriculum-based lessons and units together—which they routinely refine together on the basis of common assessment data" (p. 527). In addition to assessment data, the CCSS also provide a foundational framework for teacher collaboration. Goddard, Goddard, and Tschannen-Moran (2007) concluded that "collaboration . . . encourages teachers to move beyond reliance on their own memories and experiences with schooling and toward engagement with others around important questions of teaching and learning" (p. 892). Implementing the CCSS successfully with diverse learners is one such important question educators tackle around the country.

CORE COLLABORATIVE PRACTICES

Many teachers find engaging in ongoing professional dialogue with colleagues who share common concerns and experiences to be among the most rewarding experiences. Danielson (2009) also noted that "it's through conversations that teachers clarify their beliefs and plans and examine, practice, and consider new possibilities" (p. 1). Most teachers agree, however, that while informal interactions keep teachers connected, they are not enough to support sustained, professional collaboration. For successful collaboration—especially with the CCSS in mind—formal structures and procedures must be developed, implemented, and maintained. Such formal collaborative practices may have a more or less direct instructional or noninstructional focus, as we discussed in greater detail in *Collaboration and Coteaching: Strategies for English Learners* (Honigsfeld & Dove, 2010).

Instructional activities include (1) joint planning, (2) curriculum mapping and alignment, (3) parallel teaching, (4) codeveloping instructional materials, (5) collaborative assessment of student work, and (6) coteaching. Noninstructional activities include (1) joint professional development, (2) teacher research, (3) preparing for and conducting joint parent-teacher conferences, and (4) planning, facilitating, or participating in other extracurricular activities. The following section highlights key information needed for select collaborative activities as they pertain to aligning instruction to the CCSS.

Instructional Activities

Joint Planning

The purpose of a focused joint planning process—also referred to as cooperative or collaborative planning—is to allow special service providers and content-area teachers to share their expertise as they (a) consider the Common Core expectations, (b) discuss students' needs and the specific challenges each learner has to overcome to meet the Common Core goals, and (c) plan lessons or instructional units that they may deliver jointly or independent of each other. Sharing responsibility for the CCSS implementation through collaborative planning ensures that a sustained professional dialogue takes place. As a result, instruction offered by a team of teachers involved is aligned to the standards rather than being disjointed or fragmented. Joint planning helps ensure that the Grades 6–12 English language arts (ELA) curriculum is made accessible to all learners through scaffolding, tiering, or other differentiated instructional techniques. Joint planning opportunities must be part of the regular school schedule; lack of common preparation time is often the most frequently cited obstacle to successful teacher collaboration.

Coplanning basics. Regardless of grade level or content area, key coplanning activities include the following:

- Identifying the Common Core ELA standards (including the History/Social Studies or Science and Technical subject literacy standards) and language proficiency standards for the lesson

- Aligning language development objectives to ELA goals and students' needs based on the academic and linguistic demands of the unit or lesson
- Identifying essential questions that scaffold meaning and clarify information
- Selecting supplementary materials that help bridge new content to students' background knowledge
- Developing multilevel, tiered activities that match students' language proficiency or readiness levels
- Determining the types of instructional supports (visual, graphic, and interactive resources) needed to assist in making meaning from the required reading and assignments
- Selecting target linguistics structures (word-, sentence-, and discourse-level language features)
- Planning standards-based learning activities that integrate the four language skills—listening, speaking, reading, and writing—with content-area learning goals
- Designing formative assessment tasks and matching related assessment tools that offer data both about student progress and lesson effectiveness
- Whenever possible, using individual student profiles to further differentiate instruction

Villa, Thousand, and Nevin (2008) suggested that coplanning could be most effective when there is a set agenda used as a framework for coplanning time to guide teacher conversations between specialists and classroom teachers. When planning time is scarce, teachers need to develop communication strategies that consistently keep all parties informed and allow for shared decision making. Resourcefulness regarding planning and implementing instruction is often supplemented with creative ways to communicate with each other about students, lesson ideas, teaching strategies, and instructional materials. A shared plan book or aligned curriculum maps can serve to frame the major concepts and skills that all students must learn for a particular unit of study and assist collaborating teachers to organize lessons. Teachers can also agree on a coplanning template (see Figure 7.1) or a coplanning agenda (see Box 7.1) to ensure effective use of their collaborative time. (A full page, reproducible version of the coplanning template is available at the end of this chapter.)

Teachers engaged in regular coplanning may add additional lesson planning headings to this template. Similarly, the *Sample Common Core ELA Standards-Based Coplanning Agenda* in Box 7.1 may also be expanded and modified as needed.

Figure 7.1 Common Core ELA Standard-Based Coplanning Template

Date:	Class:	Collaborative Teachers:
Common Core Standards Addressed		
Learning Objectives (Content/Language)		
Activities/Tasks (Rigor and Engagement)		
Resources and Materials		
Technology Integration		
Accommodations/Modifications		
Assessment Procedures		
Reflections/Special Notes		

Box 7.1 Sample Common Core ELA Standards-Based Coplanning Agenda

1. Review previous unit/lesson and student assessment data.

2. Select target CCSS.

3. Determine unit or lesson goals/objectives.

4. Identify instructional procedures.

5. Differentiate instructional and assessment strategies.

6. Assign roles and responsibilities for individual follow-up planning.

Curriculum Mapping and Alignment

Curriculum mapping. Jacobs (1997), Udelhofen (2005), and others agreed that curriculum mapping is an effective procedure for collecting data about the taught curriculum in a school or district using a yearly or monthly calendar as the framework. Even when standards-based collaboration is the ultimate goal, participating teachers may first independently map their own taught curriculum. Once such overviews of students' actual learning experiences are created, teachers engage in a dialogue to ensure alignment and explore possible misalignments of essential knowledge and skills taught in the general-education, English-as-a-second-language (ESL), bilingual, or special education curriculum. As Jacobs (1999) noted, "The fundamental purpose of mapping is communication. . . . Mapping is not presented as what ought to happen but what is happening during the course of a school year" (p. 61). On the other hand, Schmoker (2009) emphasized the need for a common, coherent curriculum with collaboratively developed assessments to ensure high-quality, meaningful, standards-based instruction: "Teachers must create maps, by grading period, designating clearly which standards and objectives students will learn, with ample inclusion of higher-order, critical-thinking, reading, and writing standards" (p. 526).

In sum, with the CCSS, curriculum planning, mapping, and alignment among classroom teachers and support service professionals are receiving increasing attention. Most maps reveal five types of information: the content (essential knowledge taught), the standard that is addressed in the curricular unit, the processes and skills used to teach the content, the assessment tools, and key resources used in the unit.

Curriculum alignment. What effect has the standards reform movement had on the curriculum for English language learners (ELLs) and students with disabilities? Are districts able to incorporate the general education curriculum into the instruction of these youngsters? In our investigation of districts with an ESL curriculum, we found that there are a number of curricular options.

1. A stand-alone ESL curriculum following a locally developed scope and sequence of language and literacy development

2. A stand-alone ESL curriculum following a statewide ESL curriculum framework

3. A stand-alone ESL curriculum based on a commercially available ESL program

4. A content-support ESL curriculum based on content standards

Developing an ESL curriculum with the CCSS in mind is expected to result in an ELA standards-based curriculum aligned to grade-level English language arts and content-area literacy expectations. If the ESL program does have a strong, purposeful connection to the grade-level ELA content through curriculum alignment, instruction in the mainstream classes becomes more meaningful for ELLs. Without such curriculum alignment, the ESL services may become fragmented, the lessons delivered in each class may become disjointed, and the skills introduced and practiced may become confusing for ELLs.

In further consideration of the CCSS to create more instructional rigor for all students, special education teachers need to collaborate with general education teachers in order to align students' individual education programs (IEPs) with content curricula. The absence of knowledge of the general education curricula places both special education and ESL teachers in a position that often leads to the teaching of a narrow, skills-based curriculum for those pupils identified for these services. Furthermore, curriculum alignment through collaborative practices allows for a wider acceptance of shared academic goals and the use of differentiated instructional strategies, materials, and activities in all general education, second-language learning, and remedial programs.

Parallel Teaching

Academic intervention services (AIS), remedial reading, and ESL often continue to be implemented in the form of a stand-alone program. At the secondary level, specialists often work with small groups in their designated classrooms offering targeted interventions. One solution for more coordinated services is for specialists and general education teachers to establish and match the use of literacy objectives in content lessons that are also aligned to the CCSS. Our recommendation is to use the grade-specific standards section of the CCSS, track the standards across two, three, or occasionally more grades and *back-map* to previous grade-level expectations when working with students who need either remediation or first-time skill building as is the case with many diverse learners.

Codeveloping Instructional Materials

When teachers collaborate with students' needs in mind, their attention may be focused on not only creating CCSS-based lesson or unit plans together but also developing instructional materials, resources, graphic organizers, in-class and homework assignments, and assessment tools that make meaningful connections to the students' out-of school lives, background experiences, linguistic and academic abilities, and potentials (which can only be realized through high expectations for all). There are many already-available instructional resources that can be adapted for diverse students, teachers' own pre-Common Core materials are also well worth the attention.

The possibilities of joint ELA standards-based and content-based material development are as diverse as the lessons taught in Grades 6–12 classrooms. Some examples include the following:

- *Do Now or Warm-Up Tasks* to activate students' prior knowledge, review a previously taught lesson, or preview new information while also allowing them to make personal connections to new material

- *Anticipation Guides* that help students preview the key vocabulary and content necessary for an upcoming reading selection
- *Group Investigation Role Cards,* some of which are completed with sentence starters or language frames
- *Lab Report Outlines* and their scaffolded versions with appropriate adaptations
- *Research Project Exemplars* to offer models for students to analyze in order to understand the framework for their project's completion
- *Document-Based Analysis* templates with partially completed sample answers
- *List-Group-Label and Photo Sorts* as well as other hands-on activities that require time spent investigating resources on the Internet and preparing materials such as printing, sorting, cutting, and pasting for students to use materials in class
- *Structured Note-Taking Guides* with key words provided along with other pertinent text to scaffold the use of the guides
- *Rubrics* that specify expectations for completing a complex task with detailed information to support independent work

Collaborative Assessment of Student Work

A powerful collaborative activity that specialists and general education teachers engage in is sampling and carefully examining representative work by diverse students. In one recently developed model, *Collaborative Analysis of Student Work: Improving Teaching and Learning,* Langer, Colton, and Gott (2003) suggested the use of rubrics within a framework of collaborative conversations and inquiry. Specifically, they proposed that participating teachers focus both on students' strengths and challenges and identify appropriate strategies to respond to patterns of learning difficulties. Using a protocol, members of teacher study groups analyze student work, offer plausible explanations for student-performance levels, explore promising strategies to implement, and plan interventions. Once each teacher follows the collectively determined steps, new data are collected from the student, and the performance is assessed. This cycle is repeated, as teachers reflect on their students' learning and their own growth and needs.

In our work, we found it helpful to customize the protocol of examining student work by focusing on the challenges of specific students. For example, in order for teachers to jointly review the work of ELLs, we developed a protocol called *Sampling Work by English Language Learners* (SWELL) (Honigsfeld & Dove, 2010) as a guide for teachers to examine students' language, academic, cultural, and social-emotional development. See Box 7.2 for the entire protocol adapted for standards-based ELA instruction for academically and linguistically diverse learners.

Box 7.2 Protocol for Sampling Work by English Language Learners (SWELL)

As you collaboratively examine student literacy work samples, consider the following questions organized in four subcategories.

1. Academic Language/Linguistic Development

   a. What stage of second-language acquisition is evident (for ELLs only)?

   b. Which academic language features has the student mastered and been able to use systematically?

   c. What are two or three prominent linguistic challenges the student's work demonstrates?

   d. Other comments:

2. Disciplinary or Content-Based Academic Needs

   a. What are two to three examples of successfully acquired ELA or content-specific knowledge and/or skills?

   b. What are some noticeable gaps in the student's prior knowledge?

   c. What are some gaps in the student's new ELA skills and discipline-specific knowledge attainment?

   d. What ELA domain-specific subskills (listening, speaking, reading, writing) does the student need to work on?

   e. Other comments:

3. Cultural Experiences and Challenges

   a. In what way are the student's cultural experiences reflected in his or her work?

   b. Is there any evidence that the student was struggling with cultural misunderstandings or misconceptions?

   c. Other comments:

4. Social-Emotional Aspects of Learning

   a. Is there evidence of motivated, self-directed learning in the student's work sample?

   b. Has the learner been engaged in the task?

   c. Is there evidence of task persistence?

   d. Is there evidence of being engaged in cooperative learning (peer editing, etc.)?

   e. Other comments:

Source: Adapted from Honigsfeld, A., & Dove, M. (2010). *Collaboration and coteaching: Strategies for English Learners* (p. 71). Thousand Oaks, CA: Corwin.

Coteaching as a Framework for Sustained Teacher Collaboration

Coteaching frameworks have been presented for special education inclusion models (Friend & Cook, 2007; Murawski, 2009; Vaughn, Schumm, & Arguelles, 1997; Villa et al., 2007), as well as for English learners (Honigsfeld & Dove, 2010, 2012). In our work with ESL teachers and their general education colleagues, we have documented seven coteaching arrangements, which we refer to as coteaching models. In three of these models, both teachers work with one large group of students. In three additional models, two groups of students are split between the two cooperating teachers. In one final model, multiple groups of students are engaged in a learning activity that is facilitated and monitored by both teachers. Each of these configurations may have a place in any cotaught classroom, regardless of the grade level taught or the ELA standard targeted. We encourage our readers to consider both the advantages and challenges of each and pilot various models in their classes to see which ones allow them to respond best to the students' needs, the specific content being taught, the type of learning activities designed, and the participating teachers' teaching styles and own preferences (see Honigsfeld & Dove, 2010 for detailed discussion of each model):

1. One Group: One Lead Teacher and One Teacher "Teaching on Purpose"

2. One Group: Two Teachers Teach Same Content

3. One Group: One Teacher Teaches, One Teacher Assesses

4. Two Groups: Two Teachers Teach Same Content

5. Two Groups: One Teacher Preteaches, One Teacher Teaches Alternative Information

6. Two Groups: One Teacher Reteaches, One Teacher Teaches Alternative Information

7. Multiple Groups: Two Teachers Monitor and Teach

What Is Unique About Coteaching?

During any of the above coteaching configurations, the partnering teachers share the responsibility for planning instruction, implementing the lessons, and assessing student performance and outcomes. In a cotaught classroom, all students participate in CCSS-driven ELA or content-area lessons. When learning groups remain heterogeneous, students have the opportunity to work with others who have various academic capabilities and academic English language fluency.

In our view, there are some basic, nonnegotiable practices of a successful coteaching program. Within a general education classroom, a specialist can demonstrate strategies during a cotaught lesson, and the classroom teacher can continue to use the same strategies with students when the specialist is no longer present. Very often, the exchange of ideas between both teachers allows for more risk-taking and the use of innovative strategies on the part of each teacher to benefit all students in the classroom.

Noninstructional Activities

Joint Professional Development

All teachers may benefit from participating in joint professional-development activities based on the CCSS either at their school, within their district, or outside their own professional environment. If they attend external, off-site training programs together, they have an open forum to share their experiences with standards-based instruction, voice their concerns about the challenges the CCSS pose for diverse learners, and get feedback and responses both from colleagues who may be working at other school districts and from the course leader or workshop facilitator. Upon returning to their schools, teachers have the opportunity to share the information they gained both formally and informally with their colleagues. When they transfer the new information to their own practice and implement the new strategies in their own teaching, not only are they developing new skills, but they can also share these skills and their own classroom results with colleagues who did not attend the same training. When teachers train together, the benefit is even greater since they are able to support each other in their endeavors in the classroom.

The collaborative professional development practices that yield the most effective partnership and team building between specialists and their general education colleagues have the following common elements:

1. Regular, work-based opportunities to reflect on and improve instruction

2. Shared topics of interest

3. Team membership and participation based on self-selection

4. Focus on teachers' instructional practices and students' learning

Below we outline three possible forms of collaborative professional development activities: (a) collegial circles, (b) class visitation, and (c) collaborative coaching or mentoring.

A. Collegial Circles. Collegial circles are small groups of teachers who meet on a regular basis to discuss common questions, share concerns, offer solutions to unique or ongoing problems, and discuss appropriate instructional techniques. However, to keep professional conversations on task, protocols or formats for discussion are often beneficial. In a classic educational resource, *Looking in Classrooms*, Good and Brophy (2000, p. 490) outlined a model for group discussion. To transfer this model to the current standards-based instructional context, we renamed the stages, adjusted the goals, and gave CCSS-specific examples for each stage, as seen in Table 7.1.

Table 7.1 Phases of Group Discussion

Phases	Types of Knowledge	Goals	Examples
Phase 1	Preparation	• Share personal experiences related to the topic or problem	• Invite everyone to share his or her personal experiences • Discuss the challenges and opportunities the CCSS present for diverse student learning needs
Phase 2	External Knowledge: ↓ Review and Discover	• Explore existing, research-based information • Find out what experts say about the topic	• Find recently published articles on the CCSS and academically and linguistically diverse learners
Phase 3	Personal Knowledge: ↓ Reflect and Relate	• Engage in active listening and sharing • Connect and compare external knowledge to group members' own experiences	• Compare own challenges and successes to those documented in the literature • Reflect on own successes and lessons learned in the classroom
Phase 4	Future Actions: ↓ Revise and Devise	• Internalize new knowledge about the topic • Review and revise prior understanding of the problem • Develop a plan of action	• Evaluate recommended practices found in the literature and shared by group members • Develop a plan to experiment with and implement new CCSS-based instructional strategies

Source: Adapted from Honigsfeld, A., & Dove, M. (2010). *Collaboration and coteaching: Strategies for English learners* (p. 82). Thousand Oaks, CA: Corwin.

B. Class Visitation. One effective school-based professional-learning opportunity for specialists and general education teachers is created by visiting each other's classes. When observing the teaching-learning process and monitoring student outcomes in a diverse classroom, teachers may set a specific purpose for the visit or choose one of the following as they target the observation of specific student subgroups:

> *Student Shadowing* (Soto, 2012): With this activity, the teacher-observer focuses on one or more students in the class. Some questions to consider when observing students are as follows: What are some of the observable challenges students face as the lesson unfolds? How do they respond to the literacy tasks and language focus activities presented by the teacher? How do they interact with their classmates? What opportunities do they have to meaningfully use and, thus, develop their English language skills? What percentage of the time are students engaged? What do students do differently in the observed class?

> *Peer Observation and Coaching:* With this approach, the focus of the visit is to observe teacher practices. Some questions that might be considered during this type of observation include the following: How clearly are the standards-based goals and objectives communicated? How does each teacher approach the varied needs of students? What types of adaptations are used? What percentage of the time is the teacher talking? In what ways are the assigned texts, tasks, homework assignments, and assessment practices modified (if at all)?

It is important to note that peer observations are not meant to be evaluative or judgmental, but rather serve as an opportunity for the teacher-observer to acknowledge the challenges, share positive feedback, and offer ideas to the teacher being observed.

Allen and LeBlanc (2005) promoted a simple yet effective collaborative peer coaching system they called the *2 + 2 Performance Appraisal Model.* The name suggests that teachers who engage in this form of peer support offer each other two compliments and two suggestions following a lesson observation. Table 7.2 offers possible target areas for the 2 + 2 models used with diverse learners.

C. Collaborative Coaching/Mentoring. When teachers participate in a mentor-coaching program either as a mentor-coach or as a mentee, opportunities to improve or learn new techniques to teach diverse learners while also aligning their instruction to the CCSS abound. Collaborative coaching and peer mentoring imply that teachers support each other's practices beyond conducting peer observations. Through a framework of coaching, teachers

Table 7.2 Target Areas of Feedback in the 2 + 2 Model

General Feedback	Feedback Specific to Working With Diverse Learners	Comments
Clarity of lesson objectives	Alignment of lesson objectives to ELA CCSS standards	
Motivation	Connection to students' prior knowledge and experiences or building background knowledge	
Lesson sequence	Lesson accessibility, instructional supports	
Differentiated activities	Scaffolded and tiered activities	
Student engagement	Student participation	
Questioning techniques	Questions matched to students' language proficiency and/or readiness levels (and addressing all levels of Bloom's Taxonomy)	
Grouping techniques	Using flexible (heterogeneous and homogenous) groupings	
Assessment techniques	Differentiation of assessment for diverse learners	

Source: Adapted from Honigsfeld, A., & Dove, M. (2010). *Collaboration and coteaching: Strategies for English Learners* (p. 85). Thousand Oaks, CA: Corwin.

learn from each other, model effective instruction for one another, and benefit from sustained, job-embedded, and student-centered classroom assistance. Collaborative coaching requires an equal relationship between the two partners, such as the relationship between coteachers or those who collaborate formally in other ways to provide instruction. It is effective (a) when both participants possess knowledge about the topic or issue, such as high-stakes testing and test preparation for diverse learners, or (b) when the coach understands one part of a problem (e.g., content requirements for all students to pass a state exam) and the partner understands another part (e.g., ELL's linguistic development) (Dunne & Villani, 2007). Thus, collaborative coaching becomes a vehicle for professional growth both for the novice and experienced teacher.

Teacher Research

When teachers engage in classroom-based practitioner research, they may do so individually or collaboratively using a number of different formats. Working in research and development (R & D) teams, participating in collaborative inquiry groups, and engaging in collaborative action research or lesson studies are examples of being engaged in job-embedded explorations.

R & D teams are formed by small groups of teachers who more formally decide on a particular instructional approach that they study collaboratively. In some districts, R & D projects and accompanying teacher portfolios that document teachers' success with strategies that support CCSS implementation may be used in lieu of more traditional teacher evaluations (which are often based on observations by an administrator and may yield only limited data on the teacher's performance). After collaborating teachers review research related to the selected instructional approach, they jointly plan and implement Common Core-aligned lessons based on the approach, assess their own (and each other's) growth, and evaluate the student outcomes.

When teacher discussion groups or collegial circles elect to engage in more in-depth explorations, they may decide to form collaborative inquiry groups. They may investigate an overarching concept (such as the teaching-learning process or second-language acquisition patterns) or choose more specific topics that deal with diverse learners' instructional needs (such as using effective note-taking strategies). A form of collaborative inquiry is conducting teacher research or action research. We use Johnson's (2008) definition of action research as "the process of studying a real school or classroom situation to understand and improve the quality of actions and instruction" (p. 28). When collaborative action research is woven into the school culture and supported strongly by both the administration and the faculty, it allows teachers to examine their standards-based practices systematically and participate in the highest level of professional learning (Cochran-Smith & Lytle, 1999).

Another form of teacher research is the lesson study concept originated in Japan as a professional development movement for experienced inservice teachers who wanted to regularly engage in examining their teaching practices to improve their effectiveness (Lewis, 2002). In the classic format, participating teachers jointly plan a lesson in response to a preestablished study question or goal. One teacher teaches the lesson while others observe. Next, teachers discuss the lesson, revise it, and another team member teaches the lesson in a new class. This process of observation and discussion is repeated and ends with a written report (Fernandez & Chokshi, 2002). Yoshida (2004) emphasized that

> lesson study helps to make teachers into lifelong learners. It is especially important to think of lesson study as a professional development activity, not as teacher training and lesson develop-ment. It creates opportunities for teachers to think deeply about instruction, learning, curriculum, and education. (p. 2)

Yet another way to engage in research is by participating in a commu-nity of practice (Buysse, Sparkman, & Bwesley, 2003), which builds on the "idea that practitioners and researchers should work together to co-construct knowledge as part of a common enterprise, rather than through separate endeavors" (p. 275). The most prevalent outcome of such a partner-ship is the development of a professional community, how researchers and practitioners establish and sustain a long-term professional relationship and, as such, explore educational issues embedded in their daily practice.

Preparing for (and Conducting) Joint Parent-Teacher Conferences

When specialists and general education colleagues compare students' behavior, attitudes, and overall academic performance in their respective classes, they may observe that the same student responds to instruction quite differently in different settings.

When specialists and general education teachers write progress reports and quarterly, semiannual, or annual report cards based on collaboratively reviewed student work samples, portfolios, and test scores, multiple per-spectives are included. Such a collaborative effort is beneficial in assessing students' linguistic and academic progress since it leads to providing a clearer picture of areas of strengths and needs for both teachers and families.

Planning, Facilitating, or Participating in Other Extracurricular Activities

Breiseth, Robertson, and Lafond (2011) suggested 20 strategies for family engagement, including communicating with parents about school matters, inviting them to school events, and encouraging them to take on leadership roles. We have found that when teachers jointly prepare for and facilitate parent outreach and family engagement initiatives, as well as other commu-nity-based activities, collaboration among all stakeholders is enhanced. What are some common and uncommon collaborative practices?

1. Parent Teacher Association (PTA) meetings

2. Parent information or new family orientation night

3. Parent workshops (e.g., information about the advances/shifts presented in the CCSS)

4. Cultural events

5. Collaborative class, grade, or school newsletters

6. Class and school plays, concerts, and talent shows

ANTICIPATED OUTCOMES

The successful implementation of the collaborative practices outlined here has been observed in numerous school districts around the U.S. (Dove & Honigsfeld, 2010; Honigsfeld & Dove, 2010, 2012). Most notably, collaborations that are anchored in the Common Core State Standards allow teachers to use a shared framework and shared purpose, which leads to (re)examining not only their instructional practices and materials used in the general education and special program classes but the entire instructional service delivery system as well. The consistency and cohesion of the support services will have to be evaluated periodically to ensure that diverse students receive rigorous, research-based services that lead to both academic language proficiency development and content-specific academic achievement. The establishment of a common set of goals and a shared language to talk about goals—as intended by the CCSS—and the diversity in our classrooms contribute to effective collaborative practices.

CHALLENGES

Collaborating for the sake of diverse learners using the CCSS is no small feat! In order to establish the right context for such collaborations, school leaders—administrators, teacher- and parent-leaders together—must create an inclusive, welcoming school learning community with a shared vision of respect and acceptance of everyone's cultural and linguistic heritage and background. Building a professional learning community (DuFour & Eaker, 1998)—that continually engages in collaborative inquiry on all students' needs as it works toward meeting the CCSS—is a critical component of Common Core collaborations. Finally, addressing the logistics for these collaborative practices must include (a) using "flexible teaming" that allows for both horizontal (on grade level) and vertical (across grade level) teacher teams, as well as cross-disciplinary teamwork to support diverse students' curricular, instructional, and extracurricular needs; (b) time and place for collaborations; and (c) human and other resources that make collaborations possible in the short and long run.

COMMON CORE COLLABORATIONS—(UN)COMMON REFLECTION QUESTIONS

1. How do you define successful collaboration to meet the CCSS?

2. How do schools create the time and resources for Common Core collaborations to take place?

3. What type of school leadership is needed for collaborative practices to be implemented successfully?

4. How do schools accurately assess whether or not the CCSS are being addressed with diverse learners?

KEY RESOURCES

Professional Books

Friend, M. (2008). *Co-teach! A handbook for creating and sustaining classroom partnerships in inclusive schools.* Greensboro, NC: Marilyn Friend Inc.

Friend, M., & Cook, L. (2007). *Interactions: Collaboration skills for school professionals* (5th ed.). New York: Prentice Hall.

Jacobs, H. H. (2004). *Getting results with curriculum mapping.* Alexandria, VA: ASCD.

Murawski, W. W. (2009). *Collaborative teaching in elementary schools: Making the co-teaching marriage work!* Thousand Oaks, CA: Corwin.

Roberts, S., & Pruitt, E. (2009). *Schools as professional learning communities: Collaborative activities and strategies for professional development.* Thousand Oaks, CA: Corwin.

Online Resources

www.coteachingforells.weebly.com
www.powerof2.com

Multimedia Sources

Friend, M. (2005). *The power of 2* [DVD]. Greensboro, NC: Marilyn Friend, Inc.

St. Paul Public Schools (SPPS). (2007). *Coteaching* [DVD]. St. Paul, MN: SPPS.

Common Core ELA Standard-Based Coplanning Template

Date:	Class:	Collaborative Teachers:

Common Core Standards Addressed

Learning Objectives (Content/Language)

Activities/Tasks (Rigor and Engagement)

Resources and Materials

Technology Integration

Accommodations/Modifications

Assessment Procedures

Reflections/Special Notes

References and Further Readings

Akhavan, N. (2009). *Teaching writing in a Title I school, K–3.* Portsmouth, NH: Heinemann.

Alber-Morgan, S. (2010). *Using RTI to teach literacy to diverse learners, K–8: Strategies for the inclusive classroom.* Thousand Oaks, CA: Corwin.

Allen, D. W., & LeBlanc, A. C. (2005). *Collaborative peer coaching that improves instruction: The 2 + 2 performance appraisal model.* Thousand Oaks, CA: Corwin.

Allyn, P. (2013). *Be core ready: Powerful, effective steps to implementing and achieving the Common Core State Standards.* Boston, MA: Pearson.

Anderson, J. (2005). *Mechanically inclined: Building grammar, usage, and style into writer's workshop.* Portland, ME: Stenhouse.

Anderson, J. (2007). *Everyday editing: Inviting students to develop skill and craft in writer's workshop.* Portland, ME: Stenhouse.

Anderson, J. (2011). *10 things every writer needs to know.* Portland, ME: Stenhouse.

Angelillo, J. (2003). *Writing about reading: From book talk to literary essays, grades 3–8.* Portsmouth, NH: Heinemann.

Applebee, A. N., Burroughs, R., & Stevens, A. S. (2000). Creating continuity and coherence in high school literature curricula. *Research in the Teaching of English, 34,* 396–429.

Applebee, A. N., Langer, J. A., Nystrand, M., & Gamoran, A. (2003). Discussion-based approaches to developing understanding: Classroom instruction and student performance in middle and high school English. *American Educational Research Journal, 40,* 685–730. doi:10.3102/00028312040003685

Application of Common Core State Standards for English Language Learners. (2010). Retrieved from http://www.corestandards.org/assets/application-for-english-learners.pdf

August, D., & Shanahan, T. (Eds.). (2006). *Developing literacy in second-language learners: Report of the national literacy panel on language-minority children and youth.* Mahwah, NJ: Erlbaum.

Baker, J. (2002). Trilingualism. In L. Delpit & J. K. Dowdy (Eds.), *The skin that we speak: Thoughts on language and culture in the classroom* (pp. 49–61). New York, NY: New Press.

Beck, I. L., McKeown, M. G., & Kucan, L. (2002). *Bringing words to life: Robust vocabulary instruction.* New York, NY: Guilford Press.

Beck I. L., McKeown, M. G., & Kucan, L. (2008). *Creating robust vocabulary: Frequently asked questions and extended examples.* New York, NY: Guilford Press.

Bellanca, J. A., Fogarty, R. J., & Pete, B. M. (2012). *How to teach thinking skills within the Common Core: 7 key student proficiencies of the new national standards.* Bloomington, IN: Solution Tree.

Benson, J. (2013, March 10). *Minnesota, the next battleground state in the fight to label GMOs.* Retrieved from http://www.naturalnews.com/039420_Minnesota_GMO_labeling_legislation.html

Blachowicz, C., Fisher, P., Ogle, D., & Watts-Taffe, S. (2006). Vocabulary: Questions from the classroom. *Reading Research Quarterly, 41,* 524–539.

Block, C. C., & Pressley, M. (2002). *Comprehension instruction: Research-based best practices.* New York, NY: Guilford Press.

Breiseth, L., Robertson, K., & Lafond, S. (2011). *A guide for engaging ELL families: Twenty strategies for school leaders.* Retrieved from http://www.colorincolorado.org/pdfs/guides/Engaging-ELL-Families.pdf

Burke, J. (2002). *Tools for thought: Graphic organizers for your classroom.* Portsmouth, NH: Heinemann.

Burke, J. (2010). *What's the big idea? Question-driven units to motivate reading, writing, and thinking.* Portsmouth, NH: Heinemann.

Burns, B. (1999). *The mindful school: How to teach balanced reading and writing.* Arlington Heights, IL: Skylight Professional Development.

Buysse, V., Sparkman, K. L., & Wesley, P. W. (2003). Communities of practice: Connecting what we know with what we do. *Exceptional Children, 69,* 263–277.

Calderón, M. E. (2007). *Teaching reading to English language learners, grades 6–12: A framework for improving achievement in the content areas.* Thousand Oaks, CA: Corwin.

Calkins, L., Ehrenworth, M., & Lehman, C. (2012). *Pathways to the common core: Accelerating achievement.* Portsmouth, NH: Heinemann.

Carr, J., Sexton, U., & Lagunoff, R. (2006). *Making science accessible to English learners.* San Francisco, CA: WestEd.

Casagrande, J. (2006). *Grammar snobs are great big meanies: A guide to language for fun and spite.* New York, NY: Penguin Books.

Clay, M. (1993). *Reading recovery: A guidebook for teachers in training.* Portsmouth, NH: Heinemann.

Cloud, N., & Genesee, F. (2009). *Literacy instruction for English language learners.* Portsmouth, NH: Heinemann.

Cochran-Smith, M., & Lytle, S. L. (1999). Relationships of knowledge and practice: Teacher learning in communities. In A. Iran-Nejad & C. D. Pearson (Eds.), *Review of research in education* (Vol. 24, pp. 249–305). Washington, DC: American Educational Research Association.

Coleman, R., & Goldenberg, C. (2010). What does research say about effective practices for English learners. Part II: Academic language proficiency. *Kappa Delta Pi Record, 46*(2), 60–65.

College Entrance Examination Board. (2002). *The AP vertical teams guide for English* (2nd ed.). New York, NY: Author.

Common Core State Standards for English Language Arts & Literacy in History/Social Studies, Science, and Technical Subjects. (2010a). Retrieved from http://corestandards.org/assets/CCSSI_ELA%20Standards.pdf

Common Core State Standards for English Language Arts & Literacy in History/Social Studies, Science, and Technical Subjects. Appendix A: Research supporting key elements of the standards. Glossary of key terms. (2010b). Retrieved from http://www.corestandards.org/assets/Appendix_A.pdf

Common Core State Standards for English Language Arts & Literacy in History/Social Studies, Science, and Technical Subjects. Appendix B: Text exemplars and sample performance tasks. (2010c). Retrieved from http://www.corestandards.org/assets/Appendix_B.pdf

Crawford, J., & Krashen, S. (2007). *English language learners in American classrooms: 101 questions, 101 answers.* New York, NY: Scholastic Teaching Resources.

Cummins, J. (2001). *Negotiating identities: Education for empowerment in a diverse society* (2nd ed.). Los Angeles: California Association for Bilingual Education.

Cunningham, P., & Allington, R. (1999). *Classrooms that work: They all can read and write* (2nd ed.). New York, NY: HarperCollins.

Daggett, W. R. (2011). *The Daggett System for effective instruction: Where research and best practices meet.* Retrieved from http://www.leadered.com/pdf/DSEI White Paper 7-11.pdf

Danielson, C. (2009). *Talk about teaching: Leading professional conversations.* Thousand Oaks, CA: Corwin.

Delpit, L. (1988). The silenced dialogue: Power and pedagogy in educating other people's children. *Harvard Educational Review, 58,* 280–299.

Delpit, L. (2002). No kinda sense. In L. Delpit & J. K. Dowdy (Eds.), *The skin that we speak: Thoughts on language and culture in the classroom* (pp. 31–48). New York, NY: New Press.

Dickson, S. V., Simmons, D. C., Kameenui, E. J., & Educational Resources Information Center (U.S.). (1995). *Text organization and its relation to reading comprehension: A synthesis of the research.* Eugene: University of Oregon, College of Education, National Center to Improve the Tools of Educators.

Dove, M. G., & Honigsfeld, A. (2010). ESL coteaching and collaboration: Opportunities to develop teacher leadership and enhance student learning. *TESOL Journal, 1*(1), 3–22.

Dufour, R. (2003). "Collaboration lite" puts student achievement on a starvation diet. *Journal of Staff Development, 24*(4), 63–64.

DuFour, R., & Eaker, R. (1998). *Professional learning communities at work: Best practices for enhancing student achievement.* Bloomington, IN: Solution Tree.

Dunne, K., & Villani, S. (2007). *Mentoring new teachers through collaborative coaching: Linking teacher and student learning.* San Francisco, CA: WestEd.

Dutro, S., & Kinsella, K. (2010). English language development: Issues and implementation at grades six through twelve. In *Improving education for English learners: Research-based approaches* (pp. 151–207). Sacramento: California Department of Education.

Echevarría, J., Vogt, M., & Short, D. (2012). *Making content comprehensible for English language learners: The SIOP model* (4th ed.). Needham Heights, MA: Allyn & Bacon.

Eisenberg, M. B., & Berkowitz, R. E. (2011). *The Big6 workshop handbook: Implementation and impact* (4th ed.). Santa Barbara, CA: Linworth.

Ellery, V., & Rosenboom, J. L. (2011). *Sustaining strategic readers: Techniques for supporting content literacy in grades 6–12.* Newark, DE: International Reading Association.

Elley, W. (1996). Using book floods to raise literacy levels in developing countries. In V. Greaney (Ed.), *Promoting reading in developing countries: Views on making reading materials accessible to increase literacy levels* (pp. 148–163). Newark, DE: International Reading Association.

Elmore, R. F. (2008). *School reform from the inside out: Policy, practice, and performance.* Cambridge, MA: Harvard Education Press.

Facing History and Ourselves. (2013). *Four corners.* Retrieved from http://www .facing.org/resources/strategies/four-corners

Fang, Z., Schleppegrell, M. J., & Cox, B. E. (2006). Understanding the language demands of schooling: Nouns in academic registers. *Journal of Literacy Research, 38,* 247–273.

Fang, Z., & Wei, Y. (2010). Improving middle school students' science literacy through reading infusion. *Journal of Educational Research, 103,* 262–273.

Feldman, K., & Kinsella, K. (2005). *Narrowing the language gap: The case for explicit vocabulary instruction.* Retrieved from http://teacher.scholastic.com/products/ authors/pdfs/Narrowing_the_Gap.pdf

Fernandez, C., & Chokshi, S. (2002). A practical guide to translating lesson study for a U.S. setting. *Phi Delta Kappan, 84,* 128–134.

Fillmore, L. W. (2004). *The role of language in academic development.* Retrieved from http://www.scoe.org/docs/ah/AH_language.pdf

Fillmore, L. W. (2009). *English language development: Acquiring the language needed for literacy and learning.* Retrieved from http://assets.pearsonschool.com/ asset_mgr/current/201010/English%20Language%20Development.pdf

Fisher, D., & Frey, N. (2008). *Better learning through structured teaching: A framework for the gradual release of responsibility.* Alexandria, VA: ASCD.

Fisher, D., & Frey, N. (2010). Unpacking the language purpose: Vocabulary, structure, and function. *TESOL Journal, 1*(3), 315–337.

Fisher, D., & Frey, N. (2011). *Teaching students to read like detectives: Comprehending, analyzing, and discussing text.* Bloomington, IN: Solution Tree.

Fisher, D., Frey, N., & Rothenberg, C. (2008). *Content-area conversations: How to plan discussion-based lessons for diverse language learners.* Alexandria, VA: ASCD.

Florida Center for Reading Research. (2007). *Text structure sort.* Retrieved from http://www.fcrr.org/studentactivities/c_022c.pdf

Fogel, H., & Ehri, L. C. (2000). Teaching elementary students who speak Black English vernacular to write in standard English: Effects of dialect transformation practice. *Contemporary Educational Psychology, 25,* 212–235.

Freebody, P., & Luke, A. (1990). Literacy programs: Debates and demands in cultural context. *Prospect, 5,* 7–15.

Frey, N., & Fisher, D. (2009). *Learning words inside & out: Vocabulary instruction that boosts achievement in all subject areas.* Portsmouth, NH: Heinemann.

Frey, N., Fisher, D., & Everlove, S. (2009). *Productive group work: How to engage students, build teamwork, and promote understanding.* Alexandria, VA: ASCD.

Friend, M. (2005). *The power of 2* [DVD]. Greensboro, NC: Marilyn Friend, Inc.

Friend, M. (2008). *Co-teach! A handbook for creating and sustaining classroom partnerships in inclusive schools.* Greensboro, NC: Marilyn Friend, Inc.

Friend, M., & Cook, L. (2007). *Interactions: Collaboration skills for school professionals* (5th ed.). New York, NY: Prentice Hall.

Fullan, M. (2007). *The new meaning of educational change* (4th ed.). New York, NY: Teachers College Press.

Gallagher, K. (2011). *Write like this: Teaching real world writing through modeling & mentor texts.* Portland, ME: Stenhouse.

Gallagher, M., & Pearson, P. D. (1983). The instruction of reading comprehension. *Contemporary Educational Psychology, 8,* 317–344.

Gardner, H. (1999). *The disciplined mind: What all students should understand.* New York, NY: Simon & Schuster.

Gardner, J. W. (1995). *Excellence: Can we be equal and excellent too?* New York, NY: Norton.

Genesee, F., Lindholm-Leary, K., Saunders, W., & Christian, D. (2006). *Educating English language learners.* New York, NY: Cambridge University Press.

Gibbons, P. (2009). *English learners, academic literacy, and thinking: Learning in the challenge zone.* Portsmouth, NH: Heinemann.

Giouroukakis, V., & Connolly, M. (2012). *Getting to the core of English Language Arts, grades 6–12: How to meet the common core state standards with lessons from the classroom.* Thousand Oaks, CA: Corwin.

Goddard, Y. L., Goddard, R. D., & Tschannen-Moran, M. (2007). A theoretical and empirical investigation of teacher collaboration for school improvement and student achievement in public elementary schools. *Teachers College Record, 109,* 877–896.

Goldenberg, C. N. (1992). *Instructional conversations and their classroom application* (Educational Practice Report 2). Santa Cruz: University of California, Santa Cruz, National Center for Research on Cultural Diversity and Second Language Learning.

Goldenberg, C. N., & Coleman, R. (2010). *Promoting academic achievement among English learners: A guide to the research.* Thousand Oaks, CA: Corwin.

Good, T., & Brophy, J. (2000). *Looking in classrooms* (8th ed.). New York, NY: Longman.

Gordon-Thaxter, N. (n.d.). *How to use figurative language to convey tone.* Retrieved from http://www.ehow.com/how_7643570_use-figurative-language-convey-tone.htm

Gossard, J. (1996). Using read-around groups to establish criteria for good writing. In C. B. Olson (Ed.), *Practical ideas for teaching writing as a process* (pp. 148–151). Sacramento: California State Department of Education.

Gottlieb, M. (2011, November). *From academic language to academic success.* Workshop presented at the Iowa Culture & Language Conference, Coralville, IA.

Graham, S., & Hebert, M. A. (2010). *Writing to read: Evidence for how writing can improve reading.* A Carnegie Corporation time to act report. Washington, DC: Alliance for Excellent Education.

Grant, M. C., & Fisher, D. (2010). *Reading and writing in science: Tools to develop disciplinary literacy.* Thousand Oaks, CA: Corwin.

Graves, M. F., Graves, B., & Braaten, S. (1996). Scaffolded reading experiences for inclusive classes. *Educational Leadership, 53*(5), 14–16.

Griffin, C., Simmons, D., & Kameenui, E. (1991). Investigating the effectiveness of graphic organizer instruction on the comprehension and recall of science content by students with learning disabilities. *Reading, Writing, and Learning Disabilities, 7,* 355–376.

Hale, C. (2001). *Sin and syntax: How to craft wickedly effective prose.* New York, NY: Broadway Books.

Halliday, M. A. K. (1996). On grammar and grammatics. In R. Hasan, C. Cloran, & D. G. Butt (Eds.), *Functional descriptions: Theory into practice* (pp. 1–38). Philadelphia, PA: John Benjamins.

Harcourt Horizons. (2003). *United States History, Canada, Mexico, and Central America.* Boston, MA: Harcourt.

Hargreaves, A. (1994). *Changing teachers, changing times: Teachers' work and culture in the postmodern age.* New York, NY: Teachers College Press.

Hargreaves, A. (2011). Foreword. In Sahlberg, P., *Finnish lessons: What can the world learn from educational change in Finland?* (pp. xv–xx). New York, NY: Teachers College Press.

Harvey, S., & Daniels, H. (2009). *Comprehension and collaboration: Inquiry circles in action.* Portsmouth, NH: Heinemann.

Harvey, S., & Goudvis, A. (2007). *Strategies that work: Teaching comprehension for understanding and engagement* (2nd ed.). Portland, ME: Stenhouse.

Hill, J. D., & Flynn, K. (2008). Asking the right questions. *Journal of Staff Development, 49*(1), 46–52.

Hillocks, G. Jr. (2011). *Teaching argument writing, grades 6–12: Supporting claims with relevant evidence and clear reasoning.* Portsmouth, NH: Heinemann.

Hoffman, J. V. (1992). Critical reading/thinking across the curriculum: Using I-Charts to support learning. *Language Arts, 69,* 121–127.

Honigsfeld, A., & Dove, M. G. (2010). *Collaboration and co-teaching: Strategies for English learners.* Thousand Oaks, CA: Corwin.

Honigsfeld, A., & Dove, M. (Eds.). (2012). *Coteaching and other collaborative practices in the EFL/ESL classroom: Rationale, research, reflections, and recommendations.* Charlotte, NC: Information Age Publishing.

Illinois State Board of Education. (2012). *Common Core teaching and learning strategies: English and language arts reading informational texts, grades 6–12.* Chicago, IL: Author. Retrieved from http://www.isbe.net/common_core/pdf/ela-teach-strat-read-text-6-12.pdf

Jacobs, H. H. (1997). *Mapping the big picture: Integrating curriculum and assessment K–12.* Alexandria, VA: ASCD.

Jacobs, H. H. (1999). *Breaking new ground in high school curriculum.* Reston, VA: National Association of Secondary School Principals.

Jacobs, H. H. (2004). *Getting results with curriculum mapping.* Alexandria, VA: ASCD.

Jacobs, H. H. (2006). *Active literacy across the curriculum.* Larchmont, NY: Eye On Education.

Johnson, A. P. (2008). *A short guide to action research.* Boston, MA: Pearson.

Johnson, D. D., & Pearson, P. D. (1984). *Teaching reading vocabulary* (2nd ed.). New York, NY: Holt, Rinehart, & Winston.

Kagan, S., & Kagan, M. (1998). *Multiple intelligences: The complete MI book.* San Clemente, CA: Kagan.

Kagan, S., & Kagan, M. (2009). *Kagan cooperative learning.* San Clemente, CA: Kagan.

Kamil, M. L., Borman, G. D., Dole, J., Kral, C. C., Salinger, T., & Torgesen, J. (2008). *Improving adolescent literacy: Effective classroom and intervention practices: A practice guide.* Washington, DC: U.S. Department of Education, Institute of Education Sciences, National Center for Education Evaluation and Regional Assistance.

Keene, E. O., & Zimmermann, S. (2007). *Mosaic of thought: The power of comprehension strategy instruction* (2nd ed.). Portsmouth, NH: Heinemann.

Kessler, G., Bikowski, D., & Boggs J. (2012). Collaborative writing among second language learners in academic web-based projects. *Language Learning & Technology, 16*(1), 91–109.

Kinsella, K. (2012). Cutting to the core: Communicating on the same wavelength. *Language Magazine, 12*(4), 18–25.

Kirby, D. L., & Crovitz, D. (2012). *Inside out: Strategies for teaching writing.* Portsmouth, NH: Heinemann.

Koebler, J. (2012, December 28). 10 important scientific discoveries and achievements of 2012. *US News.* Retrieved from http://www.usnews.com/news/articles/2012/12/28/10-important-scientific-discoveries-and-achievements-of-2012

Ladson-Billings, G. (2009). *The dreamkeepers: Successful teachers of African American children* (2nd ed.). San Francisco, CA: Jossey-Bass.

Langer, G. M., Colton, A. B., & Gott, L. S. (2003). *Collaborative analysis of student work: Improving teaching and learning.* Alexandria, VA: ASCD.

Langer de Ramirez, L. (2009). *Empower English language learners with tools from the web.* Thousand Oaks, CA: Corwin.

Lapp, D., & Fisher, D. (2012). Persuasion = Stating and arguing claims well. *Journal of Adolescent & Adult Literacy, 55,* 641–644.

Larmer, J., & Mergendoller, J. R. (2012). Speaking of speaking. *Educational Leadership, 70*(4), 74–76.

Lederer, R., & Shore, J. (2005). *Comma sense: A fundamental guide to punctuation.* New York, NY: St. Martin's Press.

Lee, C. D., & Spratley, A. (2010). *Reading in the disciplines: The challenges of adolescent literacy.* New York, NY: Carnegie Corporation of New York. Retrieved from http://carnegie.org/fileadmin/Media/Publications/PDF/tta_Lee.pdf

Lehmann, C. (2012, December 11). *What good are standards, if funding varies?* Retrieved from http://www.nytimes.com/roomfordebate/2012/12/10/the-american-way-of-learning/teaching-standards-are-moot-when-funding-is-so-disparate

Lewis, C. (2002). *Lesson study: A handbook of teacher-led instructional improvement.* Philadelphia, PA: Research for Better Schools.

Lorcher, T. (2011). *Context clue challenge.* Retrieved from http://www.brighthubeducation.com/high-school-english-lessons/6323-teaching-context-clues-activity

Luke, A., & Freebody, P. (1997). The social practices of reading. In S. Muratt, A. Luke, & P. Freebody (Eds.), *Constructing critical literacies* (pp. 185–226). Cresskill, NJ: Hampton Press.

Luke, A., & Freebody, P. (1999). A map of possible practices: Further notes on the four resources model. *Practically Primary, 4*(2), 5–8.

Lukeman, N. (2006). *A dash of style: The art and mastery of punctuation.* New York, NY: Norton.

Lyman, F. (1981). The responsive classroom discussion: The inclusion of all students. In A. S. Anderson (Ed.), *Mainstreaming digest* (pp. 109–112). College Park: University of Maryland.

Manz, S. L. (2002). A strategy for previewing textbooks: Teaching readers to become THIEVES. *The Reading Teacher, 55,* 434–435.

Marinak, B. A., & Gambrell, L. B. (2009). Ways to teach about informational texts. *National Council for Social Studies, 22*(1), 19–22.

Marzano, R. (2004). *Building background knowledge for academic achievement: Research on what works in schools.* Alexandria, VA: ASCD.

Marzano, R. (2010). Teaching inference. *Educational Leadership, 67*(7), 80–81.

Marzano, R. J., & Pickering, D. J. (2005). *Building academic vocabulary: Teacher's manual.* Alexandria, VA: ASCD.

Marzano, R. J., Pickering, D., & Pollock, J. (2001). *Classroom instruction that works: Research-based strategies for increasing student achievement.* Alexandria, VA: ASCD.

Mazur, A. J., & Doran, P. R. (2010). *Teaching diverse learners: Principles for best practice.* Thousand Oaks, CA: Corwin.

McCarrier, A., Pinnell, G. S., & Fountas, I. C. (1999). *Interactive writing: How language and literacy come together, K–2.* Portsmouth, NH: Heinemann.

McKeown, M. G., Beck, I. L., & Worthy, M. J. (1993). Grappling with text ideas: Questioning the author. *The Reading Teacher, 46,* 560–566.

McNamara, D. S. (Ed.). (2007). *Reading comprehension strategies: Theory, interventions, and technologies.* Mahwah, NJ: Erlbaum.

Michaels, S., O'Connor, M. C., & Hall, M. W (with Resnick, L. B.). (2010). *Accountable talk: Classroom conversation that works* (Version 3.1). Pittsburgh, PA: University of Pittsburgh.

Miller, K. R., & Levine, J. (2003). *Biology.* Upper Saddle River, NJ: Prentice Hall.

Moore, D. W., & Hinchman, K. A. (2003). *Starting out: A guide to teaching adolescents who struggle with reading.* Boston, MA: Pearson.

Morse, W. C. (2000). Foreword. In M. Friend & L. Cook (Eds.), *Interactions: Collaboration skills for school professionals* (3rd ed., pp. xi–xii). New York, NY: Addison Wesley Longman.

Moss, B., & Loh, V. S. (2010). *35 strategies for guiding readers through informational texts.* New York, NY: Guilford Press.

Murawski, W. W. (2009). *Collaborative teaching in elementary schools: Making the co-teaching marriage work!* Thousand Oaks, CA: Corwin.

Murray, R. (2011). *Perspective, opinion, and point of view: Distinctions that matter to writers and readers.* Retrieved from http://whowritesforyou.com/2011/01/06/perspective-opinion-and-point-of-view-%E2%80%94-distinctions-that-matter-to-writers-and-readers/

Nagy, W., & Townsend, D. (2012). Words as tools: Learning academic vocabulary as language acquisition. *Reading Research Quarterly, 47,* 91–108.

National Commission on Excellence in Education. (1983). *A nation at risk: The imperative for educational reform.* Washington, DC: U.S. Department of Education.

National Council of Teachers of English. (2006). *NCTE principles of adolescent literacy reform.* Urbana, IL: Author. Retrieved from: http://www.ncte.org/library/NCTEFiles/Resources/PolicyResearch/AdolLitPrinciples.pdf

National Joint Committee on Learning Disabilities. (2008). *Adolescent literacy and older students with learning disabilities* (Technical report). Retrieved from http://www.asha.org/policy/TR2008-00304

Noden, H. R. (1999). *Image grammar: Using grammatical structures to teach writing.* Portsmouth, NH: Heinemann.

Novak, J. D., & Cañas, A. J. (2006). The origins of concept maps and the continuing evolution of the tool. *Information Visualization Journal 5,* 175–184.

November, A. (2011). Emerging roles within the knowledge community. In L. Schrum (Ed.), *The best of Corwin: Educational technology for school leaders* (pp. 59–77). Thousand Oaks, CA: Corwin.

Oczkus, L. D. (2007). *Guided writing: Practical lessons, powerful results.* Portsmouth, NH: Heinemann.

O'Hara, S., Zwiers, J., & Pritchard, R. (2013). *Framing the development of complex language and literacy.* Retrieved from http://complexlanguage.org/sites/default/files/pictures/cln_brief.pdf

Oldendorp, E. (2011). *The Zine project: Reluctant writers no more.* Retrieved from http://idiom.nystesol.org/articles/vol37-04.html

Olson, D. R., & Torrance, N. (2009). *The Cambridge handbook of literacy.* Cambridge, MA: Cambridge University Press.

Palmer, E. (2011). *Well spoken: Teaching speaking to all students.* Portland, ME: Stenhouse.

Parker, W. C. (2006). Public discourses in schools: Purposes, problems, possibilities. *Educational Researcher, 35*(8), 11–18. doi:10.3102/0013189X035008011

Paulson, F. L., Paulson, P. R., & Meyer, C. A. (1991, February). What makes a portfolio a portfolio? *Educational Leadership, 48*(5), 60–63.

Pearson, P. D., & Gallagher, G. (1983). The gradual release of responsibility model of instruction. *Contemporary Education Psychology, 8,* 112–123.

Porter-O'Donnell, C. (2004). Beyond the yellow highlighter: Teaching annotation skills to improve reading comprehension. *English Journal, 93*(5), 82–89.

Prensky, M. (2001). Digital natives, digital immigrants. *On the Horizon, 9*(5). Retrieved from http://www.marcprensky.com/writing/

Raphael, T. E. (1982). Teaching children question-answering strategies. *The Reading Teacher, 36,* 186–191.

Raphael, T. E. (1986). Teaching question-answer relationships, revisited. *The Reading Teacher, 39,* 516–522.

Raphael, T. E., Highfield, K., & Au, K. H. (2006). *QAR now: A powerful and practical framework that develops comprehension and higher-level thinking in all students.* New York, NY: Scholastic Professional Books.

Ravitch, D. (2000). *Left back: A century of battles over school reform.* New York, NY: Simon & Schuster.

Ravitch, D. (2010). *The death and life of the great American school system.* New York, NY: Basic Books.

Reeves, D. B. (2000). Standards are not enough: Essential transformations for school success. *NASSP Bulletin, 84,* 5–19. doi:10.1177/019263650008462002

Reeves, D. B. (2006). *The learning leader: How to focus on school improvement for better results.* Alexandria, VA: ASCD.

Robb, L. (2003). *Teaching reading in social studies, science, and math.* New York, NY: Scholastic.

Roberts, A., & Billings, L. (2011). *Using seminars to teach the Common Core's speaking and listening standards.* White paper. Larchmont, NY: Eye On Education.

Roberts, S., & Pruitt, E. (2009). *Schools as professional learning communities: Collaborative activities and strategies for professional development.* Thousand Oaks, CA: Corwin.

Rosen, L. D. (2011). Teaching the iGeneration. *Educational Leadership, 68*(5), 10–15.

Ross, D., Fisher, D., & Frey, N. (2009). The art of argumentation. *Science & Children, 47*(3), 28–31.

Rothstein, A., Rothstein, E., & Lauber, G. (2007). *Writing as learning: A content-based approach* (2nd ed.). Thousand Oaks, CA: Corwin.

Rowan, B., Correnti, R., Miller, R. J., & Camburn, E. M. (2009). *School improvement by design: Lessons from a study of comprehensive school reform programs* (ED507546). Philadelphia, PA: Consortium for Policy Research in Education.

Saey, T. H. (2012, September 8). RNA research may solve sick snake mystery. *Science News: Magazine of the Society for Science & the Public, 182*(5), 5–6, 8.

Sanchez, N. M., & Harper, L. D. (2012). *Intentional interaction: Research-based model for content & language learning.* Minneapolis, MN: 2030 Press.

Saunders, W. G., & O'Brien, G. (2006). Oral language. In F. Genesee, K. Lindholm-Leary, B. Saunders, & D. Christian (Eds.), *Educating English language learners: A synthesis of research evidence* (pp. 14–48). New York, NY: Cambridge University Press.

Sawyer, R. K. (2004). Creative teaching: Collaborative discussion as disciplined improvisation. *Educational Researcher, 33,* 12–20. doi:10.3102/0013189X 033002012

Schmidt, R. (2001). Attention. In P. J. Robinson (Ed.), *Cognition and second language instruction* (pp. 3–32). Cambridge, England: Cambridge University Press.

Schmoker, M. (2009). What money can't buy: Powerful, overlooked opportunities for learning. *Kappan, 90,* 524–527.

Schmoker, M. (2011). *Focus: Elevating the essentials to radically improve student learning.* Alexandria, VA: ASCD.

Seely, J. (2012). *Grammar for teachers: Unlock your knowledge of English.* Cheltenham, UK: Oxpecker.

Shanahan, T. (2013). *Strategy: Theme search.* Retrieved from http://www.learningpt .org/literacy/adolescent/strategies/themesearch.php

Shanahan, T., & Shanahan, S. (1997). Character perspectives charting: Helping children to develop a more complete conception of the story. *The Reading Teacher, 50,* 668–677.

Silver, H. F., Dewing, R. T., & Perini, M. J. (2012). *The core six essential strategies for achieving excellence with the common core.* Alexandria, VA: ASCD.

Silver, J. F. (2001). *Real-life reading activities for grades 6–12: Over 200 ready-to-use lessons and activities to help students master practical reading skills.* San Francisco, CA: Jossey-Bass.

Smith, C. B. (1991). The role of different literary genres. *The Reading Teacher, 44,* 440–441.

Smith, C. B. (1994). *Helping children understand literary genres.* Retrieved from http://www.ericdigests.org/1994/genres.htm

Smith, P., & Tompkins, G. (1988). Structured notetaking: A new strategy for content area teachers. *Journal of Reading, 32,* 46–53.

Snow, C. E. (2010). Academic language and the challenge of reading or learning about science. *Science, 328,* 450–452.

Soto, I. (2012). *ELL shadowing as a catalyst for change.* Thousand Oaks, CA: Corwin.

Spandel, V. (2005). Foreword. In J. Anderson, *Mechanically inclined: Building grammar, usage, and style into writer's workshop* (xi-xiii). Portland, ME: Stenhouse.

Sparknotes. (2013). *The grapes of wrath: Key facts.* Retrieved from http://www .sparknotes.com/lit/grapesofwrath/facts.html

St. Paul Public Schools (SPPS). (2007). *Coteaching* [DVD]. St. Paul, MN: SPPS.

Strauss, V. (2010). *What the common core standards are—and aren't.* Retrieved from http://voices.washingtonpost.com/answer-sheet/national-standards/what-the-common-core-standards.html

Taba, H. (1967). Implementing thinking as an objective in social studies. In J. Fair & F. R. Shaftel (Eds.), *Effective thinking in the social studies: 37th Yearbook* (pp. 25–49). Washington, DC: National Council for the Social Studies.

Thomas, R. M. (2002). *Overcoming inertia in school reform: How to successfully implement change.* Thousand Oaks, CA: Corwin.

Tomlinson, C. A., & Imbeau, M. B. (2010). *Leading and managing a differentiated classroom.* Alexandria, VA: ASCD.

Torgesen, J., Houston, D., & Rissman, L. (2007). *Improving literacy instruction in middle and high schools: A guide for principals.* Portsmouth, NH: RMC Research Corporation, Center on Instruction.

Trefil, J. (2008). *Why science?* New York, NY: Teachers College Press.

Truss, L. (2004). *Eats, shoots & leaves: The zero tolerance approach to punctuation.* New York, NY: Gotham Books.

Udelhofen, S. K. (2005). *Keys to curriculum mapping: Strategies and tools to make it work.* Thousand Oaks, CA: Corwin.

Understanding Language. (2013). *Six key principles for ELL instruction.* Retrieved from http://ell.stanford.edu/content/six-key-principles-ell-instruction

Vaughn, S., Schumm, J. S., & Arguelles, M. E. (1997). The ABCDEs of co-teaching. *Teaching Exceptional Children, 30*(2), 4–10.

Villa, R. A., Thousand, J. S., & Nevin, A. I. (2008). *A guide to co-teaching: Practical tips for facilitating student learning.* Thousand Oaks, CA: Corwin.

Vogt, M. E., & Echevarria, J. (2007). *99 ideas and activities for teaching English learners with the SIOP® model.* Boston, MA: Allyn & Bacon.

Walling, D. R. (2009). *Writing for understanding: Strategies to increase content learning.* Thousand Oaks, CA: Corwin.

Weingarten, R. (2012, March 2). *Implementation will move the needle* [Web log comment]. Retrieved from http://education.nationaljournal.com/2012/02/common-cores-good-bad-and-ugly.php

Wheeler, R. (2005). Code-switch to teach Standard English. *English Journal, 94*(5), 108–112.

Wheeler, R. (2008). Becoming adept at code-switching. *Educational Leadership, 65*(7), 54–58.

Whitfield, J. (1998). *Getting kids hooked on literature: A hands-on guide to making literature exciting for kids.* Waco, TX: Prufrock Press.

Wilhelm, J. D. (2007). Imagining a new kind of self: Academic language, identity, and content area learning. *Voices From the Middle, 15*(1), 44–45.

Wolsey, T. D., & Lapp, D. (2009). Discussion-based approaches for the secondary classroom. In K. Woods & B. Blanton (Eds.), *Promoting literacy with adolescent learners: Research-based instruction* (pp. 368–391). New York, NY: Guilford Press.

World-Class Instructional Design and Assessment Consortium. (2011). *Glossary of terms and expressions.* Retrieved from www.wida.us/get.aspx?id=412

World-Class Instructional Design and Assessment Consortium. (2012). *2012 Amplification of the English language development standards: Kindergarten–Grade 12.* Available from http://www.wida.us/downloadLibrary.aspx

Yoshida, M. (2004, November). *A summary of lesson study.* Paper presented at conference, Toward a Common Understanding: Implementing Lesson Study Effectively, Stamford, CT.

Zwiers, J. (2008). *Building academic language: Essential practices for content classrooms.* San Francisco, CA: Jossey-Bass.

Zwiers, J., & Crawford, M. (2011). *Academic conversations: Classroom talk that fosters critical thinking and content understandings.* Portland, ME: Stenhouse.

Zywica, J., & Gomez, K. (2008). Annotating to support learning in the content areas: Teaching and learning science. *Journal of Adolescent & Adult Literacy, 52,* 155–164.

LITERATURE CITED

Adams, J. (1776). *Letter on Thomas Jefferson.* Retrieved from http://www.bingoforpatriots.com/american-history/founding-fathers/presidents-during-the-founding-period/john-adams/letter-on-thomas-jefferson-by-john-adams-1776/

Alvarez, J. (1994). *In the time of the butterflies.* Chapel Hill, NC: Algonquin.

Angelou, M. (1969). *I know why the caged bird sings.* New York, NY: Random House.

Bellow, S. (1953). *The adventures of Augie March.* New York, NY: Viking.

Brontë, C. (2009). *Jane Eyre.* Radford, VA: Wilder.

Churchill, W. (1940). Blood, toil, tears and sweat: Address to the parliament. In W. Safire (Ed.), *Lend me your ears: Great speeches in history* (3rd ed.). New York, NY: Norton.

Cisneros, S. (1991). *Woman hollering creek and other stories.* New York, NY: Random House.

Coleridge, S. T. (2008). *Rime of the ancient mariner.* Minneapolis, MN: Chartwell Books.

Collins, S. (2010). *The hunger games.* New York, NW: Scholastic.

Dickens, C. (1980). *A tale of two cities.* New York, NY: New American Library.

Fitzgerald, F. S. (2004). *The Great Gatsby.* New York, NY: Scribner.

Franzen, J. (2001). *The corrections.* New York, NY: Farrar, Straus & Giroux.

Gaiman, N. (2009). *Stardust.* New York, NY: Harper Teen/Harper Collins.

Gladwell, M. (2002). *The tipping point: How little things can make a big difference.* New York, NY: Back Bay Books.

Goodrich, F., & Hackett, A. (1958). *The diary of Anne Frank: A play.* New York: Random House.

Greenberg, J., & Jordan, S. (2001). *Vincent Van Gogh: Portrait of an artist.* New York, NY: Random House.

Hansberry, L. (1988). *A raisin in the sun.* New York, NY: Vintage Books.

Hughes, L. (1925). *I, too, sing America.* New York, NY: Knopf.

Keats, J. (1963). Ode to a Grecian urn (1820). In A. Quiller-Couch (Ed.), *The Oxford Book of English Verse, 1250–1918.* New York, NY: Oxford University Press.

King, M. L. Jr. (1992). I have a dream—Address at the march on Washington. In J. M. Washington (Ed.), *I have a dream: Writings and speeches that changed the world* (pp. 101–106). San Francisco, CA: HarperSanFrancisco. (Speech delivered 1963)

Korman, G. (2000). *No more dead dogs.* New York, NY: Hyperion.

Lahiri, J. (2003). *The namesake.* New York, NY: Houghton Mifflin.

Lee, H. (1960). *To kill a mockingbird.* New York, NY: Harper.

Lemasolai Lekuton, J., & Viola, H. J. (2005). *Facing the lion: Growing up Maasi on the African savanna.* Washington, DC: National Geographic Books.

Martel, Y. (2001). *Life of Pi.* New York, NY: Harcourt.

McCloskey, M. L., & Stack, L. (1996). *Voices in literature: Gold.* Boston, MA: Heinle & Heinle.

Mitchell, M. (1961). *Gone with the wind.* New York, NY: Macmillan.

Mortenson, G. (2006). *Three cups of tea.* New York, NY: Viking.

Plath, S. (2004). Lady Lazurus. In S. Plath, *Ariel: The restored edition* (p. 14). New York, NY: HarperPerrenial ModernClassics.

Rowling, J. K. (2009). *Harry Potter paperback box set.* New York, NY: Arthur A. Levine Books.

Sachar, L. (2000). *Holes.* New York, NY: Dell Yearling.

Salinger, J. D. (2001). *Catcher in the rye.* New York, NY: Back Bay Books.

Shakespeare, W. (2011). *Macbeth.* New York, NY: Simon & Brown.

Steinbeck, J. (1952). *East of Eden.* New York, NY: Viking Press.

Steinbeck, J. (1993). *Of mice and men.* London, England: Penguin Books.

Steinbeck, J. (1993). *The grapes of wrath.* London, England: Penguin Books.

Tan, A. (1990). Mother tongue. In *The opposite of fate: Memories of a writing life.* New York, NY: Putnam.

Taylor, M. (1976). *Roll of thunder, hear my cry.* New York, NY: Puffin.

Tolkien, J. R. R. (1954). *Lord of the rings: Fellowship of the rings.* New York, NY: Ballentine Books.

Trumbo, D. (1984). *Johnny got his gun.* New York, NY: Bantam.

Twain, M. (2007). *The prince and the pauper.* Clayton, DE: Prestwick House.

Vaughan, J. T. (2010). *Powerful people powerful lives: Stories of champions.* Charleston, SC: BookSurge.

Walker, A. (2011). *The color purple.* Boston, MA: Houghton Mifflin Harcourt.

Whitman, W. (1860). Song of myself. In *Leaves of grass.* Oxford, England: Oxford University Press.

Whitman, W. (2005). O captain! My captain! In *The complete poems* (p. 358). New York, NY: Penguin Classics.

Wiesel, E. (1986). Hope, despair, and memory. In *Nobel lectures in peace.* Singapore: World Scientific.

Wiesel, E. (1999). *The perils of indifference.* Retrieved from http://www.historyplace.com/speeches/wiesel.htm

Zusak, M. (2005). *The book thief.* New York, NY: Knopf.

Strategy Index

CORWIN
A SAGE Company

The Corwin logo—a raven striding across an open book—represents the union of courage and learning. Corwin is committed to improving education for all learners by publishing books and other professional development resources for those serving the field of PreK–12 education. By providing practical, hands-on materials, Corwin continues to carry out the promise of its motto: **"Helping Educators Do Their Work Better."**